The Nonprofit
Sector and
Government
in a New Century

The Public Policy and the Third Sector Series

The Nonprofit Sector in Canada: Roles and Relationships
Keith G. Banting, editor

The Nonprofit Sector and Government in a New Century
Kathy L. Brock and Keith G. Banting, editors

The Nonprofit Sector and Government in a New Century

Edited by
Kathy L. Brock
and
Keith G. Banting

Published for the School of Policy Studies,
Queen's University
by McGill-Queen's University Press
Montreal & Kingston • London • Ithaca

National Library of Canada Cataloguing in Publication Data

Main entry under title:
 The nonprofit sector and government in a new century

(The public policy and the third sector series ; 2)
Including bibliographical references.
ISBN 0-88911-905-8 (bound).—ISBN 0-88911-901-5 (pbk.)

 1. Nonprofit organizations—Canada. 2. Nonprofit organizations—
Government policy—Canada. I. Brock, Kathy Lenore, 1958-
II. Banting, Keith G., 1947- III. Queen's University (Kingston, Ont.).
School of Policy Studies IV. Series.

HD2769.2.C3N65 2001   361.7'63'0971   C2001-902010-4

Contents

Tables and Figures

Tables

Figures

Preface

This book is the second contribution to the Public Policy and the Third Sector Series published by the School of Policy Studies and McGill-Queen's University Press. This series is made possible by generous support from The Nonprofit Sector Research Initiative established by the Kahanoff Foundation to promote research and scholarship on nonprofit sector issues and to broaden the formal body of knowledge on the sector.

With financial support from the Foundation, the School of Policy Studies sponsored a national research grants program. Applications for research funding were invited from researchers across the country, and grants were awarded by a peer-review panel organized by the School. This book incorporates papers funded in the second wave of projects.

The authors contributing to this book focus on the evolving relationship between the nonprofit sector and governments in Canada. The restructuring of the state in the contemporary era has had major implications for the role of nonprofit organizations, their fiscal foundations, and their relationships with both public agencies and their traditional communities. The chapters in this volume explore the synergies, contradictions and tensions that characterize these complex relationships in a period of transition. Both individually and collectively, the papers in this book extend our understanding in important directions.

A collaborative project such as this book depends on the contributions of many people. We would like to acknowledge continuing support from Shira Herzog of the Kahanoff Foundation, whose commitment was critical to the Nonprofit Sector Research Initiative, and Michael Hall, who has coordinated the various components of the Initiative with unfailing enthusiasm.

We also wish to thank the authors for their dedication to the project, and for their patience with the demands of an extended editorial process. Todd Yates of the School of Policy Studies managed the infinite number of administrative details, and contributed to the success of a workshop at which the first drafts of the papers were presented and discussed. Finally, we wish to acknowledge both the Publications Unit of the School of Policy Studies who prepared the book for publication with consummate professionalism, and McGill-Queen's University Press, our partner in the venture of publishing interesting contributions to policy studies in Canada.

Kathy L. Brock
Keith G. Banting

1

The Nonprofit Sector and Government in a New Century: An Introduction

Kathy L.Brock and Keith G. Banting

At the dawn of a new century, the third sector has become increasingly embedded in the business of government in western liberal democracies like Canada, the United States, and Britain. In part, the growing interest has flowed from governments. The redefinition and streamlining of government has caused policymakers to turn to third sector organizations to deliver services that governments no longer desire or are able to provide to citizens directly. In part, the growing interest has bubbled up from society. Disillusioned by the apparent unresponsiveness and impotence of their governments, citizens have also looked to third sector agencies to defend their rights, promote their interests, and provide needed services. Given these distinctive impulses from both the state and society, it is perhaps not surprising that the relationship between the nonprofit sector and government is complex, combining exhilarating potential and perpetual wariness. On one side, governments engage third sector organizations in the policy process, but remain uneasy about the attenuation of their own control over service delivery, the implications for political accountability, and the actual capacity of nonprofit institutions to deliver programs equitably and efficiently. On the other side, charities, nonprofit, and voluntary organizations have tried to respond by delivering services, but many are wary of the effects on their autonomy as governments demand ever more accountability, on their identities as they attempt to respond to the rising expectations, and on their viability as they stretch their resources in many directions at once.

Two events at the turn of the century seem to encapsulate both the potential and the complexities inherent in the evolving relationship between the nonprofit sector and the state. The potential was highlighted symbolically when the Canadian government and voluntary organizations warmly embraced 2001 as the International Year of the Volunteer (IYV) to celebrate the long and continuing tradition of volunteerism in this country. Events were planned across the country to promote awareness of the importance of volunteering in building a socially and economically dynamic nation. The complexity of the relationship in everyday practice was highlighted by a second process launched as a result of a decision by the federal government and representatives from nonprofit organizations to conduct a comprehensive review of the links between them. The scope and nature of this exercise are unprecedented, and the range of issues under debate is daunting. This review holds out the possibility of a more fundamental engagement of the nonprofit sector in the governance process in Canada, but it also reveals the contradictory impulses that must be reconciled before such changes can be fully realized.

This book, the second in a series on *Public Policy and the Third Sector*, seeks to contribute to our collective understanding of the underlying changes in the role of the nonprofit sector and its relationships with the state and society in Canada. The introduction to the first volume in the series (Hall and Banting 1999) provided a broad overview of the nonprofit sector in Canada. This introduction to the second volume builds on that beginning in two ways. First, it explores contemporary developments in the relationship between the nonprofit sector and government, paying particular attention to new initiatives at the federal level. Second, it outlines some of the key research concerns being identified by the ongoing dialogue about the role of the nonprofit sector and highlights the contributions of the chapters that follow to that larger picture.

THE GROWING POLICY CONSCIOUSNESS OF THE SECTOR

The UN has proclaimed 2001, the International Year of Volunteers.[1] This symbolic gesture arose out of the increasing awareness of the role of voluntary activity in building strong communities and stable polities, as well as the growing realization of the importance of nonprofit activities as forms of economic activity. Canada has been an enthusiastic supporter of the IYV. In 1999, a Leaders' Forum was held to consider Canadian participation in the celebrations. While endorsing the UN objectives, the 50 representatives from government, academia, and the voluntary sector identified five objectives for Canada: to celebrate volunteerism as a key to the quality of life in Canada; to promote volunteering for all groups in Canada; to expand the definition of volunteer action to include informal activities and encourage corporate participation; to improve the organizational infrastructure for volunteering; and to measure the contribution of volunteering to Canadian society and national progress. To achieve these objectives, the federal government appointed Human Resources Development Canada and Canadian Heritage to work with Volunteer Canada as the leader for the voluntary sector in planning activities and encouraging community participation in the IYV across the country.

Declaration of the IYV is a significant symbol. It signals the increasing appreciation of the voluntary sector among policymakers as an important social force in the country, and recognition of the sector as a dynamic environment for both paid and unpaid work. Moreover, the IYV promotes volunteer activity at a time when concerns are emerging over the long-term commitment of citizens to volunteering, declining civic consciousness, and rapid changes in the social fabric of western democracies. Celebrating volunteer action highlights its importance to building communities and bridging differences as people have become more mobile and societies have become more diverse.

Beneath the surface of this joint celebration of the voluntary impulse in Canadian life, however, lies a much more complex relationship between the nonprofit sector and governments. To understand the current debates requires an examination of the growing policy consciousness of the nonprofit sector in recent decades.

Growing Prominence, Growing Strains

Despite the long history of voluntary organizations in Canada, the third sector is a relatively new concept in the world of public policy. It was only in 1967 that the Canadian Parliament amended the *Income Tax Act* to register all organizations issuing charitable receipts to donors and to require those organizations to file annual reports on their activities (Monahan 2000, p. 11; Ontario Law Reform Commission 1996, pp. 261-65). Rather than articulating a policy presence for the organizations, however, these requirements were directed at maintaining the integrity of the tax system. It was not until the 1970s and 1980s that consciousness among policymakers of voluntary and nonprofit organizations as constituting a coherent sector began to grow. One early sign of this trend occurred in 1974 when the Secretary of State created the National Advisory Council on Voluntary Action to study issues arising out of the relationship between the federal government and the voluntary sector (Joint Tables 1999, p. 19). As the size of the sector exploded in the following years, governments came to recognize the potential of third sector organizations for policy development and service delivery.

Two trends promoted the closer interaction between nonprofit organizations and the state. Citizen activism in the 1960s and disillusionment with government in the 1970s led many citizens to pour their hopes and energies into movements and organizations challenging traditional government practices and representing their rights. As governments attempted to respond to the new pressures, they turned to these groups for advice, information, and expertise, a trend reinforced by the overall impact of the information revolution and new communication technologies (Brock 2001; Cairns 1995; Clark 1995). The second trend was driven by fiscal imperatives and "the crisis of the welfare state" experienced by a wide range of western nations, including Canada (Gidron, Kramer and Salamon 1992, p. 14; Graves 1997; Ekos 1998; Elshtain 1997; Mansbridge 1998; Hudson 1999; Caldwell and Reed 1999; Putnam 1996). During the 1980s and 1990s, the federal and provincial governments in Canada underwent significant restructuring as they attempted to bring their fiscal houses in order. In the face of rising public demands for services and declining revenues, governments began to cast about for alternative means of providing services more efficiently. While privatization was one means, off-loading services to voluntary organizations provided an attractive alternative, especially in the case of social services. However, expanded responsibilities were not always balanced with new resources. This trend was exacerbated by the concerted push of the federal government to balance its books, in no small measure by reducing transfer payments to the provincial governments who bear the primary responsibility for social services. Faced with reduced transfers and rising social costs owing to the recession of the early 1990s, provincial governments reduced payments to local governments and many social organizations, all the while encouraging them to assume greater responsibilities for services (Hall and Reed 1999; Rekart 1993). The combined burden of reduced subsidies and rising citizen expectations strained the capacity of charities and voluntary organizations. In a trenchant criticism of the federal government and spirited defence of the nonprofit sector titled, *Straight through the Heart: How the Liberals Abandoned the Just Society*, Maude Barlow and Bruce Campbell trace the effects of the Liberal government's attempts to reduce expenditures by cutting grants, increasing contractual funding, reducing welfare programs and redefining the government's role in the social sector. They concluded that the third sector felt under siege (Barlow and Campbell 1995; also Miller 1999, p. 75).

The strain was heightened by new sources of criticism. Not surprisingly, the growing importance of nonprofit organizations trained the media spotlight on the sector, and controversy soon followed. Numerous media articles emerged in the US citing examples of real and perceived malfeasance in the third sector and calling for more accountability (Chisholm 1995). These concerns soon drifted across the border. As if in reply to Barlow and Campbell, Walter Stewart published his study of the sector titled, just as revealingly, *The Charity Game: Greed, Waste and Fraud in Canada's $86 Billion-a-Year Compassion Industry* (Stewart 1996). While the book was removed from circulation after some charities threatened legal action, it had the effect of drawing attention to the use of public funds and delivery of services by third sector agencies (Juneau 1998, p. 29:1). Articles in *Maclean's* and the popular media in 1996 and 1997 profiled mistakes, funding abuses, and inadequate regulation of the industry. The Ontario Law Reform Commission added force to the criticisms in its 1996 report calling for more effective monitoring of the sector (ibid.; OLRC 1996). Perhaps most damaging of all was the publication by John Bryden, an Ontario member of the federal Parliament, of his *MP's Report: Canada's Charities – A Need for Reform* (Bryden 1996), which alleged that the organizations were unrepresentative and self-serving special interests lacking accountability and legitimate purpose. The upshot was that the Department of Finance commissioned a review of grants to so-called special interest groups, cutting their funding by $300 million within a year (Miller 1999, p. 76), and reformed the *Income Tax Act* to ensure greater transparency within the sector.

Percolating in the background of the controversies was a legal case on its way up to the Supreme Court of Canada. In the case of *Vancouver Society of Immigrant and Visible Minority Women v. Minister of National Revenue* ([1999] 1 S.C.R.), an organization which provided educational assistance to immigrant and minority women was challenging a decision by Revenue Canada not to grant it charitable status on the grounds that the society was not constituted exclusively for charitable purposes since its mandate included fundraising and political advocacy. The majority decision of the Supreme Court upheld the ruling of Revenue Canada, applying the traditional definition of charity to the Society. The dissenting judges revealed the possibilities for updating the common law understanding of charity and would have allowed the appeal. The ensuing debate over whether or not the common law definition of charity as applied by the courts and Revenue Canada was outdated prompted expectations of legislative action.

Clearly, it was time for a major review of the nonprofit sector and its relationships with government.

Two Foundational Reports

The opportunity for review opened up in the last years of the 1990s when the playing field for civil society organizations changed significantly. At the federal level, the Liberal government's intense preoccupation with the agenda of deficit reduction began to soften. By the 1997 election, the advantage of winning electoral favour in the nonprofit sector, combined with growing concerns over the health and accountability of nonprofit organizations, prompted the Liberals to promise that, if re-elected, their government would "work in partnership with the voluntary sector to explore new models for overseeing and regulating registered charities and enhancing their accountability to the public" (Liberal Party 1997).

Sensing both the underlying potential and threat embedded in this promise, national third sector organizations mobilized their case. An unincorporated group of national voluntary organizations known as the Voluntary Sector Roundtable tasked a panel of six eminent Canadians, chaired by Ed Broadbent, former leader of the federal New Democratic Party, with the responsibility of consulting widely with the voluntary sector and advising the community on methods of improving accountability and governance in a changing environment.

The Panel on Accountability and Governance for the Voluntary Sector (PAGVS) issued its report, *Building on Strength: Improving Governance and Accountability in the Voluntary Sector*, in February 1999 after the release of the controversial Supreme Court decision in the *Immigrant Women's* case. Five guiding principles animated the report: the need to encourage the sector's contribution in building social trust and social capital; the need to enhance its role in promoting democracy; the need to strengthen the capacity of the sector; the need to recognize the diversity of the sector; and the need to respect its desire for autonomy and self-governance (PAGVS 1999, p. 10).

The 41 recommendations offered by the PAGVS were sweeping. They included suggestions directed to the voluntary sector itself on the need to work collaboratively and to improve operational procedures, including the adoption of a fundraising code of ethics. The recommendations directed to donors and fundraisers suggested that they should be more supportive of the sector, but also that they should encourage good governance through such measures as more stringent outcome measures. The recommendations addressed to the federal and provincial governments ranged over a wide area and included: exhortations to collaborate more fully with the sector and provide a voice within Cabinet; suggestions for supporting better governance practices in the sector, including a code of ethics for fundraising; calls to improve the legal and regulatory framework by such things as allowing for differential reporting requirements for smaller and larger organizations, modernizing the tax system, setting more flexible requirements for advocacy, and coordinating federal and provincial links with the sector (PAGVS 1999, pp. 80-93). Among these many recommendations, the PAGVS identified four priorities: adoption of a good practices guide in the sector; establishment of a Voluntary Sector Commission to oversee the sector and act as a liaison with government; statutory enactment of a definition of "charity"; and negotiation of a compact between the voluntary sector and federal and provincial governments.

Rather than responding unilaterally to PAGVS, the federal government established a Voluntary Sector Task Force in the powerful Privy Council Office to work with organizations in the voluntary sector. Together, they created three Joint Tables with representatives from the two sectors to consider the means of building a new relationship, strengthening the sector's capacity, and improving the regulatory framework governing the sector. The Joint Tables issued their report, *Working Together: A Government of Canada/Voluntary Sector Joint Initiative* in August 1999 (Joint Tables 1999).

The Joint Tables report achieved two objectives. First, it established a working plan to guide specific changes within the sector and in its relationship with government. Second, the Joint Tables made specific recommendations in the three areas of responsibility. Like the PAGVS, the Joint Tables made extensive recommendations for restructuring the state-third sector relationship (Joint Tables 1999, pp. 9-14), including the options of closer contact for the sector at strategic levels of government, an accord to govern relations, and improvements to funding and administrative relationships. The Regulatory Table suggested clearer guidelines governing financial matters and reporting requirements in the sector, enactment of a statutory definition of charity and further consideration of a variant of a charity commission based on broader consultations (Joint Tables 1999, pp. 12, 45-53). The Capacity Table stressed the need for more information about the sector, better training opportunities, and enhanced skills, research, and technology management in the sector. The Joint Tables report extended the thinking in PAGVS and recommended further action within a reasonable time frame.

The Voluntary Sector Initiative

The work of PAGVS and the Joint Tables did not go unheeded. In June 2000, the federal government, jointly with members of the voluntary sector, announced the Voluntary Sector Initiative (VSI), which is designed to act on the recommendations of the two commissions.[2] At the time of the announcement, the federal government committed $94.6 million to a five-year plan to improve service delivery and government programs by increasing support to the sector and by enhancing its capacity to meet demands placed on it. The VSI agenda is a broad one. It will advise on relationship-building measures including the development of an accord between government and the sector ($10 million). It will initiate on capacity-building measures ($25 million), including information generation and Internet use in the sector ($10 million), a triennial national survey of giving, volunteering, and participating, and specific measures to recruit and train volunteers and staff. The agenda also includes regulatory issues ($7 million), such as making registration of charities fairer and more transparent, examining models for the reform of the regulatory institutions, and revisiting the restrictions on advocacy within the sector. Finally, the government has allocated $30 million to examine means of involving the voluntary sector more effectively in the development of government policies and programs.

The VSI is well positioned in the federal power structure and the voluntary sector. It falls under the overall stewardship of a Reference Group of Cabinet Ministers, whose role is to coordinate government activities with respect to the voluntary sector and advance the dialogue with the sector. The voluntary sector counterpart is a senior steering committee composed of members from the Voluntary Sector Roundtable and other organizations. At the operational level, a joint coordinating committee, with members drawn equally from the senior ranks of the federal government through an internal process and the voluntary sector as selected by an independent committee in an open process, oversees the public consultation process, provides feedback to the government and voluntary sector, and assists government departments, the sector and the Joint Tables in harmonizing their efforts. Complementing the coordinating committee is a set of Joint Tables with co-chairs and members drawn equally from government and the sector. The Joint Tables ensure maximum collaboration on issues relating to capacity, volunteerism, the legislative and regulatory framework, research and information management, public awareness, and the relationship between the federal government and sector (an accord). Two working groups with representation from the voluntary sector are addressing funding and advocacy issues. To ensure that the initiative reaches people beyond the actual participants and is inclusive, individual volunteers, smaller organizations and other stakeholders and citizens can engage in the dialogue on the relationship through a Web site and public hearings.

It is too early to come to a definitive evaluation of the probable effectiveness of this initiative. On the positive side, for the first time in Canadian history, the Canadian government is reaching beyond the department level to engage the voluntary sector community at a more strategic level. The two sides are certainly not equals in the VSI since the government retains primary control over areas such as the functioning of the Reference Group of Ministers and the development of legislation, but the initiative seems to place the voluntary sector in a position to influence policy development and government design in a substantive way.

Nevertheless, the VSI faces important challenges. First, it is heavily dependent on continued political enthusiasm of the government of the day, and therefore vulnerable to changing political fashion. If the initiative is to truly change the governance process, the post-election commitment of the federal government must remain strong and the VSI must become a regular feature of the Cabinet agenda. Second, the Joint Tables process must establish its capacity to handle the really tough issues in order to remain credible. There are troubling signs here. The voluntary sector pressed ahead with working groups to study the questions of funding for the sector and advocacy by agencies. Advocacy and funding are two of the most controversial areas of government and voluntary sector relations, and are vital to the long-term health and capacity of the sector. The government is not formally participating in these working groups, but it is informally discussing issues with the voluntary sector representatives, conducting an internal review of funding components, and has recently committed to talking about advocacy jointly. One of the tests of the potential effectiveness of the VSI may be whether or not the two sides can enter into a dialogue and reach an accommodation on such issues.

Third, the initiative must avoid exacerbating potential fault lines within the third sector itself. Otherwise, the process may produce agreements that serve the organizations at the table well, but do not result in an improvement of services or quality of life for Canadians. At least a couple of dimensions of the sector are critical. Given the central role of volunteerism in nonprofit organizations, it is important to ensure that citizen voices are heard in a meaningful way and incorporated into the decision-making structures of the Joint Tables. Effective use of the Web sites and public hearings is critical here. Early indications are that the Joint Tables are being responsive; but as the process wears on and becomes more demanding, real efforts will need to be made to ensure that a divide between the decisionmakers and public does not open up. Another troubling undercurrent with the potential to divide the sector flows from the fact that intermediary and larger organizations tend to drive the process. As these institutions become stakeholders in the process and final product, a gulf may be driven between these agencies and smaller ones lacking the resources to be heard. Smaller organizations may then be either critical of what they see as elitist and irrelevant arrangements on the one hand, or lapse into frustrated disengagement on the other. Balancing responsiveness with decisive leadership is no mean feat, but polarization within the community would simply damage citizen perceptions and confidence in both the third sector and government.

Beyond these more immediate challenges are larger constraints inherent in the structure of government in Canada, especially the traditions embedded in our conception of parliamentary democracy and the federal nature of government. The doctrine of ministerial accountability, which holds that ministers must be accountable in the House of Commons for policy and management in their departments, places uncertain boundaries around the openness of the governance process. These boundaries are flexible, but can tighten suddenly in the midst of political controversy. Graphic evidence of the impact can be seen in the intense political reaction to the administrative shortcomings of Human Resources Development Canada (HRDC). In the words of one experienced observer, "After the scorching debate that has taken place, the message to the public service could not be more clear ... The only way to do things is by the book, and here's a new, much thicker book to replace the one you've been using" (Kroeger 2000). This shift will be felt by thousands of community organizations across the country which annually receive funds, not just from HRDC but from a wide range of departments at all levels of government. This particular case involves service delivery rather than policy development. But the implications are relevant to the full range of governance.

Federalism also represents a constraint on the Joint Tables. Many of the most important relationships between the state and the nonprofit sector occur at the provincial and local levels. The provinces are not involved in the initiative at this stage, and the ability of the federal government to redefine the relationship is limited to its area of jurisdiction, leaving many critical issues off the various tables. The provinces are being kept informed, and there may be efforts to engage them in the process at a later date. However, the experiences of federal-provincial consultation in a wide range of policy sectors suggest that this would be a significant hurdle to surmount.

These challenges confronting the effort to engage the third sector represent echoes of earlier efforts to change the governance process in Canada. During the 1980s and early 1990s, for example, there were substantial efforts to move toward a more corporatist approach in the field of labour markets. Substantial efforts were made at both the federal and provincial levels to create multipartite councils which would engage employers, organized labour, and equity groups in the development of policy and the delivery of services. In the end, these experiments floundered on concerns about the representativeness of parties at the table, the implications of ministerial accountability and bureaucratic control over program delivery, and the fragmentation inherent in a federal system (Macintosh 2000; Sharpe and Haddow 1997).

None of these challenges is insurmountable, but managing them will require continued commitment and sensitivity on the part of both the government and the third sector. The prize of a more open, engaged process of governance in Canada is certainly worth the effort.

UNDERSTANDING RESEARCH NEEDS

In a complementary initiative to the VSI, the Coalition of National Voluntary Organisations, the Canadian Centre for Philanthropy, and the Ottawa-Carleton Centre for Voluntary Sector Research and Development organized a workshop in early September 2000 to identify and define research needs in the sector. Representatives from the third sector, the academic community, and government discussed the current state of research including gaps in our knowledge, the prospects for cooperation among academic and sector researchers, and the development of a research network of academics and practitioners. Four priorities for future research emerged from the discussions: creation of a data profile of the sector;

measurement of the impact of the sector on democratic, social, and economic development; identification of the sector's capacity in the areas of management, leadership, volunteer mobilization, and partnership links; and construction of viable research models for practitioners and academics. At the conclusion of the conference, a small "Moving Forward" working group was assigned the responsibility of drafting these ideas into a coherent action plan for network-building and knowledge creation.

The workshop process highlighted the complexities involved in developing a strong tradition of research on the voluntary sector. The diversity of research needs is significant, and poses a challenge to developing an action plan that is broadly acceptable to the larger community. There is no general consensus on the definition of research or requisite knowledge for the community as a whole. Should research be action-oriented, experiential, practical, theoretical or all of the above? collaborative or independent or a mixture of the two? based on common standards of quality or more eclectic? tied to the perceived needs of the sector or based on detached assessments or both? These questions are not easily settled even within the sector itself.

These questions play out differently across the various participants. Many third sector organizations require knowledge and research that is directly related to their functions. They accord less room to research that aims to define or target the sector as a whole. In a similar way, government officials from the central agencies may take an interest in understanding the sector as a whole while officials from individual departments may be more inclined to focus on increasing the skills and capacities of voluntary organizations that are active in areas that fall under their jurisdiction. Academics, driven by their own research agendas and by university expectations about the nature and purposes of research, may find that their interests are at variance from both government and the nonprofit sector. While the workshop participants were able to reach consensus on the need for a definition and plan of research that accommodated this diversity, any research initiative flowing from it will need to be sensitive of such differences in the implementation stages. To accommodate the differences, discrete research traditions will undoubtedly emerge, creating a danger that crucial areas of need may fall through the cracks.

Third, incorporating critical or dissenting voices into the emerging research tradition may pose the greatest difficulty in this process. To date, the community of researchers and pool of research in Canada has been relatively small, with most participants known by person or reputation and most sharing similar values and a commitment to voluntary action. As the circle of research on the nonprofit sector grows, more voices will enter the community bringing different sets of values and beliefs. Government and sector representatives have demonstrated a strong willingness to understand the strengths and weaknesses of the sector on a sectoral and organizational level. However, as nonprofit organizations are drawn further into the policy fold, more critical scrutiny may be brought to bear on them, resulting in harsher assessments of the sector, even from former allies. As governments know only too well, greater scrutiny can have long-term implications for legitimacy and public trust. In a sector so dependent upon public goodwill and a spirit of cooperation, loud dissenting voices may pose more compelling challenges than in other areas of organizational life, driving a wedge between certain sections of the academic community and the third sector. Accommodating such divides will be a difficult test of the commitment of government, the third sector, and academics to research.

Three Important Themes

Common to the VSI, the International Year of the Volunteer, and the Moving Forward Working Group is the strong desire for knowledge about the nonprofit sector in all facets. As these initiatives have unfolded, three particularly important areas of concern have emerged which are also reflected in the studies in this volume.

 First, the nonprofit sector cannot be understood in isolation from government, the for-profit sector and the communities the organizations serve. As the Joint Tables explained in *Working Together*, "The voluntary sector — which today plays an increasingly critical and complex role — has long been a vital pillar of Canadian society, working with the public and private sectors to make Canada a more humane, caring and prosperous nation" (Joint Tables 1999, p. 15). To understand the operation of the nonprofit sector and its importance, it is necessary to appreciate its relationship with other actors and organizations in society and the economy.

The chapters in this volume all contribute to an understanding of the place of the nonprofit sector within Canadian social and economic life.

Two of the chapters address specific dimensions of the relationship between the nonprofit sector and the broader Canadian environment. The team of researchers led by Jack Quarter offers an original framework for classifying organizations. Departing from past studies that classified institutions by either their form of incorporation or their type of service, they classify nonprofit organizations and cooperatives according to their underlying dimensions. These dimensions include social objectives, relationship to government, relationship to the market, democratic decision making, and volunteer participation. Through this system of classification, they are able to convey a sense of the diversity within the social economy and the complexity of the relationships between cooperatives and nonprofit agencies and other actors in the political and economic realms. From a different vantage point, the team of researchers led by James Rice place the nonprofit organizations within a community context. By studying the formal and informal social networks that support families with young children in the Hamilton area, they are able to depict the extent to which communities offer support to individuals and assess the effectiveness of nonprofit institutions in relation to government-sponsored and familial care. The chapter contributes to an understanding of the symbiotic relationship between strong communities and a healthy nonprofit sector.

A second recurring theme in the VSI, the IYV and the Moving Forward initiatives has been the need to build capacity within the nonprofit sector. When announcing the VSI, President of the Treasury Board and Chair of the Reference Group Madame Robillard proclaimed, "As a government, we have recognized that the voluntary sector represents the third pillar of our society. It is an important sector — equally important as the public and private sectors. It generates important economic spin-offs and creates hundreds of thousands of paying jobs. We need to do more — as a government and as society as a whole to support these individuals and the organizations they serve, because they contribute, without hesitation, to maintaining our social, economic and cultural fabric." As a consequence, an important priority of the VSI is to develop the resources, including financial and human resources, accountability tools, information technology, and research skills, that will improve the effectiveness of nonprofit organizations and strengthen their support networks. The IYV and Moving Forward Working Group echo this cry for in-depth study of the current strengths and weaknesses of the sector as a precursor to understanding how to build capacity within the sector so that it may serve Canadians more effectively.

Four of the essays presented in this volume highlight the struggles of nonprofit sector organizations to function effectively in a changing environment. As citizen demands increase and funding becomes more competitive, institutions are able to responding with varying degrees of success. Luc Juillet, Caroline Andrew, Tim Aubrey and Janet Mrenica investigate whether nonprofit organizations are being transformed by the need to compete in markets or submit to stricter accountability controls by government departments. They examine the impact that the changing funding environment has had on the mission statements, governance, and program delivery of eight national organizations. Darcy Mitchell, Justin Longo and Kelly Vodden shift the focus from the national level to a rural community level study of agencies concerned with economic development, natural resource management, and the environment. They chart the double impact of the government retreat from service provision and the corporate retreat from the local economy on nonprofit organizations in rural, resource-dependent communities with limited social capital. While they had anticipated that these pressures might trigger more local activity and collaborative efforts by community agencies, enhancing social cohesion, they conclude that the retreat of the government and corporate sectors strains community financial and human resources and weakens the local and regional nonprofit sector. Joseph Tindale and Erin MacLachlan also examine the specific effects of increased competition and reduced government funding in one area. They compare the experiences of three branches of the Victorian Order of Nurses as they expand their operations to include commercial activities. Luc Thériault and Sandra Salhani demonstrate how service delivery of two nonprofit homecare firms is affected by a more competitive and resource-constrained environment. All of the studies capture the resiliency of nonprofit organizations. But they also reveal the overwhelming strains placed on many organizations and communities as they struggle to adapt to a changing and more competitive environment.

A third, recurring theme is the state of volunteerism in Canada. While studies indicate that Canada has less cause for concern as a whole than the US in this regard (Jueds 1994, p. 120; Cowan 1997, p. 194; Putnam 2000, pp. 247-65; Febbraro 1999; Barnard 1998, pp. 14-24, 244-47), some fault lines are evident. Volunteers and leaders within organizations are often seen as overutilized and underpaid. As agencies strain to meet the increasing demands placed upon them for services while financial resources remain constrained, the workers and volunteers in the sector must absorb the impact of the shortfall. The long-term effects of this tension on the rate and nature of volunteerism may weaken the ability of the sector to continue to meet the needs of Canadians, let alone serve them better. An understanding of the effects of sector organizations providing services to Canadians in a competitive and resource-limited environment, is important to beginning to appreciate the long-term health of the sector.

The studies in this book highlight different facets of the volunteer experience in Canada. The Thériault and Salhani chapter offers insight into the pressures confronting both front-line service delivery agents as well as executive directors as they struggle to carry out their agencies' missions. Tindale and MacLachlan portray the challenges facing managers of nonprofit organizations as they attempt to transform their agencies to deal with new market realities. Juillet *et al.* demonstrate the pressures toward professionalism and the effects on agency personnel. Mitchell *et al.* capture, in disturbing detail, the heavy demands on capable individuals in smaller communities and the need to support volunteer efforts if agencies are to function effectively. Implicit in the Quarter study is an understanding of the variety of experiences facing volunteers in organizations operating in the social economy. Rice, Sheehan, Brown and Cuff sketch the real way that volunteers touch the lives of people in need and underscore the importance of developing processes to bring individuals and communities together in strengthening social capital.

The studies presented here contribute to a limited but growing literature on the nonprofit sector in Canada. They offer rich insights into the experiences of individuals and organizations at the community and national levels as they adapt to a changing environment. The International Year of the Volunteer, the Moving Forward Working Group, and the Voluntary Sector Initiative point to the need for a better understanding of the strengths, weaknesses and challenges facing nonprofit organizations and volunteers in Canada. These studies are intended to contribute to that goal.

Notes

[1]This section is based on information provided at <http://www.volunteer.ca/volunteer/celebrate_iyv.htm>.

[2]This discussion is based upon informal conversations with participants and especially documents provided by the federal government, National Voluntary Organisations, Voluntary Sector Roundtables and the Canadian Centre for Philanthropy at the following websites: <http://www.pco-bcp.gc.ca/volunteer/reports/>, <http://www.nvo-onb.ca/main-e.html>, <http://www.vsr-trsb.web.net/vsr-trsb, http://www.ccp.ca/>.

References

Barnard, R. 1998. *Chips & Pop: Decoding the Nexus Generation*. Toronto: Malcolm Lester Books.

Barlow, M. and B. Campbell. 1995. *Straight through the Heart: How the Liberals Abandoned the Just Society*. Toronto: HarperCollins.

Brock, K. 2001. "Executive Federalism in Canada: A Public Forum?" in *Federalism in India and Canada: A Comparative Study in History and Politics*, ed. R. Saxena. New Delhi: Indian Council of Historical Research.

Bryden, J. 1996. *MP's Report: Canada's Charities – A Need for Reform*. Ottawa: House of Commons.

Cairns, A. 1995. "The Embedded State: State-Society Relations in Canada," in *Reconfigurations: Canadian Citizenship and Constitutional Change*. Toronto: McClelland & Stewart.

Caldwell, G. and P. Reed. 1999."Civic Participation in Canada," *Inroads*, 8:215-22.

Canada. Voluntary Sector Task Force. 2000. *Partnering for the Benefit of Canadians: Government of Canada – Voluntary Sector Initiative*. Ottawa: Privy Council Office.

Chisholm, L.B. 1995. "Accountability of Nonprofit Organizations and Those Who Control Them: The Legal Framework," *Nonprofit Managemnt and Leadership*, 6(2):141-56.

Clark, J. 1995. "The State, Popular Participation, and the Voluntary Sector," *World Development*, 23(4):593-601.

Cowan, J.J. 1997. "The War Against Apathy: Four Lessons from the Front Lines of Youth Advocacy," *National Civic Review*, 86(3):193-210.

Ekos Research Associates Inc. 1998. "Public Opinion Environment," in *Lessons Learned on Partnerships: Final Report*. Ottawa: Voluntary Sector Roundtable, pp. 1-4. <http://www.web.net/vsr-trsb/publications/ekosoc98/public_opinion.html>.

Elshtain, J.B. 1997. "The Decline of Democratic Faith," in *Competing Visions: The Nonprofit Sector in the Twenty-First Century*, ed. A.J. Abramson. Washington, DC: The Aspen Institute.

Febbraro, A. 1999. *Encouraging Volunteering Among Ontario Youth*. NSGVP Online. Available at: <http://www.nsgvp.org/n-r2o-1.htm>.

Gidron, B., R. Kramer and L. Salamon. 1992. "Government and the Third Sector in Comparative Perspective: Allies or Adversaries?" in *Government and the Third Sector: Emerging Relationships in Welfare States*, ed. B. Gidron, R. Kramer and L. Salmon. San Francisco: Jossey Bass.

Graves, F.L. 1997. "Options for the Third Sector: Civic Virtue or Discount Government?" in *Filling the Gap: What Can Canada's 'Third Sector' Deliver as Governments Cut Back?* Kingston: Public Policy Forum.

Hall, M. and K.G. Banting. 1999. "The Nonprofit Sector in Canada: An Introduction," in *The Nonprofit Sector in Canada*, ed. K.G. Banting and M. Hall. Montreal and Kingston: School of Policy Studies, Queen's University and McGill-Queen's University Press.

Hall, M. and P. Reed. 1998. "Shifting the Burden: How Much Can Government Download to the Non-Profit Sector?" *Canadian Public Administration*, 41(1):1-20.

Hudson, P. 1999. "The Voluntary Sector, The State and Citizenship in the U.K.," in *Citizens or Consumers: Social Policy in a Market Society*, ed. D. Broad and W. Antony. Halifax: Fernwood.

Joint Tables. 1999. *Working Together: A Government of Canada/Voluntary Sector Joint Initiative*. Ottawa: Privy Council Office.

Jueds, V. 1994. "From Statistics to Soup Kitchens: Youth as Resources in the 1990s." *National Civic Review*, 83(Spring/Summer):120-24.

Juneau, C. 1998. "Revenue Canada Practices and Procedures Affecting Charities," in *Report of the Proceedings of the Forty-Ninth Tax Conference*. Toronto: Canadian Tax Foundation.

Kroeger, A. 2000 "The HRD Affair: Reflections on Accountability in Government." Address to the Canadian Club of Ottawa, 12 December.

Liberal Party of Canada. 1997. *Securing Our Future Together*. Ottawa: Liberal Party of Canada.

Macintosh, T., ed. 2000. *Federalism, Democracy and Labour Market Policy in Canada.* Kingston and Montreal: School of Policy Studies, Queen's University and McGill-Queen's University Press.

Mansbridge, J. 1998. "On the Contested Nature of the Public Good," in *Private Action and the Public Good*, ed. W.W. Powell and E.S. Clemens. New Haven: Yale University Press.

Miller, C. 1999. "Tough Questions Avoided: The Broadbent Report on the Voluntary Sector," *Policy Options*, 20(8):75-79.

Monahan, P.J. 2000. "Federal Regulation of Charities: A Critical Assessment of Recent Proposals for Legislative and Regulatory Reform," supported by the Kahanoff Foundation Nonprofit Sector Research Initiative.

Ontario Law Reform Commission (OLRC), 1996. *Report on the Law of Charities.* Toronto: Ontario Law Reform Commission.

Panel on Accountability and Governance for the Voluntary Sector (PAGVS). 1999. *Building on Strength: Improving Governance and Accountability in Canada's Voluntary Sector.* Ottawa: PAGVS.

Putnam, R.D. 1996. *The Decline of Civil Society: How Come? So What?* Ottawa: Canadian Centre for Management Development.

_____ 2000. *Bowling Alone: The Collapse and Revival of American Community.* New York: Simon and Schuster.

Rekart, J. 1993. *Public Funds, Private Provision: The Role of the Voluntary Sector.* Vancouver: University of British Columbia Press.

Sharpe, A. and R. Haddow, eds. 1997. *Social Partnerships for Training.* Kingston: School of Policy Studies, Queen's University.

Stewart, W. 1996. *The Charity Game: Greed, Waste and Fraud in Canada's $86 Billion-a-Year Compassion Industry.* Toronto: Douglas and McIntyre.

2

The Impact of Changes in the Funding Environment on Nonprofit Organizations

Luc Juillet, Caroline Andrew, Tim Aubry and Janet Mrenica
with the assistance of Christine Holke

Our recent political history, marked by the restructuring of state bureaucracies and their retrenchment from many areas of social intervention, has fuelled a growing debate about the proper role and contribution of nonprofit organizations to the workings of contemporary industrial societies. As nonprofit organizations are increasingly perceived as fulfilling crucial needs which cannot be met by the market and are no longer properly assured by the state, concerns about their ability to meet emerging social challenges successfully have been aired. Their ability to fulfill their mandates while maintaining their autonomy with respect to government in the midst of a turbulent and changing funding environment is being questioned (Browne 1996; Jenson and Phillips 1996).

The changing nature of the funding environment of the nonprofit sector lies at the heart of these emerging concerns. Facing a growing demand for their services, a larger number of nonprofit organizations must struggle to survive in a more competitive and changing funding environment. Moreover, as governments come to see them as an integral part of their networks of service delivery, nonprofit organizations receiving state support can also increasingly be asked to conform to modes of operation and public accountability consistent with the norms and priorities of state bureaucracies. In this new funding environment, many critics and analysts fear that, whether they are forced to compete in the market or submit to greater controls by government departments which partly fund them, nonprofit organizations are being profoundly transformed.

This chapter investigates the impact of funding practices on the nonprofit sector. We have studied the recent past of eight national nonprofit organizations from four different sectors in order to determine the impact that the changing funding environment has had on their organizational development. In order to study the aggregate impact on organizations, we examine more specifically three dimensions of the relationship between funding and organizational life. We investigated the impact that changes in funding practices have had on the way organizations maintain their mission, govern themselves, and deliver their programs. The results of our research suggest the need for some caution in thinking about the impact of the recent trends in funding. While the organizations examined experienced significant funding changes, such as a shift from core to project funding or partial cutbacks, they have also demonstrated a significant degree of resilience, showing an ability to adapt to environmental changes while remaining true to their missions. In sum, our study suggests that the dramatic view of a wholesale transformation of the third sector due to a changing funding environment is overstated.

The chapter is divided into five sections. In the next section, we briefly set the stage by discussing the changing nature of the funding environment and describing some of the prevalent hypotheses found in the academic literature on its perceived impact on nonprofit organizations. We then describe the methodology of the study. The third section provides a brief analysis of the funding trends experienced by the eight participating organizations. The following section then provides, in turn, an analysis of our results concerning the impact of funding trends on the missions of the organizations, their governance, and their program delivery. We end with a broader concluding section addressing the overall picture which emerges from the experience of the eight organizations.

FINANCIAL DEPENDENCY AND THE NONPROFIT SECTOR

How an organization finds the resources that it needs to operate its programs has an impact on most aspects of its operations and its development. Adequate resources constitute an absolute necessity for the successful fulfillment of organizational missions. And as such, even for organizations counting on the contribution of volunteers, the nature of sources of funding can have profound impacts on the way institutions structure themselves, make decisions and render accounts, deliver programs, and define their mission. Because it permeates almost all aspects of their operations, the generation and use of resources, including money, is an important structuring factor for agencies.

Because they realize its central influence on institutions, many analysts and activists of the nonprofit sector have been increasingly preoccupied with the problems associated with funding. Underlying a variety of hypotheses about the impact of changes in the nature and level of funding is the general concern that the increasingly competitive nature of their financial environment is fundamentally altering the nature of nonprofit organizations by forcing them to adopt modes of operation more akin to those found in the public and private sectors. As Herman and Heimovics point out, while those with extensive government contracts or reliance upon a few large foundation grants are especially dependent, all agencies depend on others for financial support and "a most important measure of effectiveness of the leadership of these organizations has to do with how successfully this dependency is handled" (Herman and Heimovics 1991, p. 68). The successful management of this general dependency on financial resources requires the ability to adapt to an ever-changing funding environment in order to assure an organization's survival and effectiveness while remaining true to its fundamental mission.

In this perspective, is the changing funding environment of today fundamentally or inevitably altering nonprofit organizations? Beyond the immediate (and important) concerns for an adequate level of funding, what are we to think about the broader impact of the changing funding environment on nonprofit organizations?

THE CHANGING FUNDING ENVIRONMENT

The *1997 National Survey of Giving, Volunteering and Participating* confirmed that registered charities, such as most nonprofit organizations actually depended significantly on government for their financial support. The study found that 57 percent of their revenues came from governments, mainly provincial.[1] Another 32 percent of their total revenues were provided by fees and commercial activities. Only a surprising 10 percent was actually derived from individual donations (Canadian Centre for Philanthropy, 1999). A meagre 1 percent was obtained from corporate donations (Canada. Clerk of the Privy Council 1999, pp. 3-4).

In this context of heavy reliance on government funding, it is easy to understand that much of the current concerns regarding the changing funding environment stem from the consequences of public sector restructuring in industrialized countries. Fiscal policies meant to curb public deficits and reduce the role of the state in society over the 1990s have led to significant reductions in public expenditures in many sectors. Given that in the early 1990s 14 percent of government spending was spent in supporting registered charities, these expenditures represented easy targets for budgetary cutbacks (Canadian Centre for Philanthropy 1995, p. 1). There is no doubt that, in some sectors, support for nonprofit organizations has simply fallen victim to departmental budget cuts, forcing them to engage in more commercial activities and/or struggle with reduced budgets (Browne 1996; Jenson and Phillips 1996).

But, more generally, changing governmental attitudes toward public services has been marked by a broader shift in approach in public management and program delivery. More emphasis is now placed on managerial flexibility, strategic and targeted programs, and efficiency. The emergence of this new public management and new approach to governance, in conjunction with growing budget constraints, has led governments and bureaucrats to seek to establish a new strategic relationship with the nonprofit sector (Canada. Privy Council Office, 1999*b*).

This recent restructuring of the public sector has placed significant emphasis on the importance of partnerships in pursuing the goals of public policy. Government departments have seen their workforce shrink and their roles transformed from being agents of delivery to becoming coordinators of program delivery. They increasingly see themselves as offering a strategic direction for intervention and coordinating large networks of private-public agents in the pursuit of identified objectives. In the context of this new governance, public organizations are increasingly conceived as operating within flexible networks that span the boundaries of the private, public, and voluntary sectors (Paquet 1999). In this new environment, the recognized role of nonprofit organizations in the governance of our societies has become more important and they are increasingly associated with the making of public policy and the delivery of services.[2]

The changing funding environment has contributed to changes in how nonprofit organizations relate to both the public and private sectors. With the explicit objective of exercising greater influence over the delivery of services by nonprofit agents, governments are shifting explicitly to a policy of project funding, simultaneously moving away from the core funding that has been the lifeblood of many organizations in the past. In order to ensure greater accountability for the expenditure of taxpayers' money, financial support is allegedly increasingly taking the form of detailed contractual agreements. And faced with the necessity to gain contracts and secure support for specific projects in order to survive, many nonprofit organizations must turn to the corporate sector and more generally learn to succeed in a more competitive funding environment. Others, faced with severe declines in core funding, must experiment with new forms of fundraising or risk commercial ventures in order to supplement previous funding sources.

These trends affect different nonprofit organizations to different extents; but they are unlikely to leave the sector unmarked. Given the structural importance of funding practices, these qualitative changes in the funding environment are susceptible to transforming many organizations. As such, these trends call for an examination of the nonprofit sector's responses to these changes. In recent years, such an examination has begun at least with the publication of reports by the sector itself on issues of accountability and advocacy (Panel on Accountability and Governance in the Voluntary Sector 1999). The federal government has also recently launched a process of research and consultation to examine a wide range of problems, including funding (Canada. Privy Council Office 1999*b, c*). However, the actual significance and impact of changing funding practices on nonprofit organizations remain underinvestigated in Canada, although they have been examined extensively in the academic literature of other countries.

CHANGING FUNDING ENVIRONMENT AND NONPROFIT ORGANIZATIONS: WORKING HYPOTHESES

Critics of the current trends in the funding of the nonprofit sector worry that emerging funding practices are altering nonprofit organizations in fundamental and negative ways. Historically rooted in community ties and in particular conceptions of civic engagement, many nonprofit organizations allegedly find themselves forced to alter their governance and service delivery practices as well as their mission to meet the requirements of funders who increasingly see them as mere service providers. Forced to compete in the economy of project funding, the argument goes, they must market themselves and their social contribution in business terms and adopt modes of operation that could be ill-adapted to their community roots. In sum, their dependence on external funding forces them to adapt to the changing funding environment in ways that can change (often for the worse) the very nature of their organizations.

A survey of recent literature suggests that changes in the nature and level of funding could impact their mission (particularly when political advocacy is involved), their governance practices, and their program delivery. First, in a more competitive funding environment, fearing cuts in funding, nonprofit organizations are allegedly driven to operationalize their missions through more politically neutral programs which deliver direct services. As a result, society loses important alternative voices and social agents committed to social change (Reading 1994; Abrams 1980). Other authors, such as Burton Weisbrod (1998), have argued that nonprofit missions are typically so vague and flexible that, in a changing funding environment, they enable unwarranted commercialization or they facilitate the pursuit of projects which are financially interesting but lead organizations away from their long-term objectives. In sum, it is hypothesized that the changing funding environment is leading nonprofit organizations away from their missions.

Regarding governance, the growth in contract and fee-for-service financing is also thought to be inducing many cultural and structural changes for nonprofit organizations. More formal accountability requirements and a new focus on "service to clients" and "project management" are likely to lead to greater emphasis on professionalism when hiring employees and recruiting board members. It can also lead to a move away from traditional democratic models of governance with boards made up of target populations and communities toward a more professional model where specialists oversee management (Knapp, Robertson and Thomason 1990, p. 212; Leat 1995). More simply, greater reliance on contract and project funding may result in a loss of control by boards as government contract officers and project sponsors become the main target of accountability (Salamon 1990, p. 231).

Third, the changing funding environment is also allegedly affecting the nonprofit agencies' approach to program delivery. The management of projects and contracts, as opposed to core funding, can lead many nonprofit organizations to devote a disproportionate amount of time and resources to meeting more extensive monitoring, reporting, and evaluation requirements. According to some authors, more formal accountability requirements associated with contract and project funding have also led nonprofit organizations to focus increasingly on performance measures, such as the unit price of their service (Knapp, Robertson and Thomason 1990, p. 212). Such a shift can result in less attention being paid to the quality of service and its social purpose; and it can lead to the reorientation of an agency's mission toward activities that are easier to quantify and where success is more likely (James 1989; Weisbrod 1998; Ware 1989). Moreover, constrained by established control mechanisms and with minimal core funding, organizations are also left with less room for risk-taking and innovation in service delivery (Forder and Knapp 1993). However, it can be argued that increased accountability in the not-for-profit sector will produce programs that are more effective because of the use of evaluation in their development and improvement.

These potential impacts on nonprofit agencies are matters of concern for Canadian society. In a recent speech to the Canadian Leaders' Forum on the Voluntary Sector, Mel Cappe, the clerk of the privy council and the head of the public service, admitted that the federal government faced the challenge of re-examining its approach to funding nonprofit organizations. According to him, the public service lacks adequate information about the consequences of its funding choices on nonprofit organizations, especially its admitted preference for project funding over core funding (Canada. Clerk of the Privy Council 1999). These issues are currently being addressed by joint task forces looking at the future of the voluntary sector in Canada. The public service is expecting that the results of these task forces will, among other things, lead to a more stable funding environment for nonprofit organizations. It is with the hope of contributing to this emerging debate that this exploratory study investigated how the changing funding environment during the 1990s affected the mission, governance, and program activities of eight national nonprofit institutions working in different sectors.

METHODOLOGY

Design

The methodology for the study involved in-depth case analyses of the changing funding environment faced by eight national nonprofit organizations drawn from the sectors of (i) environmental protection, (ii) health and social services, (iii) international development, and (iv) women's issues. The period of study of these organizations was 1993–98. Data collection for case analyses included an examination of documents followed by a small number of in-depth interviews with knowledgeable persons representing key stakeholder groups in each of these organizations. Information emerging from case analyses was studied in order to develop an integrated summary of the impact of the changing funding environment on mission, governance, and program delivery of the eight agencies.

Sample

A non-random sample of national nonprofit organizations was chosen for the study. The main eligibility criterion for an agency to qualify for the study was that its mission fell within one of the areas of environmental protection, health and social services, international development, or women's issues. Two organizations were sampled from each of these sectors. Some attempt was also made to sample institutions within each of the sectors that had different patterns of funding sources and that had undergone different experiences with respect to funding during the five-year period of the study. Although the sampling was not random or representative in terms of actual organizations in the different sectors, it was hoped that selecting eight agencies across four sectors would provide a window on the diverse responses of national nonprofit organizations to the changing funding environment during the 1990s. Institutions participating in the study are presented next according to the sector they represent.

Environment. The Canadian Environmental Network (CEN) is a national nonprofit organization with a mandate to assist the organizational capacity of the Canadian environmental movement. CEN serves as a networking agent helping to connect and coordinate the efforts of environmental agencies across Canada. CEN has relied heavily on funding received through a contribution agreement with Environment Canada. Other funding is obtained through contracts with members of its network (i.e., government departments and environmental agencies), membership fees, and the sale of publications.

The Canadian Nature Federation (CNF) is a national non-governmental organization with a mission to promote the conservation of Canada's natural environment through public education, advocacy, and conservation programs. The funding of CNF is derived from multiple sources including contract funding from corporations and foundations as well as public donations, partly obtained through telemarketing.

Health and Social Services. The Canadian Mental Health Association (CMHA)-National is a national nonprofit organization dedicated to promoting mental health through training, public education, advocacy, and research. CMHA-National accomplishes its mission by working collaboratively with provincial- and regional-level offices located across Canada. A major portion of CMHA-National's funding is provided by federal government ministries (e.g., Health Canada, Human Resources Development Canada) in return for developing and delivering specific national mental health programs. CMHA-National also relies on funding collected through memberships, private and corporate donations, and the sale of publications.

The Canadian Council on Social Development (CCSD) is a national nonprofit institution whose mission is to contribute to the development of progressive social policies through research, public education, and advocacy. The funding of CCSD originates from multiple sources, including research contracts, membership fees, publications, and donations.

International Development. The Canadian University Services Overseas (CUSO) is a Canadian non-governmental organization which promotes global social justice by sharing information and human and material resources through programs that send volunteers to developing countries. The large majority of CUSO's funding is provided by the Canadian International Development Agency (CIDA).

OXFAM is a Canadian non-governmental organization whose mission is to assist developing countries to address poverty, underdevelopment, and social injustice through educational and community development initiatives. Funding for OXFAM originates largely from two sources, namely CIDA and donations from the general public.

Women's Issues. The Canadian Research Institute for the Advancement of Women (CRIAW) is a national membership-based organization that coordinates and conducts research intended to advance women's equality in Canadian society. CRIAW is heavily dependent on funding from Status of Women Canada. This funding is supplemented by a small amount of revenue generated by memberships fees and the sale of publications. Funding received by CRIAW from Status of Women Canada has been converted recently from a block grant to funding tied to specific projects.

The National Council of Women of Canada (NCWC) is a federation of local and provincial councils of women intended to improve the quality of life of women, families, and society through education and advocacy. NCWC relied heavily on funding from Status of Women Canada for much of the 1990s. However, this funding was eliminated in 1998–99 and NCWC now relies on funding from its own foundation and from membership fees.

Sources of Information

Data for the study were collected by reviewing documents followed by structured interviews of a small number of staff and board members in each of the organizations. The following set of documents was requested for review from each of the organizations:

- Operational budget in its complete form
- Audited financial statements for the period 1993–98
- Organigrams
- Strategic planning documents
- Program delivery documents
- Program evaluation reports
- Annual reports for the period 1993–98

In addition, if deemed necessary for understanding an organization, researchers examined board minutes, management minutes, and any minutes from organizational planning days.

Structured interviews were conducted with key board and staff members. At least one board member and one staff member were interviewed from each organization. The choice of interviewees for the study was coordinated by the staff member in each of the organizations with the responsibility of assisting the research team with the study. The interview protocol was designed by the research team to obtain information, through open-ended questions, about funding patterns, organizational changes, and the specific impact of the funding environment on the organization's mission, governance, and program delivery during the 1990s. A copy of the interview protocol is provided in Appendix 1.

Procedure

Organizations were initially contacted by telephone to be informed about the study and invited to participate. This contact was followed up by a letter providing further information about the study, including the demands and benefits associated with participation. Information meetings were held with agencies agreeing to participate in order to discuss the study further and determine what benefits they would like to derive from their participation.

Documents obtained from organizations were initially reviewed with the intent of becoming knowledgeable about the nature of funding patterns and sources, the organization's mission, governance, and programs. A summary of each of the participating organization's finances for the period

1993–98 was developed in a spreadsheet, detailing a breakdown of revenues. An examination of these spreadsheets enabled the researchers to determine and identify any trends in financing during the period under study. Subsequent to the review of documents and development of summary spreadsheets, structured interviews were conducted. These were conducted either in person or by telephone and ranged from 60 to 120 minutes long. In total, 24 individuals were interviewed on a "not-for-direct attribution" basis.

A case analysis of each organization was developed from the information that emerged from the review of documents and interviews. Drafts of case analyses were shared with participating organizations to ensure the accuracy of their content. Case analyses formed the raw data from which an integrated summary of the impact of financial dependency across agencies was developed. Participating organizations were sent a copy of the study's final report. In addition, a meeting was set up with interested, participating agencies in order to discuss the findings.

RESULTS

The Impact of the Changing Funding Environment on Nonprofit Organizations

The eight organizations under review are primarily service organizations, and between them have experienced fluctuating, rather than stable, levels of funding in the following categories: individual donations, government grants and contributions, corporate support, income from commercial retail ventures, fee-for-service contract work, as well as income from membership fees and miscellaneous sources of funding. Each has survived these fluctuating levels of funding.

Table 1 presents the evolution of total revenues for the eight organizations during the five-year period under study (1993–98). The Canadian Nature Federation has more than doubled its revenues from 1993 to 1998. Three organizations (CEN, OXFAM, CMHA) experienced some fluctuations over the period but emerged in 1998 as having more or less the same income as in 1993. Four organizations (CCSD, CUSO, CRIAW, NCWC)

Table 1: Total Revenues of Nonprofit Organizations, 1993–98

Organization	1993 $	1994 $	1995 $	1996 $	1997 $	1998 $
OXFAM	10,814,422	11,151,185	10,825,637	12,478,131	11,105,236	11,775,244
CUSO	30,983,000	30,424,000	27,525,000	23,947,000	23,515,000	25,187,000
CEN	1,395,168	1,239,866	1,117,118	1,148,090	1,498,302	–
CNF	1,039,682	1,317,736	1,148,546	1,612,986	2,219,181	2,502,136
NCW	–	469,624	164,956	126,582	123,585	197,068
CRIAW	427,142	334,039	350,840	340,486	338,748	312,637
CCSD	2,152,933	1,816,735	1,816,626	1,517,918	1,777,663	1,672,377
CMHA	943,002	820,149	805,966	825,631	734,291	988,019

had less revenue available in 1998 when compared to their situations in 1993. The National Council of Women of Canada experienced the largest drop in income with 1998 revenues being less than half (42 percent) of that in 1994. Overall, the picture reflects a resiliency in funding for most of the organizations but with a trend toward less total funding being available for our sample of nonprofit organizations.

Figure 1 presents proportion (percent) comparisons of the years 1993 and 1998 in each organization for major categories of funding. No clear pattern emerges across the organizations in these comparisons. Three organizations (CEN, OXFAM, CRIAW) experienced relatively stable amounts of funding from the federal government in 1993 and 1998 relative to their total revenues. Although CRIAW felt a decrease in absolute dollars from federal government grants over the 1993–98 period, the share of its total revenue for this category was 80 percent in 1998 and 73 percent in 1993. This is consistent with CRIAW's overall decrease in revenues during the 1993–98 period. Contributions from the federal government decreased for

Figure 1: Comparison of Revenue Sources, 1993 versus 1998

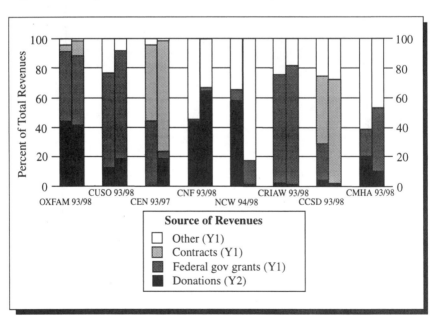

CUSO with this funding category making up 65 percent of total revenue in 1993 and 47 percent of total revenue in 1998.

Two organizations (CEN, CCSD) showed significant growth in generating revenue through contracts when comparing 1997 (CEN) or 1998 (CCSD) to 1993. CCSD generated 70 percent of its revenue in 1998 from research contracts mostly with the federal government compared to only 46 percent of its revenue in 1993. This change is in line with CCSD's organizational strategy of replacing lost block-grant revenues from the federal government with research contract revenues. CEN also experienced much less revenue from federal government grants in 1997 compared to 1993. CNF had significant growth in revenue generated through donations. Public donations made up 65 percent of its total revenue in 1998 compared to 44 percent during the 1993–98 period. The increase in donations accounts largely for the organization's significant increase in its revenues over the period. It appears that 1993 was anomalous for public donations for NCW as levels in 1994–97 are more comparable to 1998 than to 1993. CMHA also experienced a drop in public donations relative to its total revenue, with these accounting for 20 percent of total revenues in 1993 and only 11 percent in 1998.

Government Funding

All eight organizations in the study received some form of government funding throughout the five-year period. In the case of the Canadian Nature Federation, contract work for government agencies has regularly been part of their activities. However, the organization has never depended significantly on government funding. And, as a percentage of its total budget, the amount of government funding received by CNF during the period under review has actually decreased.[3] Another organization, the National Council of Women, also received minimal funding from the government, although the share of government funding in its overall budget has increased over the period.

In contrast, the remaining six organizations were given more significant government funding during the period under review, measured as a percentage of their overall budget. For most of these organizations, government funding represented a large majority of their total cash receipts in 1998. A few, such as CMHA, were more moderately dependent on government funding, but the share of government monies in their total budgets still amounted to close to 50 percent. Each of these six organizations experienced reductions in government money within key agreements during the period under review.

The organizations reported the following significant changes in government funding during the 1990s: (i) reduction in grant funding of existing programs; (ii) the move from long-term funding (program support) to short-term funding (project support); (iii) a shift from grant funding to contribution funding; (iv) increased last-minute approvals of funding by government agencies providing uncertainty in organizations' financial stability; and (v) increasing requirements tied to funding, such as accounting for volunteer contributions.

Of the four organizations receiving grant funding from the federal government, three saw their level reduced and increased efforts are now required to keep the grants. The fourth, CCSD, lost its grant funding in 1994 and has restructured itself to raise a variety of sources of contribution funding for research contracts.

During the 1990s, the federal policy regarding support for the voluntary sector also changed from a preference for grants to contribution funding. Whereas grant funding could cover all core operating costs, contribution funding provides some allowance for administrative costs, but the bulk of the funding is generally targeted to the delivery of specific programs. For affected organizations, this policy change left them with two options. They could either increase their efforts to obtain contribution funding[4] or reduce their overhead costs, cutting back on core administrative support. In our sample, among the organizations in receipt of regular government funding, all but one have tried one or the other strategies.

Last minute approvals by government agencies can also create difficulties for nonprofit organizations. This practice requires these agencies to have the flexibility to contract and expand with minimal notice. These unexpected changes can cause hardship due to short-term increases or reductions in some areas. Among the eight institutions, some nevertheless succeeded in alleviating these problems by adopting offsetting practices, such as obtaining bridge financing from financial institutions.

Among increasing requirements imposed by government agencies, we find new cost-sharing requirements, tying funding directly to services provided, more extensive requirements for gathering information, and more narrowly defined organizational priorities eligible for funding. Moreover, as OXFAM's experience illustrates, although the overall level of government funding can remain stable, the same total funding level can be tied to the delivery of an increased number of projects. In this case, this situation affected the organization by increasing its administrative burden associated with reporting requirements, leaving programming activities to suffer.

Charitable Organizations

Seven of the eight agencies are registered charitable organizations which have nurtured and maintained fundraising programs. In the case of CEN, the organization tried to obtain recognition of charitable status but was not successful. The size of these programs varied greatly among the institutions in the study, with the focus being mostly on individual donors rather than corporate donors. Due to the changing funding environment, there have been increased fundraising activities undertaken by the agencies in the study. The maintenance and expansion of such fundraising programs have resulted in an increased need and use of resources, and therefore higher cost in the short term coupled with uncertainty as to achieving desired results.

Revenues from individual donations declined in absolute dollars for five (CCSD, CRIAW, CUSO, CMHA, NCW) of the eight organizations. For the cases where fundraising costs can be partitioned from other administrative costs, the loss in donations was accompanied by a (less than proportional) decrease in fundraising costs. In speaking about their public fundraising programs, organizations identified (i) the sophistication of fundraising programs needed in order to reach potential donors, (ii) the need to develop and maintain a database on existing and potential donors in order to sustain a constant donation flow, and (iii) the need to respond to individual donor inquiries as being particular factors increasing the resource requirements of these programs.

Commercialization

As government and donation revenues have decreased in absolute dollars, nonprofit organizations have looked to other means for additional revenue sources, namely in areas traditionally reserved for the commercial sector.

In its broadest form, commercialization incorporates revenues from sales and fees.[5] Using this simple definition, all eight of the organizations under review have some direct commercial activity. These revenue sources include sales of merchandise and fees for membership and conferences. Of the eight organizations, five (CCSD, CEN, CNF, CUSO, OXFAM) also generated some of their revenues by contracting their services to clients.

Three of the organizations (CNF, OXFAM, CUSO) also established separate incorporated structures as commercial ventures, such as a bookstore, which can be interpreted to be the purest form of commercialization of the sector. However, the commercial ventures of two of these organizations, CNF and OXFAM, both in the retail market, actually contributed to the financial difficulties of their parent organizations by generating deficits. Both organizations no longer support these ventures. The third organization, CUSO, has not yet begun the operation of its enterprise.

After this brief analysis of the financial situation of the eight organizations over the period reviewed, we now examine the impact that the changes in funding had on their mission, governance, and program delivery.

IMPACT OF THE CHANGING FUNDING ENVIRONMENT ON THE CAPACITY OF NONPROFIT ORGANIZATIONS TO MAINTAIN AND DEVELOP THEIR MISSIONS

In thinking about the interrelationship of funding and the mission of the organizations studied, one can reflect on the ways in which the mission was influenced by the funding context, but also about the ways in which the mission had an influence on how the organizations reacted to the changing funding context.

It might have been assumed that such a changed funding context would have led to dramatic shifts in organizational missions. However, such was not the case. The missions of the organizations studied showed little or no change over the period reviewed. One of the few examples of noteworthy change was CEN's decision to add education to their objectives. The change was undertaken for the explicit purpose of gaining charitable status. Since the attempt was unsuccessful, there is now a move by CEN to remove education from its mission. CRIAW added "initiate" to the list of activities it would undertake in relation to research, but this is not a major change of focus but rather the addition of another type of research activity. Finally, CNF added a statement in its mission about financial stability.

In *To Profit or Not to Profit*, Burton Weisbrod provides an interpretation of the stability of missions even in the face of financial uncertainty in his analysis of what he calls "mission vagueness." His argument is that many, if not most, nonprofit organizations define their mission in such broad terms that it can accommodate a wide diversity of activities. However, at the same time, these mission statements offer very few guidelines from which to relate revenue-generating activities to mission. Interested by the commercialization of the nonprofit sector, Weisbrod's argument is that "mission vagueness" has meant that the missions of nonprofit agencies do not act as deterrents to commercialization since almost any activity can be justified given their very general mandate.

> As our research proceeded, it became increasingly apparent that mission vagueness is fundamentally important in predicting and evaluating nonprofit organization behaviour. It makes the operational definition of an "unrelated" business activity inherently problematic; it explains why nonprofits can undertake an ever widening array of revenue-enhancing activities that the organization can argue are related to mission, and that the IRS finds difficult to term "unrelated" and, hence, taxable. Mission vagueness permits managers and trustees to alter behaviour in response to changing financial constraints while — at least arguably — continuing pursuit of the same goals. Means and ends are easily confused when goals are vague, and the wider the scope of mission, the greater is the challenge to organization leadership, prospective donors, and regulations to determine whether a profitable activity is mission related (Weisbrod 1998, p. 290).

However, as Weisbrod points out, it is often difficult to distinguish between vagueness of mission and flexibility of resource use. Drawing this distinction is nevertheless important in order to predict the responses of nonprofit agencies to exogenous changes in regulatory, financial, and technological constraints, and to assess their accomplishments in achieving their goals (ibid.).

Weisbrod's analysis suggests that we can review our case studies by examining the mission vagueness of the organizations and by seeing how it is related to the extent and growth of a variety of forms of revenue-generating activity. Regarding mission vagueness, it seems possible to put our agencies into two groups: one with missions framed in vague terms and the other with mission statements that are specific, at least in terms of undertaken activities.

Table 2: The Mission Statements of Organizations

Organizations with **Vague** Missions	Organizations with **Specific** Missions
OXFAM "Committed to the equitable distribution of wealth and power through fundamental social change."	CFN "Dedicated to promoting the conservation of Canada's natural environment (fauna and flora) through education programs, advocacy and conservation initiatives."
CUS CUSO "Supports alliances for the promotion of global social justice and works with people striving for freedom, self-determination, gender and racial equality and cultural survival."	CEN "Dedicated to building the organisational capacity of the Canadian environmental movement."
NCWC "Empower all women to work towards improving the quality of life for women, families and societies through a forum of member organisations and individuals."	CRIAW "Encourage, communicate, co-ordinate and initiate research in order to advance women's equality in Canada."
CMHA "Exists to promote the mental health of all people."	CCSD "Develop and promote progressive social policies inspired by social justice, equality and empowerment of individuals and communities through research, consultation, public education and advocacy."

The main element that characterizes the vagueness of mission statements is that the last four comprise some description of the selected methods of intervention whereas the first four do not. We can therefore divide the organizations into two groups, the vague (1–4) and the more specific (5–8). The sector of the organization would seem to play a role here, at least half our cases, the two international development agencies having very general missions and the environmental organizations being at the less general end of the ranking. Organizations representing the women's and health and social service sectors had representation in each of the two types of missions.

Having established this grouping, it is interesting to see to what extent Weisbrod's hypothesis is borne out by our organizations, by seeing whether those organizations with the highest mission vagueness have moved more easily into the diversification of their revenue-generating activities. It is, of course, important to be aware of the limitations of our analysis and therefore, of our ability to "test" Weisbrod's hypothesis. First of all, as we have stated earlier, the explicit commercialization of activities, understood in its purest form in our agencies was both limited and unsuccessful. On the other hand, there has clearly been a diversification of revenue-generating activities which does in fact lead the organizations studied into operations fairly similar to those found in the private sector. A rigorous testing is clearly beyond the possibilities of this study, but even a more descriptive examination requires a somewhat subjective evaluation about the degrees of changing funding strategies, what constitutes profitable activities, and whether the fact that the profitable activities were unsuccessful should be taken into account. CRIAW, CEN, NCWC, and possibly CUSO would seem to be on the low end in terms of the diversification of revenue-generating activities, whereas OXFAM, CMHA, CCSD, and CNF would appear to have more actively moved in the direction of diversification. The four organizations with the most generally formulated missions divide in two: two are on the low end of the diversification of revenue-generating activities and two are on the high end. The following diagram illustrates that the specific formulation of Weisbrod's hypothesis is not borne out by our organizations.

Table 3: Mission Vagueness and Diversification of Activities

Mission Statement	Diversification of Activities		By Sector	
Less Vagueness	**Less** CEN CRIAW	**More** CCSD CNF	Environment Women's Issues	Health and Social Services Environment
More Vagueness	CUSO NCWC	Oxfam CMHA	International Development Women's Issues	International Development Health and Social Services

The clearest link would seem to be by sector rather than by mission vagueness; women's groups have moved less into diversified revenue-generating activities and social welfare groups have done so to a greater extent. But a precise link between degree of mission vagueness and movement into diversified activities is not apparent. However, this does not mean that Weisbrod's overall analysis of mission vagueness is not useful to our understanding of our organizations. By linking the generalness of missions and their stability with what can either be seen as flexibility in reacting to new circumstances or a desire not to articulate the mission in ways that are measurable, Weisbrod's analysis allows us to think of mission stability not as a passive reaction to external change, but as a particular form of organizational adaptation.

Mission vagueness can be seen as a tool of resilience or as a lack of direction. It remains true that the organizations studied have generally worded mission statements and that these missions remained remarkably unchanged throughout the period studied, despite the changes in the funding environment. Where changes were made to the missions, they did tend to relate to the funding question. For instance, the CNF amended its mission statement in 1996 to add "To achieve our overall mission, the CNF will develop and maintain a strong financial base to ensure continuity of operations, organizational viability, and an active presence within Canada." However, these changes were made in the direction of mission stability and continued mission vagueness. Our agencies do seem to conform to Weisbrod's analysis in that the generality of their missions certainly did not prevent the organizations taking on new activities and, indeed, facilitated this process. By allowing any and all activities to be seen as compatible with the mission of the organization, diversification of activities, often related to a search for new sources of funding, was not seen as causing problems for the direction of the organization.

We could even ask whether mission vagueness could actually have contributed to a lack of direction in the organizations. Certainly one of the strong hypotheses in the literature on grass-roots organizations is that contact with the state and particularly with state funding leads to the de-radicalization of the groups, to a service orientation denuded of ideological commitment. If mission vagueness allows and encourages the diversification of activities, does this not mean that it would allow, and, indeed, facilitate development of service activities and therefore depoliticize the groups? On the one hand, this point of view is compatible with authors such as Lamoureux (1997), who dichotomize political advocacy and service delivery. State funding leads to service delivery and therefore to the lessening of advocacy. On the other hand, other authors, such as Masson (1998, 1999), argue that service delivery is not necessarily incompatible with advocacy and/or ideological commitment and that the two must be investigated separately.

How do our findings relate to these different positions? How do mission vagueness and the diversification of activities relate to the importance of advocacy activities and the sense of the importance of a commitment to social change within the organizations? Before directly answering these questions, it is important to recognize that the overall context for advocacy and a commitment to social change is increasingly difficult. Jenson and Phillips have clearly described some of the complex, and at least partially contradictory, pressures on the relations between state and nonprofit organizations visible in what they see as a regime shift:

> The devolution of service delivery means that the state will need the third sector more than ever. Nonetheless, the discourses and practices which delegitimize advocacy as the expression of "special interests" make it more difficult for groups to function. They have always been advocates, intervening to claim programs and policies which they deem necessary. Moreover, those groups are also the basis for civic engagement; by encouraging individual participation, they contribute to the development of communities and civil society. They cannot easily separate their activities to become simply the service providers the government seems to want. Moreover, funding cuts, threats to their existence and assaults against their legitimacy, as well as the difficult financial times, have already stretched them to the limit. The anti-interest discourse and enthusiasm for removing the so-called "public trough" may undercut the third sector's capacity to perform these new roles and deliver services by damaging its credibility and institutional capacity. The current assumption in government is that groups will respond to government priorities and, as the state downsizes, the third sector will pick up the slack. This assumption may be misplaced. The mismatch in the expectations of citizens and the state has not yet been eliminated (Jenson and Phillips 1996, p. 129).

This quotation does remind us of several of the major parameters of the changed context in which our groups function. "Special interests" have been attacked strongly, undermining the sense of legitimacy of advocating measures of social change. Governments have tended to want service delivery to the exclusion of all other kinds of activities. The organizations are doing things that clearly governments no longer want to do. Interestingly, there are recent declarations that seem to recognize the need to re-examine certain elements of the state-nonprofit relationship. For instance, a May 1999 speech by the clerk of the privy council, Mel Cappe, entitled "Building a New Relationship with the Voluntary Sector," states: "We also need to be aware of the long-term impact that our current preference for project versus core funding is having on the sector's capacity. So one of the challenges we face is to re-examine our approach to funding" (Canada. Clerk of the Privy Council 1999) This quote increases the sense of an unstable environment. The context within which our organizations function has changed dramatically within the last ten years and it is still changing.

Having established the difficulties of comparing the role of advocacy within our agencies over the recent past, we return to our results and the ways in which activity diversification, service delivery, and advocacy are interrelated. In a number of cases, there has been increasing emphasis on service delivery (CCSD, CMHA, CNF, OXFAM) but does this mean that commitment to social change has been reduced? This is not so clear. For example, CNF maintains an objective of lobbying despite a recognition that this activity does not increase revenues (and can even make it difficult to raise funds from some sources). CCSD recognizes the necessity to be financially self-sustaining, but argues that it can influence public policy and public opinion through doing quality research and making sure the results of that research are widely accessible. The NCWC tries to develop a sustainable financial base but always within the context of maintaining its autonomy so as to be able to lobby the government for the kind of measures the organization feels will improve the lives of Canadian women.

Advocacy activities have not increased in the studied agencies for the period examined, but neither have they disappeared. If mission vagueness has facilitated the diversification of activities, as Weisbrod has suggested, it cannot be concluded that it has led to a total lack of direction or to the abandonment of the social change commitment that is common to all the organizations studied. The patterns are much more complex and must include an understanding of the overall context. Mission vagueness certainly is associated with the diversification of activities (and this to the changing funding environment), but in the case of the organizations studied, there is no clear indication that growth in service delivery is necessarily linked to a reduction or an elimination of advocacy. Reduction of advocacy is more clearly linked to changes in the political context and the organizations studied have not eliminated their commitment to social change or to activities destined to demonstrate this commitment.

THE IMPACT OF THE CHANGING FUNDING ENVIRONMENT ON THE GOVERNANCE OF NONPROFIT ORGANIZATIONS

The comparative analysis of our eight cases reveals a complex relationship between the funding of nonprofit organizations, its patterns of change, and the organizations' governance practices. In this section, we focus on three dimensions of this relationship. First, our data suggest a positive relation between the confrontation of funding difficulties and a decline in the size of boards of directors of nonprofit organizations. While this relationship appears as a result of cost-saving measures (and the desire of boards to set an example), it can raise challenges for assuring adequate representation of diverse memberships and can create problems of legitimacy for community-driven nonprofit institutions.

Second, our eight cases throw considerable doubt on the prevalent hypothesis that the increasingly competitive and contract-driven funding environment of nonprofit organizations leads them to assemble more "corporate" or "professional" boards of directors. Such a shift from the recruitment of committed member activists to a greater reliance on members with professional expertise has not been observed in participating agencies. Many institutions have even clearly rejected such an approach.

Finally, while we did not find evidence of a trend toward the recruitment of "professional" or "corporate" board members, there is some evidence that a more competitive funding environment led nonprofit organizations to reform their governance practices to attribute more autonomy to their senior management. The tasks and roles of the board of directors tend to be increasingly confined to setting policy, formulating organizational development strategy, and assuring the accountability and performance of executive directors. In other words, many of the nonprofit organizations that we studied were moving toward a more "business model" of board-management relations in the hope of clarifying lines of accountability and providing managers with more autonomy to respond to financial challenges.

Before engaging in a more detailed discussion of these results, we should state the need for some prudence. Our interviewees often warned us about inferring a simple causal relationship between funding issues and changes in governance. Organizations are complex entities evolving in a turbulent environment. As a result, organizational changes are often the result of multiple factors. While financial concerns have an impact on governance practices, they are frequently accompanied by other factors, such as changes in personnel and concerns for adequate representation in decision making by stakeholders. While financial issues are important, in practice, our interviewees often found it difficult to isolate the effect of funding from other factors affecting the evolution of the organization.

Board Size and Operation

The first significant finding concerns the effect that financial difficulties can have on the size and operation of the boards of directors.[6] Five of the organizations participating in our study reduced the number of seats on their boards in an explicit attempt to respond to financial pressures and to reduce costs. For example, CMHA moved from a board of 36 to a board of 24 directors in the late 1980s, partly to reduce the costs of governance. CCSD reduced the number of board seats from 39 to 17 in the early 1990s, partly as a cost-saving measure. CEN has cut its board from 12 to 6 members.

Moreover, all eight organizations have modified the operation or structure of their boards of directors in order to cut operating expenses. A typical development across our cases was a greater reliance on teleconferencing for meetings as a way to save on travel expenses of board members. Other cost-saving measures included the elimination of some board committees, a reduction in the number of meetings per year, and the cancellation of real-time translation during board meetings.

One of the principal functions of governance practices is to assure the legitimacy of the organization's activities and orientations in the eyes of its members and stakeholders. As Wood points out, boards provide a forum for the consultation of stakeholders which serve both to air and mediate differences of opinions. They play a crucial role in the legitimization and institutionalization of organizational changes, both internally and with respect to their relationship with stakeholders (Wood 1996, pp. 4-5). In this context, changes in the size of a board and its mode of operation cannot be perceived strictly as a matter of economy. Modifications originally driven by financial concerns have important and direct impacts on the effectiveness of the boards in assuring representation and fostering legitimacy for the organization's decisions.

The cases of CEN and CCSD illustrate this indirect impact of funding problems on representation. Following the loss of its sustaining grant in the early 1990s, CCSD's board underwent a turbulent and difficult period. In an effort to reduce its costs, CCSD not only eliminated board seats but also terminated the use of interpretation services at its board meetings and other functions. Coupled with the closing of the Montreal office, the termination of interpretation services led to the resignation of all directors from the province of Quebec. They later decided to establish their own provincial council. While CCSD succeeded in regaining a full contingent of Quebec directors following these events, the case demonstrates the important impacts that funding matters can have on adequate governance from the perspective of legitimacy and stakeholder representation. In reflecting on these events, interviewees considered them to be representing a "traumatic" period in the organization's history.

CEN underwent similar problems with its own board of directors. While the organization had been struggling with issues of regional and cultural representation for a long time, the reduction in the size of the board has not facilitated a resolution of these ongoing tensions. After several board members resigned in the early 1990s partly over issues of cultural and regional representation, CEN decided to restructure its board in the hope of resolving some of these tensions at the same time as generating some savings. The new smaller board assures one seat to each "region" of the country, including the territories, as well as a seat for First Nations' representation.

However, interviewees told us that there are no indications that the changes have succeeded in alleviating representational problems. In contrast, the smaller number of seats seems to leave less room for the adequate representation of local needs. As one of our interviewees argued, when the number of seats is reduced, there is a tendency to keep board members coming from large, professional organizations who have more clout in national debates and are more widely recognized in the community. As a result, there is typically less room for smaller local groups on the board, which makes the articulation of these particular local needs much more difficult. And at the time of resource allocation, these inequities in representation can make a difference.

In sum, while the actual impacts will vary according to the particular circumstances of individual groups, our analysis suggests that the reduction of board size due to funding pressures can entail significant challenges for the representational functions of boards. More generally, our evidence leads us to hypothesize the existence of the following paradoxical impact of decline in funding: a more difficult and turbulent funding environment can lead nonprofit agencies to weaken the boards' representative features which are most needed to validate and legitimize changes necessary to adapt to this new environment. For example, if the reduction in board size or in the frequency of meetings leads to an effective lessening in the legitimacy of decisions in the eyes of some stakeholders, these stakeholders are less likely to support the implementation of these decisions and to approve of the more general orientation adopted by the organization.

In recent years, the importance of appropriately consulting stakeholders has grown. The complexity of problems, the growing number of partnerships and alliances, and a more active citizenry typically call for more inclusive governance practices. Inclusion and consultation are not only seen as measures of more democratic practices. They are also increasingly understood as guarantors of greater effectiveness by generating the cooperation and support of stakeholders. To the extent that financial trends bring organizations to lessen the representativeness of their boards, financial difficulties may hamper nonprofit boards from moving in this direction. And for organizations that are typically built on community ties, this may have particularly negative consequences for their effectiveness and legitimacy.

The impact of the reduction in board sizes and economies in operation was not exclusively negative. In some cases, the elimination of some board seats was also seen as a means to improve the decision-making process. Organizations with very large boards often found that the diversity and number of members impeded the prompt resolution of problems. Consensus was often difficult, debates dragged on for a long time. In times of difficulties and change, a smaller board was seen as potentially more responsive to rapid changes and more likely to provide decisive directions. Moreover, for some organizations, the greater use of technology, such as teleconferencing, provided a means to discuss the organization's development more frequently than when meetings occurred only face-to-face. As a result, there was an improvement in communication, at least for the members of the executive committee. These positive attributes associated with the governance reforms brought about by financial difficulties may suggest that there is indeed a need for reaching a balance between equitable representation and effective decision making.

The "Professionalization" and "Corporatization" of Boards

With the notable exception of the two organizations operating in the health sector, the board members of our sample organizations do not participate in major ways in fundraising activities. While they can be occasionally called to participate in meetings with donors or while they may refer funding opportunities to the staff, board members rarely engage actively in raising revenues for their organizations. This reality seems to be consistent with American findings which suggest that nonprofit boards are not heavily involved in fundraising (Duca 1996, p. 83). In a recent survey, less than 5 percent of nonprofit executives interviewed cited fundraising as a strength of their board (Slesinger and Moyers 1995, p. 5).

Fundraising appears to remain clearly a staff matter. For example, when faced recently with the challenge of seeking new sources of funds, the CNF chose to hire a new staff member dedicated to corporate fundraising. OXFAM has also recently hired a fundraising manager to pilot its new targeted fundraising initiatives. Moreover, when CNF was confronted with a financial crisis in the mid-1990s, the organization did not turn to board members to raise more revenues but hired a professional telemarketing firm. Overall, we found no indication of a growing reliance on board members for raising revenues. Again, the health organizations are an exception. Their board members were traditionally more involved in fundraising and, in the last few years, CMHA's board members have been playing a growing role with respect to fundraising in the corporate sector.

In addition, our cases do not reveal a trend toward the recruitment of corporate executives to boards of directors as a strategy to facilitate raising corporate donations. The scholarly literature on funding and governance often argues that the shift toward private funding and the decline of government grants will lead organizations to court the corporate sector through their board members. As we noted above, we found little evidence of greater involvement in fundraising by board members within our cases. However, even within organizations pressured to diversify their funding sources or having explicitly adopted a corporate fundraising strategy, there were no articulated intentions of moving this way in the coming years. While the matter was often discussed, organizations have rejected this strategy as a result of fears that it would threaten the actual control by members or compromise their founding philosophy. For example, in our environmental cases, ethical considerations and philosophical orientations prevented such moves as members feared that such changes would threaten the organization's control by grass-roots members or betray its founding philosophy.

Also in contrast to an hypothesis prevalent in the literature, our study did not find a trend toward the recruitment of professionals as directors. The scholarly literature dealing with the development of the "contracting regime" in nonprofit-government relations has generally argued that this new funding environment has brought about a "professionalization" of nonprofit boards (and management). As the level of legal and administrative expertise required for getting and managing contracts calls for a more professional approach, nonprofit agencies are influenced to recruit board members with the professional skills likely to further the organization's interests in this new environment, even if they do not share the organization's philosophy and commitment with the same intensity as activist members.

The cases reviewed for this study do not support this hypothesis. Some agencies spoke of their passing desire to recruit a new board member with marketing, legal or fundraising expertise. But generally, selection criteria have not changed. Commitment to the organization's mission and philosophy as well as some recognized experience or potential by peers remain more important factors. It is needless to point out that many committed activists who sit on boards also have significant professional expertise; but this expertise is generally seen as secondary to their qualities as committed social activists. Moreover, in most organizations, democratic procedures tend to limit the potential for directing the choice of members.

Executive-Board Relationships

The nature of executive-board relationships varies significantly across organizations. The traditional theories of organization tend to stress the separation of board and management. Boards are clearly conceptualized as setting priorities and exercising leadership while managers are concerned with daily operations and policy implementation. But even a casual observer of nonprofit organizations knows that this model often clashes with reality. Particularly in small organizations, board members can be heavily involved in managerial and operational issues. And vis-à-vis a board of volunteers, the executive director is often the determinant source of organizational leadership. In fact, many studies suggest that an executive-centred model is a generally more realistic description of governance in the nonprofit sector. (See, e.g., Herman and Heimovics 1991, pp. 54-55, 68.)

Patterns and sources of funding are likely to have an impact on the practice of executive-board relations and the division of tasks between them. However, it remains to be determined whether wide-ranging shifts in the patterns of funding, a decline in government funding or a move to project/ contract funding actually enhances or weakens the power of executives in relation to boards. On this issue, the literature tends to predict a shift in power in favour of managers and executives. In particular, the shift to a contracting regime would seem to favour the professional, nonprofit manager with experience over the transitory part-time, board volunteer.

Examining our eight participating organizations, instead of a clear shift in favour of managers, we note a significant trend toward the clarification of respective roles and responsibilities among staff, executive directors, and board members in many of the eight organizations. Financial difficulties and the funding environment led several organizations to adopt governance practices that increase the autonomy of the executive director and its staff while also emphasizing formal accountability to the board. As a result, the boards of directors tend to concentrate more clearly on setting broad policies, monitoring financial practices, and assessing performance.

In several of our organizations, this change took the form of an explicit adoption of the Carver model of board leadership[7] (Carver 1990).

In the case of the CNF, a period of serious financial difficulty and a successful recovery had illustrated the need for clear lines of accountability and decisive decision making by the executive. But members of other organizations also spoke of the need for greater autonomy by the executive director and senior management in the context of the new funding environment. It was stressed that, as organizations are forced to respond quickly to a greater number of funding opportunities, managerial flexibility and discretion become more important. Too much involvement of the board of directors in the daily operations was perceived as potentially detrimental to organizational performance in this new context of rapid change.

A common assertion in the literature on nonprofit governance is that greater reliance on government funding leads to greater control by the executive director to the detriment of the leadership of the board of directors (Wood 1996, p. 10; Kramer 1984, p. 195; Gronbjerg 1993; Smith and Lipsky 1993). The hypothesis asserts that managers typically know more about the inner workings of government financial, policy, and managerial processes than volunteer board members. As a result, in the intimate relations with bureaucrats entailed by their financial reliance on the attribution of government funds, managers have an expertise and information advantage that allows them to dominate board members in providing leadership. Moreover, government funding can increase the administrative demands for managing contracts and reporting, which will typically add to the complexity of controlling management for board members and empower the managers with the expertise (Smith and Lipsky 1993, p. 88).

Without speaking directly to this hypothesis, our findings nevertheless suggest that, in contrast, a decline in government reliance does not necessarily lead to a return to more powerful boards. The more general shift toward contract/project funding arguably contributes as much to a need for greater managerial autonomy as does government reliance. Dealing with the management of multiple contracts and projects, whether these projects are funded by government, foundations or corporations, is what ultimately helps shift authority from the board to the executive. In fact, the management of a single source of core government funding often entails less complexity than multiple sources of funding and arguably allows boards to exercise better control over their organizations.

In our sample of cases, it is the complexity entailed by multiple sources of funding, the gain and management of multiple projects, and the associated requirements for greater entrepreneurship and expedient actions that called for granting managers more autonomy and authority. As a result, while greater government reliance (at least as long as it takes the form of contract funding) may lead to a lessening of board control, the current competitive funding environment is not likely to return more control to executive directors.

THE IMPACT OF THE CHANGING FUNDING ENVIRONMENT ON PROGRAM DELIVERY

Our analyses of program delivery in the eight organizations studied were framed by two working hypotheses suggested by the research and literature. Our first hypothesis suggested that changes in funding in the nonprofit sector would prompt agencies to alter and reduce the program activities they offered (Gutch 1992; Weisbrod 1998). Our second hypothesis predicted that the move to contract funding for discrete projects would result in greater accountability requirements for organizations by funders, including an increase in the use of program evaluation (Knapp, Robertson and Thomason 1990; Ware 1989).

Changes in Program Delivery

In the face of a shifting funding environment which included reductions in funding and changes in funding sources and requirements, program delivery of the eight organizations in our study remained remarkably stable. Agencies were able to continue the delivery of the majority of their core activities. As well, several launched new projects that corresponded to their missions and took advantages of new funding opportunities.

In the domain of international development, CUSO increased its level of overseas placements, a key indicator of programmatic activities by its donors. OXFAM was also able to maintain most of its programming activities in developing countries at a similar level of intensity during the period under study. Similarly, the two women's agencies continued to deliver the same core activities, albeit with some varying intensity from year to year. For CRIAW, these included conducting research projects, funding external research, developing and disseminating publications, organizing conferences, and administering an awards program. NCWC, in its role as a federation of local and provincial councils of women across Canada, has continued its advocacy activities at much the same level throughout the 1990s as well as delivering a small number of special events which can best be described as educational activities (e.g., national forum on girls and young women as victims and perpetrators of violence).

The two environmental organizations (CNF and CEN) also continued to deliver more or less the same programmatic activities. Although CNF experienced significant changes in the nature of its funding during the 1990s, its major programmatic activities, which included advocacy and the operation of conservation projects, remained much the same. CEN has continued to serve as a coordinating agency and clearinghouse of information for environmental agencies across Canada. The health and social service organizations (CMHA and CCSD) were also able to maintain many of their core activities in public education and advocacy even in the face of losing significant block funding from the federal government.

A number of reasons seemed to contribute to minimal changes in program delivery across organizations. Many of the agencies responded to the loss of government funding by successfully diversifying their revenue generation. The most striking example of this diversification was CCSD which replaced the loss of block funding from the federal government with revenue produced by undertaking contracted research work with a wide range of governmental institutions. Another noteworthy example was the success of CNF in generating revenue through an ongoing telemarketing campaign.

A second reason for the maintenance of programmatic activities by organizations appeared to be the reduction in certain expenditures to address lowered funding while protecting those most closely associated with program delivery. Cutbacks in expenditures included downsizing staffing (CNF, CEN, CCSD), reducing the size of the board (CEN, CCSD), and cuts to the budget in such areas as travel and administrative expenses (CEN, CMHA).

The flexibility of the program mission of organizations also enabled them to adapt to the changing funding environment by altering certain specific activities yet maintaining their overall programs. For example,

CMHA has been able to fulfill its mission of "promoting mental health of Canadians" by initiating new fundable programs in the areas of public education, advocacy, and service. CCSD fulfilled its role as an agency that provides social policy analysis and advocacy by undertaking research projects to help inform the social policy debate.

Although agencies in our study were able for the most part to maintain their programmatic activities, there were instances where core activities had to be terminated or reduced in intensity because of funding cutbacks. In response to cutbacks and financial reorganization, CCSD closed its self-help resource centre and library and terminated its provision of international consulting on social policy to developing countries. CEN reported the termination of its environmental youth internship because of loss of funding after only one year of operation. OXFAM closed its Canadian regional offices because of the loss of developmental education funding.

CEN also terminated the Environment and Development Support Program after five years of operation (1990–95) because of changes in the funding practices of CIDA. This program funded conservation and environmental education partnerships among Canadian and southern environmental, non-governmental organizations. CRIAW responded to its loss of funding by continuing to deliver its core programs but in a reduced manner. For instance, it reduced the number of research grants that it awarded from ten to four and changed the cycle of its conference from annual to biennial.

Conversely, some organizations experienced the initiation of new activities and the creation of new structures because of funding opportunities. CMHA's programmatic activities in 1998 reflected greater diversity and an increased number of discrete time-limited projects as compared to those in 1993. As part of a major restructuring in response to funding cutbacks, CCSD created the Centre for International Statistics on Economic and Social Welfare for Families and Children, a unit within CCSD whose primary purpose was to conduct revenue-generating research that could impact on the development of social policy. The centre has proven to be very successful and has led to a significant increase in and broadening of the research being produced by CCSD.

Another example of programmatic changes of an opportunistic kind is CUSO's focusing of activities on two main areas of work, namely sustainable economic alternatives and the cultural survival of indigenous peoples.

Similarly, CEN established international program teams with a mandate to develop packages of activities and partnerships for international environmental projects. This was also initiated in response to changes in CIDA funding and was intended to replace the Environment and Development Support Program.

Use of Program Evaluation

In the context of shrinking resources in the nonprofit sector, program evaluation is being increasingly expected by funders to ensure that they are receiving value for their money. All of the organizations were aware of the importance of program evaluation and indicated an interest on the part of their agencies to use it as a program development tool. However, our review of eight national organizations across four different sectors suggests that this interest has not been translated into widespread practice.

There is some use of evaluation by different institutions with certain programs but it tends to be in a time-limited manner on a specific program wherein funders have provided some resources for this purpose. In addition, there appeared to be some evidence of increased reporting requirements by funders at least as related to financial processes and products of services. This was identified by some organizations as producing a greater administrative burden at a time when they were experiencing a cutback in administrative resources. It is noteworthy that there was no indication that any of the organizations were examining the impact or outcomes of their programs.

The most commonly cited reasons for the paucity of program evaluation being undertaken by organizations were a lack of resources (i.e., time and/ or funding that can be dedicated to program evaluation) and lack of in-house expertise. In addition, it was noted by some organizations that their programmatic activities can be considered indirect services and are not easily evaluated. For example, CCSD's main activities involve producing research; NCWC engages mostly in advocacy activities; CEN serves to assist with the coordination of environmental agencies. Organizations from the international development sector appeared to be the most advanced in terms of engaging in systematic program evaluation activity. This is not surprising given the long-standing use of program evaluation in international development projects over the past two decades. A recent development in this sector is the move away from specific time-limited program evaluations by external evaluators. These are being replaced by the development of internal evaluation systems which are intended to support ongoing quality assurance and program improvement processes commonly known as results-based management.

Our study revealed that internal systems of evaluation supporting results-based management were being increasingly expected by funders of CUSO and OXFAM programs. However, both CUSO and OXFAM were experiencing difficulty in implementing these evaluation systems for their programs. Again, the lack of resources and expertise combined with the presence of organizational restructuring has made it difficult to successfully implement this kind of evaluation in both organizations.

CONCLUSIONS

The study was intended to investigate the impact of the changing financial landscape in the nonprofit sector on nonprofit organizations' missions, governance, and programs. These areas were chosen based on arguments in the literature that allegations in funding conditions over the past decade had fundamentally changed the nature and operation of nonprofit organizations.

What we discovered was less dramatic than that suggested in the literature. Indeed, the agencies we encountered experienced significant financial pressures during the 1990s. However, they all appeared to have responded to this pressure with a certain organizational resilience. The changes initiated by the agencies were certainly important, but they were not as dramatic nor as clear-cut as much of the literature would contend.

Our study of eight national nonprofit organizations from diverse areas suggested that there was a decline in funding in the third sector in addition to changes in the forms of funding. These changes have often been more qualitative than quantitative. For instance, there is a clear shift from core funding to project funding and this has required adaptations on the part of the agencies. In some cases, the move from core to project funding has involved real changes in activities, in other cases much less.

An unequivocal finding from our analyses was the clear maintenance of missions in all the examined organizations in the face of the changing financial environment. The elasticity of how missions of nonprofit organizations are operationalized contributed to this maintenance. As well, a strong commitment to their missions appeared to be a common characteristic encountered in all the organizations we studied. Looking now at the impact in terms of programs and structures, once again our results yield more complex and more qualified conclusions than the hypotheses from the literature suggest. There is a move, at least in some of the organizations, toward service delivery and there is probably in general a lessening of advocacy activities, but there is no necessary relationship between increased service delivery and lessened advocacy and, in addition, despite the much more difficult political climate, advocacy had not disappeared in the institutions we examined.

From the standpoint of governance, there were tendencies to professionalization and bureaucratization but more in the direction of an increased role for the professional staff and particularly the executive directors. Indeed, the boards have not professionalized and the suggestions in the literature that funding restrictions would increase the professionalization of boards were not borne out in our organizations. Once again, there were changes but they are less dramatic than those suggested as well as more complex. Boards have become smaller, often at least in part justified for financial reasons, but they have generally not taken on fundraising responsibilities.

The organizations that we investigated reported feeling under pressure to make changes and to adapt to new funding realities. At the same time, it was quite clear that they also resisted these changes; they maintained old patterns of activity and the stability of their program activity was more noteworthy than their changes. The resilience of the agencies needs to be included in our understanding of the nonprofit sector as do the pressures for change. Our study suggests that the dramatic view of a wholesale transformation of the third sector is overstated. At the same time, our study raises a variety of other questions related to the financing of nonprofit organizations that need further examination.

Notes

[1]The federal government also supports the voluntary sector through its tax policies providing incentives for charitable donations. In 1998 alone, tax expenditures related to individual charitable donations represented over $1 billion (Privy Council Office 1999a, p. 1).

[2]According to a recent federal survey, there are already approximately 300 official joint initiatives between nonprofit organizations and federal departments for the making and delivery of public policy in Canada (Canada. Clerk of the Privy Council, 1999, p. 1).

[3]This situation will probably change in the years ahead because CNF will participate, with two other conservation organizations, in a large conservation program funded by the federal government.

[4]On this point, previous research suggests that it can require an increased effort to obtain the same level of contribution funding. The shift can consequently result in increased costs which may not be covered under the administrative allowances of contribution agreements. This argument is examined in Weisbrod (1998).

[5]The whole question of trying to define commercialization of the nonprofit sector is a large and extremely complex one, one we cannot do justice to in this paper. We only wish to acknowledge the complexity of the issue.

[6]We should point out that, in some cases, the savings from these changes can be modest compared with the size of the organizations' operational budgets and the actual cuts required to meet declining funding. However, in addition to genuinely participating to the organization's financial efforts, these cuts are often seen as setting an example and ensuring that everything is done to avoid affecting programs.

[7]The Carver model, also called the Policy Governance Model, is developed in detail in Carver (1997). It insists on a clear distinction between the roles and responsibilities of the board of directors and the executives of the organization. Board members, argues Carver, should be conscious of their responsibility as the representatives of the community "owning" the organization (whether these be shareholders or otherwise) and ensure that they provide adequate accountability of the executives' behaviour to this community. Accordingly, board members should strive to effectively control the "ends" (results, mission) of the organization through affirmative and prescriptive actions and the "means" of achieving these ends only through limitative actions and interdiction of certain practices. The result should be a board-executive relationship in which the board sets objectives and policies as well as controls performance while the executives benefit from as much freedom as possible in meeting the board's expectations. Despite its popularity, the model contrasts with the practices of many organizations (especially small ones) where board members tend to be involved to a greater extent in daily operations.

References

Abrams, P. 1980. "Social Change, Social Networks and Neighborhood Care," *Social Work Service*, 22: 12-23.

Browne, P. 1996. *Love in a Cold World? The Voluntary Sector in an Age of Cuts.* Ottawa: Canadian Centre for Policy Alternatives.

Canada. Clerk of the Privy Council. 1999. "Building a New Relationship with the Voluntary Sector," Speech to the Third Canadian Leaders' Forum on the Voluntary Sector, 31 May.

Canada. Privy Council Office. 1999a. "Federal Government and Voluntary Sector Seek New Strategic Relationship," *Press Release*, 15 June.

_____ 1999b. "Le processus des tables conjointes," *Press Release*, 15 June.

_____ 1999c. "Joint Work: Federal Government and Voluntary Sector," *Press Release*, 15 June.

Canadian Centre for Philanthropy. 1995. "Funding Charities: Dependency on Government and Implications of Cutbacks," *Research Bulletin*, 2:1.

_____ 1999. "Much Comes from the Few: The Thin Base of Support for Charitable and Nonprofit Organizations," *Research Bulletin*, 6:2.

Carver, J. 1990. *Boards that Make a Difference.* San Francisco: Jossey-Bass.

Duca, D.J. 1996. *Nonprofit Boards: Roles, Responsibilities and Performance.* New York: John Wiley & Sons.

Forder, J. and M. Knapp. 1993. "Social Care Markets: The Voluntary Sector and Residential Care for Elderly People in England," in *Researching the Voluntary Sector*, ed. S. Saxon-Harrold and J. Kendall. Tonbridge: Charities Aid Foundation.

Gronbjerg, K. 1993. *Understanding Nonprofit Funding.* San Francisco: Jossey-Bass.

Gutch, R. 1992. *Contracting: Lessons from the US.* London: National Council for Voluntary Organizations and Bedford Square Press.

Herman, R.D. and R.D. Heimovics. 1991. *Executive Leadership in Nonprofit Boards.* Oxford: Jossey-Bass Publishers.

James, E. 1989. "Sources of Charity Finance and Policy Implications: A Comparative Analysis," in *Sources of Charity Finance*, ed. N. Lee. Tonbridge: Charities Aid Foundation.

Jenson, J. and S. Phillips. 1996. "Regime Shift: New Citizenship Practices in Canada," *International Journal of Canadian Studies*, 14:111-35.

Knapp, M., E. Robertson and C. Thomason. 1990. "Public Money, Voluntary Action: Whose Welfare?" in *The Third Sector: Comparative Studies on Nonprofit Organizations*, ed. H. Anheier and W. Seibel. Berlin: Walter de Gruyter.

Kramer, R. 1984. "A Framework for the Analysis of Board-Executive Relationships in Voluntary Agencies," in *Voluntarism and Social Work Practice*, ed. F. Schwartz. New York: University Press of America.

Lamoureux, D. 1997. "Les services féministes – de l'antiétatisme à l'intégration subsidiaire," in *Women and the Canadian State*, ed. C. Andrew and S. Rodgers. Montreal and Kingston: McGill-Queen's University Press.

Leat, D. 1995. "Funding Matters," in *An Introduction to the Voluntary Sector*, ed. J. Smith, C. Rochester and R. Hedley. London: Routledge.

Masson, D. 1998. "With and Despite the State: Doing Women's Movement Politics in Local Service Groups in the 1980's in Quebec." PhD thesis. Ottawa: Carleton University.

_____ 1999. "Repenser l'État: Nouvelles perspectives féministes," *Recherches feministes*, 12(1):5-24.

Panel on Accountability and Governance in the Voluntary Sector. 1999. *Building on Strength: Improving Governance and Accountability in Canada's Voluntary Sector.* Ottawa: Supply and Services Canada.

Paquet, G. 1999. *Governance through Social Learning.* Ottawa: University of Ottawa Press.

Reading, P. 1994. *Community Care and the Voluntary Sector: The Role of Voluntary Organizations in a Changing World.* Birmingham: Venture Press.

Salamon, L. 1990. "The Nonprofit Sector and Government: The American Experience in Theory and Practice," in *The Third Sector: Comparative Studies on Nonprofit Organizations*, ed. H. Anheier and W. Seibel. Berlin: Walter de Gruyter.

Slesinger, L. and R. Moyers. 1995. *A Snapshot of America's Nonprofit Boards: Results of a National Survey.* Washington: National Center for Nonprofit Boards.

Smith, S. and M. Lipsky. 1993. *Nonprofits for Hire: The Welfare State in the Age of Contracting.* Cambridge, MA: Harvard University Press.

Statistics Canada. 1998. *Caring Canadians, Involved Canadians: Highlights from the 1997 National Survey of Giving, Volunteering and Participating.* Ottawa: Minister of Industry.

Taylor, M. 1990. *New Times, New Challenges: Voluntary Organizations Facing 1990.* London: National Council for Voluntary Organizations.

Ware, A. 1989. *Between Profit and State: Intermediate Organizations in Britain and the United States.* Cambridge: Polity Press.

Weisbrod, B. 1998. *To Profit or Not to Profit.* Cambridge: Cambridge University Press.

Wood, M., ed. 1996. *Nonprofit Boards and Leadership.* San Franscisco: Jossey-Bass.

3

An Analytic Framework for Classifying the Organizations of the Social Economy

Jack Quarter, Betty Jane Richmond,
Jorge Sousa and Shirley Thompson

INTRODUCTION

In general terms, the social economy can be used as a catch-all for the area between the private and state sectors. Researchers (Defourny 1988; Defourny and Monzon 1992; Jeantet 1988; Quarter 1992; Snaith 1991) have tended to include the following organizational types: nonprofits, including those with charitable status; unincorporated formal associations (typical examples being labour and professional associations, home and schools, tenants and neighbourhood groups), and cooperatives and credit unions (caisses populaires in francophone regions) (Quarter 1992). Mutual insurers, particularly small companies dealing with property and casualty insurance in farm areas (Canadian Association of Mutual Insurance Companies 1999),[1] also may fit the tradition of the social economy. Like nonprofits, they are companies without shareholders and each policyholder is allowed one vote in their affairs.

This study begins from the premise that even though the organizations within the social economy might have a particular type of incorporation, neither nonprofits nor cooperatives are part of a unified sector, but rather both contain a variety of forms that affect the relationship between them. These forms are also correlated with type of service for both nonprofits and cooperatives. For example, cooperatives in such contexts as housing, childcare and health care are also nonprofits (that is, cooperatives without share capital), whereas others such as credit unions, and cooperatives in farm marketing and food retailing typically have share capital. These are commercial enterprises that have some similarities to nonprofits with a commercial focus (Dees 1998). Therefore, it appears that neither form of incorporation nor type of service are adequate in classifying the organizations of the social economy.

In general, the classification systems for organizations within the social economy are based upon the type of incorporation and they also tend to be one-dimensional. For cooperatives, it is most common to classify them according to the type of members, for example, producers, consumers or workers (Craig 1993) or by the type of service, for example, financial, retail food, farm marketing (Co-operatives Secretariat 1998). Similar one-dimensional classification systems are used for nonprofits (for a summary, see Febbraro, Hall and Parmegiani 1999). There are at least two major multi-dimensional classification systems for nonprofits (ibid.; Jansen, Senecal and Thompson 1982). The latter is complex and based upon 16 possible dimensions, subdivided into two categories: organizational characteristics (for example, size and funding sources) and action dimensions (for example, type of service, target population for service). The Febbraro, Hall and Parmegiani model, which is designed for nonprofit health services in Canada, uses five categories (major area of activity, beneficiaries of the service, function of the organization, legal status, and size). These categories were developed after a thorough analysis of one-dimensional models and a critique of their limitations. While these categories deal with important organizational characteristics, they do not get at the underlying characteristics of nonprofits, and particularly dynamics that might be used in a social economy framework. Moreover, both of these classification schemes, as well as the one-dimensional schemes, are strictly conceptual. They have not been subjected to an empirical test of their utility.

By comparison, the current study not only attempts to visualize the underlying conceptual dimensions which might link organizations of the social economy but also subjects them to an empirical test. Some of the organizational characteristics included in Febbraro, Hall and Parmegiani and Jansen, Senecal and Thompson (1982) are used as background variables. However, the primary dimensions used in the analytic framework are drawn from the social economy theorists (Defourny 1988; Defourny and Monzon 1992; Jeantet 1988; Quarter 1992; and Snaith 1991).

Five dimensions are presented as a preliminary framework for analyzing the data. These dimensions are social objectives, relationship to the state, relationship to the market, democratic decision making, and volunteer participation. They differ from the aforementioned descriptive characteristics of the nonprofits and cooperatives in that they are dynamic and can be applied to any type of organization, including private sector businesses and organizations in the public sector. To take social objectives as an example, it is used because nonprofits and cooperatives are founded to fulfill a social purpose, as presented in their mission statements. However, private sector businesses may also have social objectives, perhaps to a lesser degree. Some private sector businesses (e.g., The Body Shop [Roddick 1991], Ben & Jerry's [Lager 1994]) emphasize their social objectives, but in general these are secondary to their commercial goals. Nevertheless, the dimension of social objectives can be used as a basis for measuring the degree of commonality between organizations, and it is not limited to one organizational type. The same is true of each of the dimensions that are utilized in this study. Nevertheless, the study is exploratory in that the survey used to measure the dimensions is developed anew, and even though the five dimensions that follow are from the social economy theorists, it could be argued that other dimensions might be used. This study hopefully begins a process that can be taken forward by other researchers.

We begin with an elaboration of the dimensions that will serve as the initial basis for analysis.

Dimensions

Social Objectives. Both nonprofits and cooperatives start from a social purpose that defines an organization's objectives and how they are put into practice. For that reason, it is appropriate to label them as social organizations. The social tradition surrounding nonprofit organizations is rooted in the religions of the Middle Ages that gave rise to institutionalized forms of charity (Hansmann 1986; Martin 1985). Members of religious groups believed that they were furthering the purpose of their religion by assisting those in need. While charity has religious roots, the concept has been broadened to include motivations that are largely secular; that is, the responsibility of a community to support the services that its members require. Nonprofits (some of which have a charitable status) may be viewed as a secular expression of this philosophy.

The concept of charity and the objectives of charitable organizations have been broadened from the original notion of relief of poverty and now include such social objectives as international aid, education, youth programs, health, family services, culture and the arts, heritage, and environmental protection. Therefore, a distinction can be made between charity as a community's response to those in dire need and organizations with charitable objectives (meeting the criteria required for charitable status under the taxation laws) and often serving a broader public. Although modern charities are of both types, organizations serving a broader public are more typical. This might be referred to as the universalization of charity. In the modern world, charity has been both secularized and universalized, although the more traditional arrangements directed toward those in dire need are still quite prominent.

While charitable organizations often involve the delivery of assistance by the more fortunate to the less fortunate, nonprofits serving a membership (that is, mutual associations), cooperatives, and mutual insurers are based on the principle of self-help (Craig 1993). The members of these institutions share a common bond association (e.g., a common heritage, occupation or location) and a need that they attempt to meet through providing a service to themselves. These organizations have their roots among exploited groups in society (MacPherson 1979) but, unlike the recipients of charity, they have sufficient strength to help themselves. Some of the oldest associations were mutual benefit societies in which people, often of common religious or ethno-cultural heritage, would arrange services like insurance and burials for members. In rural areas, farmers formed mutual property and casualty insurers because foreign companies were uninterested in insuring them. Similarly, credit unions (or financial cooperatives) were started in Canada at the beginning of the twentieth century, first through Catholic parishes in Quebec, because of either the unavailability of consumer loans or because of usurious interest rates (Kenyon 1976). Farm marketing cooperatives were also started about the same time, initially in western Canada and in Ontario, in order to enable their members to obtain a fair price for their products and to make basic purchases that they required (MacPherson 1979).

Over the years, people with common bonds such as a place of work, profession, business, religion or ethnic identity have formed a broad array of mutual associations and cooperatives. While some of these adhere to the tradition of being organized around exploited groups, others simply involve a common social interest, a profession or some other commonality, including a privileged status, such as the members of a golf club or an elite business association. The bonds of association might differ, but such organizations are set up to meet a social objective.

It could be argued that by satisfying their customers, a private sector company also meets social objectives. While this argument has some validity, particularly in the service sector, capital invested in the private companies, and particularly in mature companies as opposed to small owner-operated firms, has weak social commitments. With the exception of small owner-operated enterprises which are tied to a particular neighbourhood or larger firms which depend upon a particular location for their products (e.g., resource extraction), private sector companies will normally remain loyal to a community as long as they obtain a competitive rate of return. When a greater return is possible from other investments, or from manufacturing products elsewhere, private companies are likely to shift their loyalties. By comparison, social organizations (i.e., the organizations of the social economy) not only set the service first but also have loyalties to either a defined community or a defined membership. An apparel manufacturer, for example, may move production to countries where labour rates are cheap, but a social organization is guided by its social objectives in determining where it is located. In that respect, social organizations differ from the rootless, impersonal structures of mature private sector corporations.

Although the social purpose is a given within the social economy, the extent to which it is realized in practice may vary. Commercial objectives may colour how either a nonprofit or a cooperative pursues its social objectives. For example, one of the frequently voiced criticisms of credit unions is that they are scarcely different from banks. Without attempting to address this criticism, it does raise the question as to what extent social objectives define an organization's activities.

Relationship to the State. In Western Europe, where the social economy concept has broader acceptance, "independence from the state" is one of the defining criteria. There is logic to this criterion, in that it is important to differentiate the social economy from the government sector. Co-operatives, for example, have included independence from government as one of their defining principles. The most recent version of the International Co-operative Alliance's principles uses the words autonomy and independence, with the admonition that co-operatives must not jeopardize their independence through agreements with government (Wilkinson and Quarter 1996). However, some forms of co-operatives (housing) are dependent upon government assistance for financing, and health-care co-operatives operate within the framework of government-sponsored medicare plans. Thus, the principle of autonomy from government must be qualified.

The same point must be made for nonprofits. Some forms of nonprofits (e.g., heritage institutions, hospitals, extended care settings, and universities and colleges) depend heavily upon government financing, and are also influenced by government policies. Therefore, they can be viewed as an extension of the state and excluded from the social economy. However, such an argument seems overly simplistic because in the modern world the foundation underlying social organizations, a strong geographic community (Milofsky 1987), has been weakened and supplanted to a large extent by highly impersonal groupings based upon common interests (Christenson 1994; Wilkinson 1994). Government institutions have, to a degree, stepped into this breach caused by weaker geographic communities, and have come to play a vital role in sustaining a reconstructed sense of community, based less on local neighbourhoods and more on vaguely defined regions. Some might argue that a "reconstructed sense of community" is not a community, but rather the anomie of urban life propped up by government institutions providing necessary services. Without attempting to resolve that debate, it is doubtful that without the social support resulting from government institutions, existing communities would be sustained. Within this context, social organizations providing services to the public operate at arm's length to government and in effect, enter into a partnership (Salamon 1995).

Martin traces this change in the role of government through four distinct stages. Stage one, which he describes as personal service, occurs in a society "with a high degree of personal involvement" (Martin 1985, p. 26), and without significant government participation in service provision. With urbanization which concentrated the population in cities and led to less personal relations, formal institutions such as hospitals, schools, soup kitchens, and museums evolved, but funding still was viewed as an individual responsibility (stage two). As services increased in response to the problems of urban societies, and as the demand for financing outstripped what individuals were prepared to donate, government became involved and began to take up a significant share of the financing (stage three). In the final stage, government (through using the tax revenues it receives) becomes a major player and even more so with the introduction of universal social programs, such as medicare. Indeed many of the largest nonprofit organizations such as hospitals and universities which in their origins might have been supported by private donors like religious institutions, have become highly dependent upon government financing and therefore can be influenced by government policy. While this characteristic is part of their distinctiveness, and important to understand, it seems inappropriate to use it as a basis for exclusion from the social economy. They are still nonprofits fulfilling a social purpose, but are also different in some respects in that they receive their funds from other sources.

Relationship to the Market. In general, social economy theorists have not used this criterion, but because the market has become such a dominant force in the modern world, it cannot be ignored. Even charitable organizations, which are highly dependent on various levels of government as well as private donors, earn 19 percent of their revenues from market-based services (Sharpe 1994).

Other nonprofits vary in the extent to which they earn their revenues from services. Some (albeit a small subset of the total) are commercial outfits which receive their revenues from the sale of services. Blue Cross, the Canadian Automobile Association, and Travel Cuts are examples of such nonprofits. Except for their ownership arrangements and their origins, they are indistinguishable from a private sector firm.

There are other nonprofits, not as explicitly commercial in their focus, but nevertheless they earn the majority of their revenues from the sale of services. These include the YMCAs, Boy Scouts and Girl Guides, and competitive sports programs, such as those offered by the various local branches of the Canadian Amateur Hockey Association and the other sports affiliated with the Sports Federation of Canada. The performing arts, in general, make about half their revenues from ticket sales and a variety of paid services (Cromie 1990). Other organizations, such as homes for the aged, nonprofit housing, and nonprofit daycare, also involve substantial payments by the users of the service.

Nonprofits serving a membership earn a portion of their revenues from membership fees supplemented by donations from members. It is a matter of interpretation whether these fees should be considered as payment for a service, analogous to a commercial arrangement. In some cases, members of such organizations also pay for specific services. The payment for services by members is more characteristic of co-operatives, both those with and without shares. In the case of co-operatives, the membership fee is usually a small part of the overall revenues and the payment for services is the largest part. In general, co-operatives not only receive revenues from services but also operate in competitive markets that include private sector firms. The same is true for some nonprofits, such as YMCAs and daycare centres.

Increasingly, the term entrepreneurship is being applied to the commercial activities of social organizations (Dees 1998; Ellerman 1982). However, entrepreneurship takes on a different meaning among nonprofits and co-operatives because of their distinctive ownership arrangements. Such organizations are not property to enhance their members' personal wealth. Whereas personal gain is the hallmark of ownership in the private sector, and share values are a primary consideration in whether firms are bought, sold, merged, restructured or downsized, social benefit is the defining characteristic for institutions in the social economy. Their purpose is to provide a service either to members or to the public, and organizational rearrangements are undertaken with that objective in mind, not personal gain for shareholders.

Even where social organizations have shares, as in most co-operatives, they do not serve the same purpose as a private sector firm. Such shares do not reflect either the book value of the organization or what speculators are prepared to pay on the stock market, but rather they have a relatively constant value and are comparable to a membership fee (Ellerman 1990). They can go down in value if the co-operative has financial difficulties, but in general they stay at a constant value (or an initial value adjusted for

inflation). When members leave, the reimbursement normally is the original contribution plus a modest interest rate agreed to by the organization.

Similarly, when a social organization has a year-end surplus, the use of
that income is guided by its primary objective: improving and broadening
the availability of the service. For co-operatives with shares, surplus
revenues may result in a patronage dividend, not based on shareholdings
as in the private sector, but either on the use of the service by members or
on an egalitarian basis. When organizations in the social economy lose
money (that is, have a year-end deficit), unless the loss can be absorbed
through reserves either the service is reduced or the cost to patrons is increased. If the losses become too great, the institution might have to close.

Therefore, even for social organizations engaged in commercial activities, their financial dynamics differ from that of a private sector firm. As
such, the term "social entrepreneurship" (Ellerman 1982) seems more appropriate than entrepreneurship per se. Commercial activities, where they
are undertaken, serve the organization's social objectives not the shareholders' desire for personal gain. For highly commercial nonprofits and
co-operatives, the social objectives might be weakened over time. And there
are some private sector firms (The Body Shop) that highlight their social
mission. However, both of these cases might be viewed as atypical devia-
tions from a norm. In general, the entrepreurial dynamics of nonprofits
and co-operatives are based on social benefit, whereas the entrepreneurial
dynamics in the private sector are based on personal gain.

Governance. Social organizations have a membership that is entitled to
one vote each in the governance. While this may seem like a recipe for
democratic governance, there is much variability in the extent to which the
ideal is realized in practice. Within some social institutions, particularly
those with an active membership, democracy is a central feature of the
organizational culture. Such organizations would include some forms of
co-operatives, particularly worker, housing and farm marketing co-operatives, and many types of mutual associations, neighbourhood groups, and
social clubs. These agencies might be described as a social democracy, not
in the sectarian political sense, but quite literally as democracy within a
social institution. The vision associated with the social economy is to extend democratic control beyond the political domain to society at large.

Voting rights in such organizations are accorded to members on the basis of one member/one vote, rather than on property holdings as in private sector firms (Ellerman 1990). There are private sector firms, for example, an equal partnership, that also have equal voting rights among owners. However, unlike social organizations, these rights are based on property rather than membership, and therefore can be altered as property is bought and sold. An equal partnership, or to use another example, an equal shareholding arrangement in a limited company, are anomalous arrangements within the private sector.

Similarly, some organizations within the government sector, such as boards of education, are based on direct democratic control. Citizens living within a particular jurisdiction, each having one vote, elect trustees who have legal responsibility for the board. A board of education, albeit a government-created institution that may have the power to tax as well, is much the same as organizations in the social economy. It provides a service to a public that has the opportunity to democratically elect its governance. In one case the voters are citizens living within a particular jurisdiction; in the other case they are members of an institution.

But most government organizations and private companies lack the democratic opportunities of boards of education. The exceptions in the private and government sectors are more usual in the social economy. In a mature social organization (that is, with a formal structure that includes a board, bureaucracy, and administrative staff), members, each with one vote, elect a board that in turn appoints management. This circumstance bears direct parallels to a political democracy, in which citizens, each having one vote, elect a government that in turn appoints deputy ministers to act as senior management. The parliament or legislature of social organizations is the board of directors and the deputy ministers are senior management appointed by the board. As in a political democracy, there is tension between these two levels of governance, with senior management often assuming greater control because of its technical competence.

The aforementioned discussion is based upon an ideal type, but in practice there are variations from the ideal. First, there are grass-roots voluntary associations that often use direct rather than a representative democracy in their decision making. Such organizations are usually small and not incorporated, so rather than a board that is the legal representative of the organization, there is a less formal arrangement with broader participation in decision making (Rothschild-Whitt 1982). The small size often leads to a "face-to-face" form of democracy, as is found in feminist collectives, for example. Social relations are highly personal, roles are flexible and interchangeable, decisions are arrived at through consensus, and management (to the extent that it exists) is often a shared responsibility. While such arrangements are not necessarily a recipe for harmony, in that decision making can be emotionally charged and conflictual (Mansbridge 1982), they do reflect a direct form of democracy with a high level of member participation.

A second variation from the ideal occurs in member-based associations that make available the opportunity for participation but whose members are uninvolved or passive. One reason for this is that the service of the organization is not very important to the members or, in the words of Kurt Lewin, is a small part of "their life-space." A passive membership is typical of such member-based organizations as credit unions, retail food co-operatives or professional and labour associations, and many social clubs. Essentially, a small group (senior management and the board of directors or executive) runs the organization with the tacit consent or tolerance of the larger group. On occasion this group may resort to proxy voting because they require the membership to participate to satisfy the constitution. This is most likely where the membership is widely dispersed.

When an organization depends upon voluntary efforts from members in addition to their fees, members who do not take on this responsibility can be classified as "free riders" (Olson 1965) because they obtain the service for only part of the true cost. However, even in this type of arrangement, members may on occasion choose to exercise their franchise, such as when they are upset with a particular decision, or if they suspect financial mismanagement or if there is some external threat to the organization. In some respects, there are parallels between these arrangements and a political democracy where the electorate is uninvolved but are galvanized by a particular issue.

A third variation occurs among social organizations with a closed membership defined around its board of directors. These can be family foundations, universities, hospitals and social service agencies. The board becomes a self-perpetuating group — beholden to government regulation and large external funding sources — and nominates new members as vacancies arise. The members may be labelled as representatives of a particular stakeholder group, but in actual practice it is the board, not the legitimate representatives of the stakeholder group in the community, who nominates the appointee.

The source of financing is a major influence in whether a social organization actively engages in democratic decision making. Where funding comes from members, it is more likely that they will either participate actively or participate under particular circumstances. Where the funding comes from a large group of donors, it is also likely that a subset of that group will become active participants in the affairs of the organization. Where the funding comes from government, perhaps in combination with a small group of wealthy benefactors, it is more likely that the board will be synonymous with the membership.

These variations from the ideal type notwithstanding, it appears that organizations in the social economy do afford their members the opportunity for democratic decision making. They not only contribute to the pluralism which is a hallmark of a democratic society, but by engaging in the practice of democracy they acculturate their members with decision-making skills, knowledge about organizations which can be generalized to the political domain, and expectations as to how their representatives in the political realm ought to function.

Volunteer Participation. The label "voluntary" is often applied to organizations in the social economy because most rely on the contribution of volunteers to provide their services. All nonprofits have volunteers who serve on their boards and who are responsible for the governance of the organization. However, Sharpe (1994) found that about 70 percent of nonprofits with charitable status use volunteers for tasks other than serving on the board of directors. It is noteworthy, however, that 30 percent use none. In other words, not all charitable organizations rely upon volunteers, but most use a lot. Charities reported using 4.5 million volunteers or about 63 per organization. Nor is volunteering limited to nonprofits with charitable status; as noted above, 7.5 million Canadians over age 15 volunteered in 1996–97, according to the national survey conducted by Statistics Canada (1998). A survey conducted for the Canadian Centre for Philanthropy in 1991 came up with an estimate of 8.5 million. The Statistics Canada survey indicates that volunteer contributions were important to such areas as social services, recreation, sports and social clubs, religious congregations, and health organizations.

However, in spite of that, it might be misleading to refer to institutions that use volunteers as voluntary because the term implies spontaneous groupings without either a permanent administrative structure or paid staff. Such an impression would be quite misleading. Rather volunteers, in the main, fit into bureaucratized, mature social organizations often crossing many locales, and these organizations reserve for the volunteers specific positions with expectations that exist apart from the individuals who fill them. In other words, these positions are not voluntary in the sense that they are created by volunteers, but rather pre-defined by staff for volunteers to fit into them.

Even volunteers for permanent roles can be differentiated according to their degree of involvement — some having tasks that involve substantial time and a strong organizational identification (a Scout troop leader) and others having a passive affiliation such as a membership. Putnam (1995) refers to such a role as "tertiary" because it involves a weak link to an organization that might include membership fees and possibly financial donations, but no other involvement. Nevertheless, these nominal forms of involvement are important to organizations because they assist with financing and may be used to enhance their influence. For social movement agencies in particular, having a large membership may influence the public's perception of the initiatives. Only 6,000 of the 67,000 who pay for memberships to Amnesty International (Canada) are active, but having the larger group enhances the strength of Amnesty's efforts. Similarly, the labour movement in Canada has a membership that is largely inactive, but the fact that about one-third of the workforce belongs to a union is a significant factor in the perception of initiatives undertaken by labour leaders. Moreover, passive members of an organization can be mobilized for specific campaigns such as letter writing, petitions, and demonstrations. With the advent of the Internet and other forms of modern communication, such mobilizations have become easier.

In addition to mature social organizations operated by permanent staff, volunteers also participate in voluntary associations. Smith refers to voluntary associations as "grass roots," and defines them as: "locally-based, significantly autonomous, volunteer-run, formal, nonprofit groups that have an official membership of volunteers and that manifest significant voluntary altruism" (1997, p. 115). Unlike mature social organizations, voluntary associations rely upon volunteers not only for their activities but also for maintaining their organizational framework, which tends to be simple.

Milofsky describes voluntary associations as "neighborhood-based organizations" and argues that they should be "treated as subordinate parts of a larger social system, the community" (1987, p. 278). It is difficult to know what proportion of the social economy consists of voluntary or grassroots associations. Such associations (protest groups, neighbourhood and tenants groups, some social clubs and self-help groups) tend to be most difficult to assess because they may be more transient than mature organizations with paid employees and a formal organizational structure. By Smith's own account, many of the voluntary associations exist in relation to mature social organizations and might not survive without them.

But at the same time that the role of voluntary associations has been diminished because of the weakening of local communities, modernization has stimulated a contradictory trend. Modern forms of communication have increased the opportunities for people to form voluntary associations through the Internet, albeit associations based on very weak interpersonal connections. Baym (1996) estimates that there are over 100,000 discussion groups on the Internet, including a large number of online self-help groups for concerns related to physical and mental health and social problems such as addictions (Cooper 1999; Ferguson 1997). In addition, voluntary issue-based associations are evolving, in some cases facilitated by mature social organizations and in other cases spontaneously in response to concerns shared by their members. The Internet, therefore, may be reconstructing the notion of voluntary association from its original roots in stable neighbourhoods to a non-geographic cyberspace. Whether these interactions satisfy the meaning of community is open to debate. However, they are a form of voluntary association that is on the rise at a time when geographically-based voluntary associations are on the decline and volunteering is occurring primarily in mature, social organizations.

Summary

The aforementioned discussion has elaborated on the five dimensions that serve as the basis for the analysis that follows. The discussion brings out the underlying rationale for the dimensions that form the basis for the social economy, but also presents the complexity of the issues related to these dimensions. Although there is a basis for arguing that these dimensions can be used to explain the social economy concept, the complexity surrounding these dimensions suggests that the organizations within the social economy might not be homogenous, but rather might fall into some distinct clusters. This study therefore proceeds to explore the basis for those clusters.

METHODOLOGY

Participants and Procedure

In order to conduct the study, a sample of nonprofits and co-operatives in the province of Ontario was drawn. Ontario has a broad array of both organizations and therefore seemed appropriate for the purpose of the study. Mutual insurers were not included in the sample because they represented such a small number in relation to the other two types of organizations.

For nonprofits, the directory *Associations Canada 1998–99* containing 7,354 listings for Ontario was used to draw the sample. This appeared to be the most comprehensive sampling frame available in that it contained a range of organizations in many different fields, a range of size, and also of those with and without charitable status. For co-operatives, a list was obtained from the Co-operatives Secretariat of the Government of Canada. The Co-operatives Secretariat compiles an annual statistical profile of co-operatives in Canada and provides a list of all such organizations in Ontario. In total, there were 2,056 on the list, including 601 financial co-operatives (that is, credit unions/caisses populaires). The list of co-operatives was an ideal sampling frame in that it contained all of the co-operatives in Ontario. However, there was no similar list available for nonprofits. *Associations Canada* appeared to be best possible alternative, albeit one that was open to bias in that it did not include all nonprofits in the province. Therefore, it seems more appropriate to describe the sample as purposive rather than representative. Nevertheless, the sample was comprehensive and effort was taken to choose the participants in a non-biased manner. Yet, they were volunteers and we had no way of checking whether there was a particular bias in which organizations volunteered.

Given that we were unable to know in advance what portion of the organizations would agree to participate, a larger pool was employed than it was expected would be needed. For nonprofits, the pool consisted of 300 organizations, or every twenty-fourth one in the directory. Using this procedure guarded against any possible bias related to alphabetical position, for example, organizations beginning with Canadian might have different characteristics than the overall group. Similarly for co-operatives, a pool of 300 was drawn, or approximately every seventh one on the list.

With the exception of a small number of institutions that, upon being contacted, stated that they wanted to do the survey without an interview, three telephone interviewers collected the information for the study. They asked to speak either to the general manager or another key participant who was sufficiently knowledgeable to answer the questions in the survey. The participation rate was 84 percent, somewhat higher among nonprofits than among co-operatives, and particularly credit unions.

The final sample consisted of 212 social organizations, 66.5 percent were nonprofits, including both incorporated organizations and unincorporated associations, and 33.5 percent were co-operatives. For the purposes of data analysis, the co-operatives were subdivided into those without share capital (19 percent of the sample) and those with shares (14 percent). The co-operatives without share capital, predominantly in the housing and childcare sectors, could also be labelled as nonprofits, but to avoid confusion that reference will be reserved for corporations without shares. Forty-eight percent of the organizations had a charitable status. These were predominantly among the nonprofits, where two-thirds had a charitable status. The organizations in the study had the following median descriptors: 25 years of age, 6 employees, 30 volunteers (that is a ratio of five volunteers to one employee), and just over $500,000 of revenues.

Measures

The interviews were based upon a 37-item survey (see Appendix A) which elicited information related to the five dimensions and in addition some background information on each organization such as the form of incorporation, whether the organization had a charitable number, its age, and number of employees. The items related to the five dimensions were developed by the research team and before being finalized were piloted on four organizations. The primary structure for these items was a Likert scale, and after each item participants were offered the opportunity to add supplementary information.

Data Analysis

There were three primary steps in the data analysis. First, to determine whether each of the hypothesized scales was sufficiently reliable and whether any of the items should be dropped because of an inconsistent relationship with the other items on a particular scale. To meet this goal, Cronbach's alpha for internal consistency was computed for each hypothesized scale. Once the scales were finalized, the second step in the data analysis, a cluster analysis, was undertaken to divide the sample into homogenous clusters based on these scales. Third, once the clusters were established, chi-square tests were undertaken to determine whether particular background variables differed significantly in their relationship to the clusters. The relationship to the background variables will be presented with each of the clusters.

For all of the analyses, only organizations with complete data were included. The number of missing cases was highest for the cluster analysis because it included five scales simultaneously.

RESULTS

Scale Reliabilities

The scale items referred to in this section are from the survey in Appendix A. Items 14 to 17 in the survey were designed to measure the strength of each organization's social objectives. This scale had an alpha coefficient of 0.67.

Two items were used to measure the degree of dependence upon government. The response that organizations gave to item 18f and g (that is, the percentage of revenues from government contracts and grants) was converted to a five-point scale, ranging from highly independent to highly dependent. Item 19 was also used. This scale had an alpha coefficient of 0.54.

For relationship to the market, the percentage of revenues derived from the sale of services and products as well as contracts from non-governmental sources (18b, c, and e) was converted to a five-point scale and combined with item 20. Items 21 and 22 were originally part of the scale but were dropped because of their lack of positive relationship with the other items. The alpha coefficient for this scale was 0.59.

The democratic decision-making scale was set up to measure the extent to which the organizations engaged in democratic decision-making practices. In its final form, the scale included items 28, 31, 32, and 33, and had an alpha coefficient of 0.51. Four items were dropped from this scale because of their lack of relationship to the core items.

The final scale was designed to measure the extent of volunteer participation. The items consisted of: the ratio of volunteers to employees (item 34 over item 11) converted to a five-point scale; the percentage of revenues from donations from individuals, businesses, and foundations (item 18h, I, and j) converted to a five-point scale; the number of activities in which volunteers participate (items 35) converted to a five-point scale; and 36. Item 37 was dropped because of too much missing data. The alpha coefficient for the scale was 0.52. Overall, the scale reliabilities were low, but sufficient to proceed.

Cluster Analysis

Each of the five scale scores was standardized to have a mean of zero and a standard deviation of one. A cluster analysis was undertaken which included all organizations with complete data. The following algorythms were used: agglomerative hierarchical clustering; average linkage between groups and the squared Euclidean distance. These are the most commonly used algorythms and generally serve as a default. The best model for describing the data was the one with six clusters (Table 1). This model made the greatest sense since with seven clusters there was a jump in the distance between clusters. Of the sample of 154 organizations with complete data, 140 fell within the first three clusters. Even though the three smaller clusters represented only 9 percent of the sample, they were suggestive of distinct groupings that were worth exploring. To further test for the distinctiveness of the six clusters, a MANOVA was employed to determine whether or not the clusters varied according to their mean scores on the five dimensions. Cluster membership was the independent variable and

Table 1: Results of the Cluster Analysis

			CLUSTER															
SCALE	1 Volunteer			2 Publicly-Oriented			3 Market-Based			4 Volunteer-Social			5 Volunteer-Democratic			6 Commercial-Nonprofit		
	N	Mean	SD	N	Mean	SD	N	Mean	SD	N	Mean	SD	N	Mean	SD	N	Mean	SD
SOCIAL	72	−0.21	0.79	36	0.74	0.71	32	−0.83	0.99	8	0.82	0.65	3	0.86	0.83	3	0.41	0.72
GOVERNMENT	72	−0.35	0.59	36	1.41	0.79	32	−0.62	0.48	8	0.18	0.80	3	1.76	0.99	3	−0.79	0.28
MARKET	72	−0.26	0.76	36	−0.52	0.58	32	1.34	0.58	8	−0.99	0.38	3	−0.23	0.54	3	1.18	0.20
DEMOCRACY	72	0.06	0.90	36	0.04	0.70	32	0.40	0.74	8	−1.93	0.41	3	0.91	0.61	3	−2.70	0.00
VOLUNTEER	72	0.47	0.85	36	−0.52	0.57	32	−0.94	0.54	8	0.69	1.03	3	1.38	0.29	3	−0.56	0.17

the five scales were the dependent measures. The F value was significant (p = 0.000).

The first cluster (N = 72) is labelled as Volunteer because of its high scores on the scales for volunteer participation (mean = 0.47) (Table 1). Given that 47 percent of the sample fall into this cluster, its scores had a heavy weighting on the mean of the overall sample. The first cluster was also below the norm both for its dependence on government (–0.35) and on the market (–0.26).

Although this cluster appears to be a catch-all for volunteer organizations, there are some patterns in their characteristics: 74 percent are nonprofits and another 24 percent are cooperatives without share capital, that is, cooperatives that are also nonprofits (Table 2); they over-represent organizations with a charitable status (Table 3); and they over-represent organizations that serve a membership (Table 4). The overall pattern suggests that organizations within this cluster derive their revenues primarily

Table 2: Form of Incorporation by Cluster

| | | CLUSTER | | | | | | |
FORM OF INCORPORATION		1	2	3	4	5	6	TOTAL
CORPORATION	N	53.00	28.00	6.00	8.00	2.00	3.00	100.00
WITHOUT	Expected	46.75	23.38	20.78	5.19	1.95	1.95	100.00
SHARE	Row %	53.00	28.00	6.00	8.00	2.00	3.00	100.00
CAPITAL	Column %	73.61	77.78	18.75	100.00	66.67	100.00	64.94
CO-OPERATIVE	N	17.00	7.00	8.00	0.00	1.00	0.00	33.00
WITHOUT	Expected	15.43	7.71	6.86	1.71	0.64	0.64	33.00
SHARE	Row %	51.52	21.21	24.24	0.00	3.03	0.00	100.00
CAPITAL	Column %	23.61	19.44	25.00	0.00	33.33	0.00	21.43
CO-OPERATIVE	N	2.00	1.00	18.00	0.00	0.00	0.00	21.00
WITH	Expected	9.82	4.91	4.36	1.09	0.41	0.41	21.00
SHARE	Row %	9.52	4.76	85.71	0.00	0.00	0.00	100.00
CAPITAL	Column %	2.78	2.78	56.25	0.00	0.00	0.00	13.64
TOTAL	N	72.00	36.00	32.00	8.00	3.00	3.00	154.00
	Expected	72.00	36.00	32.00	8.00	3.00	3.00	154.00
	Row %	46.75	23.38	20.78	5.19	1.95	1.95	100.00
	Column %	100.00	100.00	100.00	100.00	100.00	100.00	100.00

Table 3: Charitable Status by Cluster

CHARITABLE STATUS		CLUSTER						
		1	2	3	4	5	6	TOTAL
YES	N	38.00	25.00	4.00	8.00	2.00	3.00	80.00
	Expected	37.40	18.70	16.62	4.16	1.56	1.56	80.00
	Row %	47.50	31.25	5.00	10.00	2.50	3.75	100.00
	Column %	52.78	69.44	12.50	100.00	66.67	100.00	51.95
NO	N	34.00	11.00	28.00	0.00	1.00	0.00	74.00
	Expected	34.60	17.30	15.38	3.84	1.44	1.44	74.00
	Row %	45.95	14.86	37.84	0.00	1.35	0.00	100.00
	Column %	47.22	30.56	87.50	0.00	33.33	0.00	48.05
TOTAL	N	72.00	36.00	32.00	8.00	3.00	3.00	154.00
	Expected	72.00	36.00	32.00	8.00	3.00	3.00	154.00
	Row %	46.75	23.38	20.78	5.19	1.95	1.95	100.00
	Column %	100.00	100.00	100.00	100.00	100.00	100.00	100.00

from donations and membership fees. These institutions were well above the norm in their ratio of volunteers to employees (9.7 to 1) and had less revenues and fewer employees than the norm (see Table 5). These latter characteristics suggest a smaller size and a purer volunteer form.

Cluster 2 (N = 36) consists of organizations that are highly dependent on government (mean = 1.41), a score on the dependence-on-government scale that is the highest of any cluster. Given that these organizations tend to serve the public at large rather than a membership, this cluster is referred to as Publicly-Oriented (Table 4). The organizations in this cluster were low on their relationship to the market (mean = –0.52) as well as volunteer participation (mean = –0.52). They were, however, well above average for their social objectives (mean = 0.74).

About 78 percent of the organizations within cluster 2 were nonprofits, and another 19 percent were co-operatives without share capital (Table 2). Sixty-nine percent of these organizations had a charitable status (Table 3), a figure that was much higher than the sample norm of 48 percent. Therefore, this cluster might be viewed as a charitable grouping as well. The organizations within this cluster had nearly five times the number of

Table 4: Form of Service Delivery by Cluster

FORM OF SERVICE DELIVERY		CLUSTER						
		1	2	3	4	5	6	TOTAL
NON-PROFIT	N	24.00	20.00	2.00	8.00	1.00	2.00	57.00
SERVING THE	Expected	26.65	13.32	11.84	2.96	1.11	1.11	57.00
PUBLIC	Row %	42.11	35.09	3.51	14.04	1.75	3.51	100.00
	Column %	33.33	55.56	6.25	100.00	33.33	66.67	37.01
NON-PROFIT	N	29.00	8.00	4.00	0.00	1.00	1.00	43.00
SERVING A	Expected	20.10	10.05	8.94	2.23	0.84	0.84	43.00
MEMBERSHIP	Row %	67.44	18.60	9.30	0.00	2.33	2.33	100.00
	Column %	40.28	22.22	12.50	0.00	33.33	33.33	27.92
CO-OPERATIVE	N	17.00	7.00	9.00	0.00	1.00	0.00	34.00
WITHOUT	Expected	15.90	7.95	7.06	1.77	0.66	0.66	34.00
SHARE	Row %	50.00	20.59	26.47	0.00	2.94	0.00	100.00
CAPITAL	Column %	23.61	19.44	28.13	0.00	33.33	0.00	22.08
CO-OPERATIVE	N	2.00	1.00	17.00	0.00	0.00	0.00	20.00
WITH SHARE	Expected	9.35	4.68	4.16	1.04	0.39	0.39	20.00
CAPITAL	Row %	10.00	5.00	85.00	0.00	0.00	0.00	100.00
	Column %	2.78	2.78	53.13	0.00	0.00	0.00	12.99
TOTAL	N	72.00	36.00	32.00	8.00	3.00	3.00	154.00
	Expected	72.00	36.00	32.00	8.00	3.00	3.00	154.00
	Row %	46.75	23.38	20.78	5.19	1.95	1.95	100.00
	Column %	100.00	100.00	100.00	100.00	100.00	100.00	100.00

employees of cluster 1 and a ratio of volunteers to employees of only 1.43 to 1, or less than the overall sample (Table 5). In other words, the organizations in this cluster were nonprofits and nonprofit co-operatives dependent upon government, with strong social commitments and had a lower ratio of volunteers to employees than most of the other organizations. They were much less self-sufficient than the organizations in the Volunteer cluster and even more so in the Market-Based cluster (cluster 3) that follows.

Cluster 3 (N = 32) are market-based organizations in that their score on that scale is more than one Z-score above the mean (Table 1) — and the highest of any cluster on that scale. These organizations also function with a high degree of independence from government (mean = –0.62). They are

Table 5: Background Information by Cluster

BACKGROUND VARIABLES	CLUSTER											
	1		2		3		4		5		6	
	N	Median	N	Median	N	Median	N	Median	N	Median	N	Median
AGE OF ORGANIZATION	72	26.00	36	20.00	32	42.50	8	24.50	3	21.00	3	37.00
NUMBER OF VOLUNTEERS	72	29.00	36	20.00	32	30.00	8	120.00	3	16.00	3	6.00
NUMBER OF EMPLOYEES	72	3.00	36	14.00	32	10.00	8	7.50	3	12.00	3	325.00
RATIO OF VOLUNTEERS TO EMPLOYEES	72	9.70	36	1.43	32	3.00	8	16.00	3	1.30	3	0.02
GROSS REVENUES	72	$362,500.00	36	$1,050,000.00	32	$1,936,830.50	8	$412,500.00	3	$68,050,000.00	3	16,500,000.00

relatively high on democratic decision making (mean = 0.40), but low on volunteer participation (mean = –0.94) and social objectives (mean = –0.83). More than 56 percent of the organizations within this cluster are co-operatives with share capital (more than four times greater than their share of the overall sample) and another 25 percent are co-operatives without share capital (Table 2). Nonprofits, 19 percent of this cluster, are grossly under-represented in relation to their share of the overall sample.

Nonprofits serving a membership have a stronger presence in this cluster than those serving the public (Table 4). Not surprisingly, only 12.5 percent of the institutions with a charitable status are within the cluster (Table 3), suggesting that the cluster might also be called publicly-oriented charitable organizations. Compared to the first two clusters, the organizations within cluster 3 are older (median = 42.5) and have about four times the revenues (median = $1.9 million). They also have a surprising number of volunteers (median = 30), but the ratio to employees is less than the norm because they also have a higher number of employees (that is, ten) (Table 5).

Clusters 4 to 6 are small, involving from three to eight cases (Table 1), and therefore will not carry the same weight in the discussion. However, these clusters might be suggestive of unique groupings which are worth exploring.

Cluster 4 (N = 8) is distinguished by its high social commitment and volunteer participation scores (Table 1). Therefore, it is labelled as Volunteer-Social. The cluster also has very low scores for both relationship to the market (mean = –0.99) and democratic decision making (mean = –1.93). All of the organizations within this cluster are nonprofits serving the public (Tables 2 and 4) and all have a charitable status (Table 3). These organizations have an extraordinarily high number of volunteers (120) and a ratio of 16 volunteers to each employee (Table 5). Their revenues are about a $100,000 less than the norm. Therefore, this cluster might be viewed as a purer volunteer grouping than cluster 1 — stronger on both volunteer participation and its social objectives — but unlike cluster 1, not particularly democratic.

Cluster 5 with only three cases was a bit difficult to interpret. It had the highest scores on all the scales except dependence on the market (Table 1).

The scores on dependence on government (mean = 1.76) and volunteer participation (mean = 1.38), suggest that the organizations involved supported themselves from a combination of donation and government grants. The high scores on democratic decision making (mean = 0.91) and the social commitment measure (mean = 0.86) reflect highly democratic organizations with strong social commitments. The cluster consisted of two nonprofits (one serving a membership) and one cooperative without share capital (Tables 2 and 4). Two of the three organizations also had charitable status (Table 3). The organizations in the cluster had the largest revenues of the clusters ($68 million) and the second largest number of employees (12) (Table 5). Cluster 5 is the third cluster with a high score on the volunteer participation scale. This pattern suggests that volunteer organizations are heterogeneous, with varying degrees of commitments to social objectives and democratic decision making.

Cluster 6 (N = 3), a second grouping of market-based organizations (mean = 1.18) (Table 1), also indicates that there is variation among social organizations tied to the market. Unlike cluster 3, which had a low score on social objectives and a high score on democratic decision making, the organizations in this cluster are relatively high on social objectives (mean = 0.41) and very low on democratic decision making (mean = −2.70). The three organizations in this cluster are large non-profits with a charitable status (Tables 2 and 3), all in the arts, which derive their revenues primarily from ticket sales. They have medians of 325 employees, only six volunteers, and revenues of $16.5 million (Table 5). They might be described as commercial nonprofits, and therefore that label will be applied to cluster 6.

In summary, there are three clusters with high volunteer participation scores, two made up of market-based organizations, and two of organizations aligned with the public sector. Although the subsequent discussion will focus on the three large clusters, the smaller ones are important because they indicate that volunteer organizations, market-based groupings, and those that are dependent upon government are heterogeneous in their characteristics. Therefore, with a larger sample, it is possible that these small clusters would become more meaningful.

DISCUSSION

This study makes three contributions to research in this field. First, rather than simply focusing on nonprofits, it utilizes the social economy concept that has little use outside Quebec and Western Europe. In the introduction, a rationale for using the social economy was developed by suggesting that nonprofits share characteristics in common with other organizations in the social economy, that is, social organizations. Although there are classification systems for nonprofits (Febbraro, Hall and Parmegiani 1999; Jansen, Senecal and Thompson 1982), in general such systems have tended to view nonprofits as distinct from other organizational types.

Second, this study not only develops an approach for classifying the organizations in the social economy, but it also does this empirically rather than intuitively as is the general practice in the field. In order to conduct empirical research, a survey was developed for this study. Even though the survey was carefully tested prior to its use here, it was necessarily experimental. As such, the study is exploratory. However, viewed positively, it has produced an instrument that other researchers in the field can utilize and improve upon.

Third and perhaps most importantly, this study employs a multi-dimensional approach for classification. Other researchers have utilized multiple dimensions for classifying nonprofits (ibid.), but this work has not involved the social economy concept nor an empirical approach. Through utilizing five empirically determined dimensions, this study arrived at six clusters or groupings of organizations within the social economy. There were three major groupings and three smaller ones. With a larger sample, it might be possible to determine whether these smaller groupings actually represent a significant number of organizations within the social economy. The following discussion will focus on the multi-dimensional issue as it bears particular significance to research both on nonprofits and the social economy.

The results confirm the working assumption underlying this study that the social economy is heterogeneous and it would be better to characterize this heterogeneity in terms of underlying dimensions than simply the form of incorporation. The three main clusters were composed of organizations with all three incorporation types. Nevertheless, there was a highly significant relationship between the clusters and the form of incorporation (chi-square=59.9, p<.005)[2] (Table 2), suggesting that organizations with a particular form of incorporation were more likely to end up in one cluster than another. However, a reasonable interpretation of the data suggests that this occurred not because of the incorporation type but rather because of the characteristics of these organizations, as reflected by their scores on the five scales.

For example, cluster 3 consisted of market-based firms, and grossly over-represented co-operatives with share capital, that is, credit unions, farm marketing, and retail food co-operatives. It would be tempting to argue that organizations were in this cluster because they were co-operatives with share capital, but nearly half of this Market-Based cluster were either co-operatives without share capital and nonprofit corporations. This pattern suggests that co-operatives with share capital are more market-based in their orientation than either of the other two forms of incorporation, and particularly more so than nonprofits. However, such a conclusion is tempered by the make-up of cluster 6 (Commercial Nonprofits), which also had a very high score on the market scale. Therefore, it appears that market-based firms are more likely to be co-operatives with share capital, but could also be co-operatives without share capital (for example, childcare co-operatives) and nonprofits. The nonprofits were either arts organizations that had a commercial orientation or nonprofits selling a service through the market, such as credit counselling.

This same pattern is apparent in the other major groupings. The organizations that were highly dependent upon government (cluster 2 and also 5) over-represented nonprofits and grossly under-represented co-operatives with shares. Nearly 70 percent of the organizations in these clusters had a charitable status (much higher than the overall mean of 48 percent). However, it would be overly simplistic to refer to this cluster as either nonprofits or charities. More than 20 percent of these clusters consist of co-operatives without shares and about 30 per cent of the organizations lack a charitable status. Similarly, nonprofits serving the public are more heavily represented than those serving a membership. Focusing on one dimension only does not lead to a proper understanding.

Therefore, we propose that a multi-dimensional approach to classifying the organizations of the social economy is more useful than focusing on their form of incorporation or their type of service. In the taxonomy literature, multi-dimensional or polythetic approaches are viewed as a conceptual advance (Sokal 1974). In this study, the dimensions that were used for classification purposes were derived from the social economy concept discussed earlier in the introduction. These are dynamic variables that apply in varying degrees to all organizations in the social economy. By applying these five dimensions, it was possible to establish clusters that were descriptive of the underlying characteristics. Volunteer or Market-Based, for example, are descriptive of characteristics that organizations of the social economy share.

Moreover, the clusters indicate that these underlying dimensions can lead to interesting variations. For example, organizations with high volunteer participation scores end up in three distinct clusters. The organizations in two of these groupings operated independently of government, although one did not. They also differed in the degree to which they embraced democratic decision making and the strength of their social objectives. Whereas the primary grouping (cluster 1) was high only on volunteer participation, both smaller clusters (4 and 5) were high on social commitments, but cluster 5 was the only one high on democratic decision making. In other words, organizations based on volunteer participation can also differ, not only on that dimension but also in the extent to which they engage in democratic practices and the strength of their social objectives.

One of the difficulties in a multi-dimensional model is that categorization can become too complex. It is easier to focus on simple categories such as nonprofit or co-operative, and to ignore the obvious variations. Inevitably, in a multi-dimensional approach, one focuses on the most salient characteristics and tends to downplay others. Nevertheless, if heterogeneity exists, it should be presented in the research. Not all social organizations are alike, and the differences go beyond their form of incorporation, their charitable status, and such obvious characteristics as their type of service and size. In fact, the differences are so profound that, to a degree, they call into question the unifying concept of the social economy. However, the same can be said of most unifying concepts. Within the private and public sectors this same heterogeneity also exists. Private sector firms can range from huge international corporations to owner-operated micro-enterprises, and public sector organizations can range from Crown corporations that compete in the market to government agencies. In both cases, the unifying thread is quite thin.

Part of the reason that this study drew out the heterogeneity within the social economy was that the sample was limited to social organizations. The unifying dimensions of the social economy would become more apparent if the analysis included private sector firms as well as government agencies. That mix would likely alter the relative positioning of social organizations on the standardized scores, and would in all probability accentuate the unifying dimensions of social organizations. For example, for each of the scales, organizations received a standardized Z-score, which was used to determine their relative positions in the overall sample. Changes in the composition of the sample can affect the relative positioning of any one institution, or for that matter any group of organizations. Let us illustrate the point by reference to the market scale. One of the items on this scale asks: "To what extent does your organization have to compete in the market with private sector companies to earn its revenues?" The mean of the raw scores for this item is 2.76, or just under the mid-point response of "somewhat." If the sample also included private sector firms, the actual mean would increase, as they would in all probability mark "a lot," or the final point on the scale. Moreover, if the mean were to increase, the relative positioning of social organizations would decrease.

This same point can be made with respect to each of the items on the five scales. With a broader sample, the unifying dimensions among social organizations are more likely to emerge, but a sample consisting only of social organizations highlights the heterogeneity and downplays the unifying dimensions.

A CONCLUDING COMMENT

While the measures used in this study can be refined and the sampling can be improved, the general approach of using multiple dimensions to understand the heterogeneity within the social economy appears to be sound. The appropriateness of the conceptual dimensions used is open to debate; perhaps other dimensions might be more useful. However, a multidimensional model based upon the underlying dynamics of the organizations within the social economy appears to be the most logical approach to understanding this sector and raising issues for further research.

Notes

Recognition is also due to Sandra Anthony and Paul Raun for undertaking the interviews, and Tahany Gadalla for her helpful advice with respect to the data analysis.

[1] There are also insurance companies (primarily life insurers) bearing the name mutual that have been organized in this way by management to block a hostile takeover. Therefore, these have been excluded from the social economy framework.

[2] Given that there were so many cells in clusters 4 to 6 with fewer than five cases, the chi-square was done with only clusters 1 to 3.

References

Amnesty International (Canada). 1999. Personal communication. May.

Baym, N.K. 1996. "Agreements and Disagreements in Computer-Mediated Discussion," *Research on Language and Social Interaction*, 29 (4):315-45.

Canadian Centre for Philanthropy. 1999. Personal communication. May.

Canadian Association of Mutual Insurance Companies. 1999. Personal communication. May.

Christenson, J. 1994. "Themes of Community Development," in *Community Development in Perspective*, ed. J. Christenson and J. Robinson. Ames, IA: Iowa State University.

Cooper, G. 1999. "Online Assistance for Problem Gamblers." Unpublished doctoral dissertation proposal. Toronto: University of Toronto.

Co-operatives Secretariat. 1998. *Co-operatives in Canada (1996)*. Ottawa: Government of Canada.

Craig, J. 1993. *The Nature of Co-operation*. Montreal: Black Rose.

Cromie, M. 1990. "Performing Arts," *Canadian Social Trends*, 28 (Winter):301-04.

Dees, J.G. 1998. "Enterprising Non-Profits," *Harvard Business Review*, 76(January/February):55-67.

Defourny, J. 1988. "De la coopération à l'économie sociale," in *Proceedings of the Congreso de Co-opertivisimo*. University of Duesto and the World Basque Congress, pp. 71-88.

Defourny, J. and C.J. Monzon, eds. 1992. *The Third Sector: Co-operative, Mutual and Nonprofit Organizations*. Brussels: CIRIEC, DeBoeck University.

Ellerman, D. 1982. *The Socialization of Entrepreneurship*. Boston: Industrial Cooperative Association.

_____ 1990. *The Democratic Worker-Owned Firm*. Boston: HarperCollins.

Febbraro, A. R., M. Hall and M. Parmegiani. 1999. *Developing a Typology of the Voluntary Health Sector in Canada: Definition and Classification Issues*. Toronto: CPRN for Canadian Centre for Philanthropy.

Ferguson, T. 1997. "Health Care in Cyberspace: Patients Lead a Revolution," *The Futurist*, 31 (6):29-33.

Hansman, H. 1986. "The Role of Nonprofit Enterprise," in *The Economics of Nonprofit Institutions: Studies in Structure and Policy*, ed. S. Rose-Ackerman. New York: Oxford University Press.

Jansen, J., F. Senecal, F.G. Thompson. DPA Consulting. 1983. *The Development of a Typology of the Voluntary Sector in Canada*. Ottawa: Social Trends Analysis Directorate, Policy Coordination Analysis and Management Systems Branch.

Jeantet, T. 1991. "Économie sociale et coopératives." France: n.p.

Kenyon, R. 1976. *To the Credit of the People*. Toronto: Ontario Credit Union League.

Lager, F. 1994. *Ben & Jerry's: The Inside Scoop*. New York: Crown.

Mansbridge, J. 1982. "Fears of Conflict in Face-to-Face Democracies," in *Workplace democracy and social change*, ed. F. Lindenfeld and J. Rothschild-Whitt. Bountiful, UT: Horizon Publishers.

Martin, S. 1985. *An Essential Grace: Funding Canada's Health Care, Education, Welfare, Religion and Culture*. Toronto: McClelland & Stewart.

MacPherson, I. 1979. *A History of the Co-operative Movement in English-Canada: 1900-1945*. Toronto: MacMillan.

Milofsky, C. 1987. "Neighborhood-based Organization: A Market Analogy," in *The Nonprofit Sector: A Research Handbook*, ed. W.W. Powell. New Haven: Yale University Press.

Olson, M. 1965. *The Logic of Collective Action*. New York: Schocken.

Putnam, R. 1995. "Bowling Alone: America's Declining Social Capital," *Journal of Democracy*, 6(1):65-78.

Quarter, J. 1992. *Canada's Social Economy: Co-operatives, Non-profits and Other Community Enterprises.* Toronto: James Lorimer.

Roddick, A. 1991. *Body and Soul:* New York: Crown.

Rothschild-Whitt, J. 1982. "The Collective Organization: An Alternative to Bureaucratic Models," in *Workplace Democracy and Social Change,* ed. F. Lindenfeld and J. Rothschild-Whitt. Bountiful, UT: Horizon Publishers.

Salamon, L. 1995. *Partners in Public Service: Government-Nonprofit Relations in the Modern Welfare State.* Baltimore, MD: The Johns Hopkins University Press.

Sharpe, D. 1994. *A Portrait of Canada's Charities.* Toronto: Canadian Centre for Philanthropy.

Smith, D.H. 1997. "The Rest of the Nonprofit Sector: Grassroots Associations as the Dark Matter Ignored in the Prevailing "Flat Earth" Maps of the Sector," *Nonprofit and Voluntary Sector Quarterly,* 26(2):114-31.

Snaith, I. 1991. "The économie sociale in the New Europe," *Yearbook of Co-operative Enterprise.*

Sokal, R. 1974. "Classification: Purposes, Principles, Progress, Prospects," *Science,* 185(4157):1115-23.

Statistics Canada. 1998. *Highlights from the 1997 National Survey of Giving, Volunteering and Participating.* Ottawa: Minister of Industry.

Wilkinson, K. 1994. "The Future of Community Development," in *Community Development in Perspective,* ed. J. Christenson and J. Robinson. Ames, IA: Iowa State University.

Wilkinson, P. and J. Quarter. 1996. *Building a Community-Controlled Economy: The Evangeline Co-operative Experience.* Toronto: University of Toronto Press.

Appendix A

CONFIDENTIAL NON-PROFIT/CO-OPERATIVE SURVEY

Background Information

1. Your name: _____

2. Your position in the organization: _____

3. Organization name: _____

4. Address: _____

5. Phone: _____ Fax: _____ Email: _____

6. How old is your organization? _____ Years

7. Which of the following best describes your organization:
   1. Corporation without share capital (non-profit)
   2. Co-operative without share capital (non-profit)
   3. Co-operative with share capital
   4. Unincorporated association
   5. A trust
   6. Other (specify): _____

8. Circle the jurisdiction(s) in which your organization is registered: (Circle one number)
   1. British Columbia   2. Alberta   3. Saskatchewan
   4. Manitoba   5. Ontario   6. Quebec
   7. New Brunswick   8. Nova Scotia   9. Prince Edward Island
   10. Newfoundland   11. Federal

9. Does your organization have a charitable registration number?
   1. YES   2. NO

10. If YES, for how many years? _____

11. Total number of employees in the organization: _____

Social Objectives

12. Why was your organization formed originally?

_____
_____
_____
_____

13. What is its current mission?

_____
_____
_____
_____

14. How would you rate your organization's social objectives relative to its commercial objectives?

My organization's social objectives are:

1	2	3	4	5
Much Less Important	Less Important	Of Equal Importance	More Important	Much More Important

14a. Please Elaborate

_____
_____
_____

15. To what extent does your organization view itself as part of one or more social movements?

1	2	3	4	5
Not At All	A Little	Somewhat	Moderately	A Lot

15a. If you circled either points 1 or 2, please indicate which social movement or movements:

_____
_____
_____

16. To what extent does your organization view itself as an agency of social change?

1	2	3	4	5
Not At All	A Little	Somewhat	Moderately	A Lot

16a. If you circled either points 1 or 2, please elaborate:

_____
_____
_____

17. Relative to service to its consumers, how important are your organization's social movement goals? (Circle one number)

1	2	3	4	5
Much Less Important	Less Important	Of Equal Importance	More Important	Much More Important

17a. Please elaborate:

_____

_____

_____

Relationship to Government and Private Sector:

18. In the last fiscal year, approximately what were your organization's gross revenues?

_____

Approximately what percentage of those revenues came from the following sources:

a) Sales of services   _____

b) Sales of products   _____

c) Membership fees   _____

d) Contracts with non-government sources   _____

e) Government contracts   _____

f) Government grants   _____

g) Donations from individuals   _____

h) Donations from businesses   _____

i) Donations from foundations   _____

j) Other sources (specify)   _____

_____

_____

19. Apart from the financial relationship, which of the following best describes your organization's relationship to government?

1	2	3	4	5
Highly Independent	Mostly Independent	Equally Independent & Dependent	Mostly Dependent	Highly Dependent

19a. Please elaborate:

_____

_____

_____

20. To what extent does you organization have to compete in the market with private sector companies to earn its revenues?

1	2	3	4	5
Not At All	A Little	Somewhat	Moderately	A Lot

20a.Please elaborate:

_____

_____

_____

21. To what extent does your organization utilize partnerships with private sector companies?

1	2	3	4	5
Not At All	A Little	Somewhat	Moderately	A Lot

21a.Please elaborate:

_____

_____

_____

22. Even though your organization's incorporation differs from private sector businesses, to what extent do you view your organization as similar to them?

1	2	3	4	5
Not At All	A Little	Somewhat	Moderately	A Lot

22a.Please elaborate:

_____

_____

_____

Governance:

23. Are there general meetings of the membership (as distinct from the board meetings)?
    1. YES   2. NO

23a.If YES, how many members (people who are eligible to vote at meetings) would usually attend? _____

24. How many members does your organization have? _____

25. Who is eligible for membership?

_____

_____

_____

26. Describe the process for becoming a member?

_____

_____

_____

27. How many board members does your organization have? _____

28. Describe the process for becoming a board member?
    1. Election by the general membership   2. Appointment by the board
    3. Appointment by government   4. Other (specify): _____

29. How long is a board member's normal term of service?
    1. 1 year   2. 2 years   3. 3 years
    4. More than 3 years   5. Other (specify) _____

30. How often does the board meet?
    1. Annually   2. Quarterly   3. Bi-monthly
    4. Monthly   5. Bi-weekly   6. Weekly
    7. Other (specify) _____

31. To what extent does the general membership influence the decisions of the board of directors/trustees?

1	2	3	4	5
Not At	A	Somewhat	Moderately	A
All	Little			Lot

31a. Please Elaborate:

_____
_____
_____

32. To what extent does the board of directors/trustees influence the decisions of senior management?

1	2	3	. 4	5
Not At	A	Somewhat	Moderately	A
All	Little			Lot

32a. Please Elaborate:

_____
_____
_____

33. To what extent does the general membership influence the decisions of senior management? (Circle one number)

1	2	3	4	5
Not At	A	Somewhat	Moderately	A
All	Little			Lot

33a. Please Elaborate:

_____
_____
_____

Volunteers:

34. How many volunteers does your organization have?

35. Describe the types of activities undertaken by volunteers?
    1. Board of directors   2. Board committees
    3. Other committees   4. Fundraising
    5. Other service (specify): _____

36. To what extent is your organization referred to as a volunteer organization?

1	2	3	4	5
Never	Rarely	Sometimes	Often	Always

36a. Please Elaborate:

_____
_____
_____

37. To what extent do volunteers (other than board members) influence the decisions of management?

1	2	3	4	5
Not At All	A Little	Somewhat	Moderately Lot	A

37a. Please Elaborate:

_____
_____
_____

4

Capturing Community Capacity: The Role of Informal and Formal Networks in Supporting Families with Young Children

James J. Rice, Debbie Sheehan,
Suzanne Brown and Marney Cuff

INTRODUCTION

The early years of a child's development sets the stage for learning, socialization and health throughout the life cycle (McCain and Mustard 1999). Many factors affect this early developmental period. There are contextual risk factors and conditions such as poor family relationships, family conflict, inconsistent or ineffective parenting, abuse, adolescent parenthood, single parenthood, recent immigration, lack of social supports, poverty, or social assistance dependence that can negatively affect a child's ability to function (Thomas *et al.* 1997).There are environment factors such as poor nutrition and inadequate stimulation that have a greater influence on infant brain development than previously suspected, and the effects are long lasting (Hertzman 1995; Statistics Canada 1996; Nash 1997; National Council of Welfare 1997). These multiple risk factors are difficult to address and single-strategy programs supporting vulnerable families are likely to be ineffective.

Social policy theorists have introduced the idea that all individuals, families and neighbourhoods have gifts and assets that can be engaged to help mothers deal with these risks and build healthier families (Kretzmann and McKnight 1993). The transmission of these gifts and assets can take place through the family's social networks. Social networks are made up of *informal relationships* with family, friends, co-workers, partners, and neighbours; and *formal relationships* with professional people such as social workers, nurses, family home visitors or other social service agency staff. Together, these relationships create the social context in which families live and provide the "mediating structures" to help families meet their needs (Eng and Young 1992). The promotion of social support activities has emerged as an important strategy in meeting the needs of families. These strategies have been conceptualized as community-based activities which provide less formal interventions in the lives of families and use more natural social activities as the foundation of change. The newly released *Early Years Study* recognizes the importance of these mediating structures and recommends that investment in early child development and parenting be key priorities for the province of Ontario (McCain and Mustard 1999).

Theories related to community capacity-building do not preclude the necessity of outside resources from government or private business from being introduced into the community (Kretzmann and McKnight 1993). Indeed, capacity-building argues that the assets of individual people and neighbourhoods can be mobilized, in part, for the purposes of identifying and acting to bring much needed outside resources into low-income neighbourhoods. Some communities are unable to provide the social support needed by mothers without the help of those outside resources.

There is empirical evidence that demonstrates a positive association between social support for mothers and positive health outcomes such as breast-feeding duration (Matthews *et al.* 1998; Oakley 1992) and infant birth weight (Turner, Grindstaff and Phillips 1990). Supports such as individual opportunities, close family ties, and external support systems (formal and informal) have been shown to improve the health and developmental outcomes of children who face chronic stressors (Garmezy 1991). Social support and supportive environments are important concepts in both the health promotion and community capacity literature (Hamilton and Bhatti 1996; Kretzmann and McKnight 1993). On the other hand, lack of social support has been associated with increased risk of child abuse and family violence (MacMillan, MacMillan and Offord 1993).

Researchers have identified four domains of informal network support: emotional support (affect, esteem, and concern); appraisal support (feedback, affirmation); information support (suggestion, advice, and information); and instrumental support (labour, money, time, etc.) (Eng and Young 1992). Researchers have also identified three characteristics of informal networks which can be used to categorize the relationships among individuals: the structures of the network (size and density of the network), interaction process between people within the network (frequency, reciprocity), and functional outcomes of the interactions within the network (functions provided by the network members). (See Israel 1985.)

In the same way, researchers have identified three distinct roles that formal organizations play within social networks. They can provide social support, counselling services, and education to increase the ability of families to connect with appropriate resources (Eng and Young 1992). This "hidden system" has been variously defined as: the mobilization of community resources to meet identified needs, the use of transferable knowledge and skills to meet goals and objectives, or the strengths of the community that enable it to affect change (Abelson 1999; Baker and Teaser-Polk 1998; Goodman *et al.* 1998). These resources represent some elements of our community's capacity to support families and can be categorized into four groups: informal care-givers and neighbourhood networks, mutual aid groups (strangers with common issues), volunteers (individuals offering their time and services), and formal voluntary organizations (Cox 1993).

The formal relationships that make up part of a person's social network consist of interactions with people from the public, private, and nonprofit sector. *Public organizations* are operated by governments and provide programs that are mandated by legislation. *Private organizations* are privately owned and return profits to the owners or directors of the enterprise. For this study we used Salamon and Anheier's structural/operational definition of *nonprofit organizations*.

Table 1: International Classification of Nonprofit Organizations

Criteria	Characteristic
	The organizations
Formal	• must be institutionalized to some extent
Private	• must be separate from government
Nonprofit distributing	• do not generate profits
Self-governing	• have their own internal procedures for governance
Voluntary	• have a significant degree of voluntary participation

Source: Adapted from Salamon and Anheier (1992).

In seeking help, families often use government agencies such as public health, social assistance programs, and youth-serving agencies for assistance. They turn to the private sector for health services, child care or care of the elderly. And they turn to nonprofit organizations for support such as information, counselling or friendly advice, advocacy, housing, aid, or comfort, etc. (Rice 1990).

In an earlier period of social network analysis, Caplan identified three roles that networks might play in providing help: helping to mobilize resources and manage emotional problems, sharing tasks, and providing material assistance to help deal with a particular stressful situation (Caplan 1974). These resources represent some elements of our community's capacity to support families.

In recent years we have witnessed the growth of formalized community initiatives to support families with young children. Hamilton-Wentworth has benefited from large-scale public sector initiatives such as the federal Community Action Program for Children[1] and the Province of Ontario's new Healthy Babies, Healthy Children (HBHC) Program.[2] There has been a corresponding growth in other community responses, including work by local foundations (Hamilton Community Foundation) and community advocacy groups (Voices for Children and Connections for Kids). These initiatives all support the formation of networks through which agencies attempt to coordinate services and supports for families. At the same time funding to the nonprofit sector has not expanded or in fact has been decreased (e.g., maternity homes) over the past number of years, as witnessed in our community by declining United Way resources and major financial cuts to social services agencies like Second Stage Housing, which provides transitional housing and support for women and their children leaving abusive situations.

These changes, both positive and negative, pose important questions about how families use their informal and formal networks in supporting their endeavors to raise their children.

PURPOSE OF THE RESEARCH

The objective of this study is to examine how families with young children (0–6 years) use formal and informal networks to assist them in their roles as parents. The research examines two components of social networks: informal relations with family, friends, co-workers, partners, and neighbours; and formal relationships with professional people such as social workers, nurses, family home visitors or other social service agency staff.

The research questions are:

- What are the patterns of families' use of informal and formal supports?

- What are the experiences families have in receiving support from their informal and formal support networks?

- What type of formal networks (public, nonprofit or private) do families turn to?

- How does the community context influence support utilization?

The results of this study are used to generate policy recommendations for the volunteer/nonprofit sector and the social services system.

METHODS

Study Setting

Hamilton-Wentworth, with an approximate population of 480,000, has an ethnically diverse community with its population spread over urban and rural areas (Statistics Canada 1996). There are approximately 6,000 births annually. Hamilton-Wentworth has the highest prevalence of socio-economic risk factors, and the highest rate for most of the adverse pregnancy outcomes in Central West Ontario (Lee *et al.* 1999). Adolescent pregnancy rates increased from 43 pregnancies per 1,000 teens (15 to 19 years of age) in 1989 to 51 pregnancies per 1,000 teens in 1995. In 1996, single pregnant women and pregnant adolescents were more likely to give birth to low birth-weight babies than older and married pregnant women.

Compared with other Central West Ontario districts, Hamilton-Wentworth has a high number of low-income families (19 percent) and lone parent families (13 percent) (Hamilton-Wentworth. Social and Public Health Services Division 1999). Since 1991, there has been an increase in the local poverty rate by 4.5 percent with a parallel increase in the number of single parent families receiving social assistance benefits (Hamilton-Wentworth. Social Planning and Research Council 1999). The number of children (0–18 years) brought under protective care by the local children's aid societies increased from 4.3 per 1,000 children in 1996 to 4.8 per 1,000 children in 1997 (Hamilton-Wentworth. Social and Public Health Services Division 1999).

Hamilton-Wentworth has a diverse network of almost 800 social service agencies as well as strong faith communities and neighbourhood associations (Community Information Services 1998). Many local community groups offer both support and advocacy to members of the community. In Hamilton-Wentworth there are approximately 100 self-help groups identified in the Self-Help Centre/Community Information Services directory, with names that range from "Grandparents Raising Grandchildren" to "Quoc Viet" a support group for Vietnamese women.

Study Design

This exploratory study gathered information about the nature and use of the families' social networks, the way they viewed their community, and the risk factors that exist in their communities. Three tools[3] were used to collect data about the families. The Social Network Inventory examined the family's social networks. The daily diaries documented the use of networks over a six-month time period. The Perceived Level of Neighbourhood Social Capital Scale explored the way families perceived their community.

Data from the 1996 Statistics Canada Census were used to describe socio-demographic characteristics of the communities in which the families lived. Formal networks identified by the families were classified as public, private, or nonprofit using the definitions identified in the introduction of this chapter. At the end of the study a subsample of the families participated in a focus group.

Study Sample and Recruitment

The study population consisted of families referred by the HBHC program from September to December 1998, who resided in the City of Hamilton. Public health nurses described the research project to all eligible families and obtained their (written) agreement to be involved in the research process. Families recruited into the study were referred to the HBHC program for a variety of reasons, including: premature birth, recent immigration to Canada, language barriers, difficulty accessing prenatal care, and self-referral for family history of depression. A research assistant contacted the family either by phone, a brief home visit (if no telephone), or through the public health nurse. During the initial contact this individual arranged a time to meet the family in their home for the initial interview.[4]

DATA COLLECTION

An initial individual interview was conducted in the home to collect baseline data using the Social Network Inventory (see Appendix 1). Each family was then asked to fill out a series of diaries which recorded their daily use of social networks (see Appendix 2). The diary was designed to examine the use of social networks over time as well as the nature of the relationship between the families and the people in their networks as they occur in everyday life. Diaries were translated into the language spoken at home for non-English-speaking families. Cultural interpreters assisted the research assistant during the individual interviews when required. After families had been in the study for six months, the individual interview was repeated and families also completed the "Perceived Level of Neighbourhood Social Capital Scale" (see Appendix 3).

At the completion of the project, ten study families were invited to participate in a focus group to provide input into the data analysis and further explore emergent themes observed during the project. The process was intended to encourage the families to identify their own issues and discuss how they perceived using their support systems.

We were interested in looking at the distribution of known community risk factors within the communities where the families lived (by postal code) and comparing these with the region of Hamilton-Wentworth as a whole. This would assist us in determining how important community context is in relation to the use of social networks. The study used Statistics Canada 1996 Census data to develop a risk index for each local community. The methodology used to develop the index is described in Appendix 4.

DATA ANALYSIS

All data were directly entered from the study instruments into SPSS 9.0 for Windows data entry system. Descriptive statistics were used to describe services used and the characteristics of participants. Frequency counts and percentages were calculated as appropriate. Data from the focus groups were analyzed using an inductive approach. Using the constant comparative method, data were grouped into categories as they emerged (Maykut and Morehouse 1994).

RESULTS

The preliminary analysis of these data is presented in ten sections: study completion rate, changes in families' networks over time, changes in informal networks over time, frequency of contacts, number of daily contacts, proximity of people in the network, helping nature of the network, types of network support, families' use of formal networks, and the community context. Each section provides an overview of the concepts and a description of the data.

Study Completion Rate

Forty families were recruited into the study, with 25 completing all of the diaries and questionnaires. Three families completed partial diaries, seven dropped out of the study because of a crisis in the family, two moved out of the community, two did not respond to phone calls after the initial interview, and one withdrew at the request of the partner. At the time of entry into the study six women were pregnant. The youngest child of the other families ranged from newborn to seven years of age. Nine families did not speak English as their first language at home, with five requiring interpreters throughout the study. The findings are based on the 25 families who completed the study. The study families had a variety of living arrangements: 60 percent lived with a partner; 20 percent lived with their family of origin; and 20 percent lived on their own.

Changes in Families' Networks over Time

The families were asked in the initial and exit interviews to identify people who provided support and with whom they currently had a relationship. In the initial interview families identified people they thought were in their networks. This required them to answer questions asked by the research assistant and to think about the people who had interacted with them over the past month. In the exit interview the same questions were asked. The names identified in these interviews were then categorized into informal or formal networks (as defined in the section of the chapter on study design).

Families identified a total of 567 potential members in their networks, of which 399 were categorized as "informal" and 167 "formal" (Table 2). The average size of a family's total network was 22.7 people (range 10 to 51). The average size of the informal network was 15.9 people (range 3 to 48) and the average size of the formal network was 6.7 people (range 1 to 19). There appeared to be no pattern of relationship between the size of the informal and formal networks or the balance of informal to formal supports. Of the "potential" members available to them, families only had contact with 40.6 percent of the members of their informal network (N=162/ 399). There was a similar trend for their formal networks, with families having contact with 44.3 percent (N=74/167) of the members. There was little change in the total number of members in their informal networks over time (N=162 at initial interview, 168 at exit).

The most dramatic change in the use of networks occurred within the formal network. There was a substantive decline in contacts with formal agencies from 74 initially to 26 at exit. Formal connections decreased over the six-month period while informal networks remained steady. This shifted the proportions of formal to informal networks from 2.2:1 initially to 0.8:1 at exit. When asked about this finding in the focus group, families explained that as agencies decreased their services to families, friends stepped in to fill the gaps. Focus group participants identified that "agencies left too early." In fact, some families who had just had their babies felt that there was not enough formal support as "hospitals discharge moms way too early." They also felt that it was often difficult to get a rapid response from agencies when it was needed. Families made many calls to agencies to find out about breast-feeding, infant nutrition, and to ask about their baby's health. The mothers reported that many agencies would not/could not help them, or were slow in returning calls. Some respondents felt that agencies left too early in their child's development and said that the support would have been beneficial on a more long-term basis.

Table 2: Changes in Social Networks over Time

Type of Relationship	Potential Members in Networks		People Identified in Initial Interview		People Identified in Exit Interview	
	N	%	N	%	N	%
Informal Network	399	70.4	162	68.4	168	86.2
Formal Network (agency)	167	29.5	74	31.2	26	13.3
Other	1	0.2	1	0.4	1	0.5
Total	567	100	237	100	195	100

Changes in Informal Networks over Time

There was little change over the six months in the total number of contacts within their informal networks: 162 at the initial interview and 168 at exit (Table 3). However, over the length of the study, there was a shift toward identifying more friends (67 initially to 82 at exit) and fewer family members (71 initially to 61 at exit). Contact with neighbours and co-workers declined slightly but remained small throughout the study (range 5–10 initially to 2–7 at exit). There was an increase in contacts with boyfriends and the babies' fathers (5 initially to 11 at exit), although the total number of contacts remained small.

The parents in the focus groups reported that except for the first week, they saw friends and families less frequently in the beginning of the project and slightly more near the end. This is not supported by the data from the diaries which indicate that contacts with extended family, co-workers, and neighbours decreased over time. However, it is evidenced by the increase in the number of contacts with friends, boyfriends, and babies' fathers over the period of the study. The mothers identified that "in the beginning [i.e., after they had their babies] you are too tired and don't want to go out." These feelings of isolation also reflect the fact that the study was conducted during the winter months and Hamilton-Wentworth had experienced a bus strike during this time. The mothers reported that winter snow often kept families housebound because baby strollers are "no good" on snow-filled sidewalks, and public transportation was not available. As spring approached and the weather got better parents said they got out more with the baby in a stroller and they saw more of their friends. Other families which were newcomers to the city (and country) had not yet had the opportunity to make friends and so had few people to visit. Language barriers kept families with diverse ethnic backgrounds from making personal connections in the beginning of the study. The families also reported that by the end of the study, many of the mothers had returned to work or gone back to school (English as a Second Language or secondary school). Not surprisingly, this increased the number of friends in their informal networks.

Table 3: Changes in Families' Informal Network over Time

Members of Informal Network	People Identified in Initial Interview		People Identified in Exit Interview	
	N	%	N	%
Family	71	43.8	61	36.3
Friend	67	41.4	82	48.8
Co-worker	10	6.2	7	4.2
Neighbour	5	3.1	2	1.2
Boyfriend/baby's father	5	3.1	11	6.6
Other	4	2.5	5	3.0
Total	162	100	168	100

Frequency of Contacts

Table 4 describes how often the families saw people in their networks. Over time, there was little change in contact with informal and formal supports on a daily basis. Families saw more of their formal networks on a weekly basis (35.7 percent at initial interview, to 48.4 percent at exit) with a parallel decline in contact to once or twice a month (47.6 percent at

Table 4: Frequency of Contact by Informal and Formal Networks

Frequency of Contact	Initial Interview						Exit Interview					
	Informal Network		Formal Network		Other		Informal Network		Formal Network		Other	
	N	%	N	%	N	%	N	%	N	%	N	%
Not at all	15	10.3	9	10.7	0		11	6.9	1	3.2	0	
Once or twice a month	44	30.1	40	47.6	1	100	48	30.2	13	41.9	1	100
About once a week	44	30.1	30	35.7	0		47	29.6	15	48.4	0	
About every day	43	29.5	5	6.0	0		53	33.3	2	6.5	0	
Total	146	100	84	100	1	100	159	100	31	100	1	100

initial interview, to 41.9 percent at exit). There was as a decline in the number of networks with whom they never had contact (10.3 percent initially to 6.9 percent at exit for informal; 10.7 percent initially to 3.2 percent at exit for formal networks).

Number of Daily Contacts

Families recorded the number of contacts they had with people on selected days in their diaries (Table 5). The sampling methodology is described in Appendix 2. In the first week of recording the diaries, families chronicled a total of 270 contacts with people in their networks (there could be multiple contacts with one person), for an average of 10.8 contacts per family. By the mid-point of the study (at 13 weeks) that number had fallen to 207 contacts, with an average of 8.3 contacts per family. By the end of the study (week 26), total contacts recorded were 131 or an average of 5.2 contacts per family. Over the six months of the study, there was a decrease in the total number of contacts by 51.5 percent.

Informal contacts included family, boyfriend/partner, friends, neighbours and co-workers, but did not include those members of their network with whom they lived. In the first week, a total of 209 informal contacts were recorded. At week 13 this number had dropped to 167 contacts, and by week 26, contacts were down to 116.

Families also recorded the number of contacts they had with formal organizations. Initially, families identified a total of 60 formal or agency contacts (average 2.4/family). This declined to 40 contacts by week 13 and was down to 15 per week by the end of the study. The total number of agency contacts is small even at the beginning of the study, which is dissonant with families' perceptions of "a lot" of initial agency involvement. Focus group participants identified that they felt that they had a lot of contact with agency staff at the beginning of the study and that this tapered off quickly and in many cases, too early. There is a more rapid decline in agency contact (75 percent) than informal networks (44.5 percent) over the six months.

The ratio of formal to informal contacts is approximately 1:4 at the beginning of the study, 1:6 by midpoint and 1:11 by the end of the study, clearly demonstrating a shift in reliance from formal to informal networks.

Over time there is a steady decline in both networks, however this is not a smooth transition (Figure 1). Focus group participants identified that when filling out the diaries in the beginning they were not sure whom they had talked to or had contact with. The act of filling out the diaries made them aware of whom they talked to on a regular basis. As the warmer weather approached toward the end of the study, families in the focus group reported that it was harder to remember to fill out the diaries as they were outside more and had more things to do. This may account for some of the irregularities toward the end of the study.

Table 5: Total Number of Contacts over the Twenty-Six Weeks

	No. of Informal Contacts	No. of Formal Contacts	No. of Other Contacts	Total No. of Contacts	Average No. of Contacts	Ratio Informal: Formal
Week 1	209	60	1	270	10.8	3.48
Week 2	201	54	2	257	10.28	3.72
Week 3	193	39	1	233	9.32	4.95
Week 4	182	56	0	238	9.52	3.25
Week 5	176	43	2	221	8.84	4.09
Week 6	191	47	2	240	9.6	4.06
Week 7	187	46	0	233	9.32	4.07
Week 8	186	41	0	227	9.08	4.54
Week 9	200	42	1	243	9.72	4.76
Week 10	182	40	0	222	8.88	4.55
Week 11	183	39	0	222	8.88	4.69
Week 12	178	41	0	219	8.76	4.34
Week 13	167	40	0	207	8.28	4.18
Week 14	174	39	2	215	8.6	4.46
Week 15	157	31	0	188	7.52	5.06
Week 16	154	38	0	192	7.68	4.05
Week 17	171	24	0	195	7.8	7.13
Week 18	149	22	0	171	6.84	6.77
Week 19	143	21	0	164	6.56	6.81
Week 20	159	18	0	177	7.08	8.83
Week 21	172	17	0	189	7.56	10.12
Week 22	137	24	0	161	6.44	5.71
Week 23	138	23	0	161	6.44	6.00
Week 24	149	20	0	169	6.76	7.45
Week 25	120	25	0	145	5.8	4.80
Week 26	116	15	0	131	5.24	7.

Note: Diaries were "sampled" three days per week (see Appendix 2).

Figure 1: Total Number of Contacts over the Twenty-Six Weeks

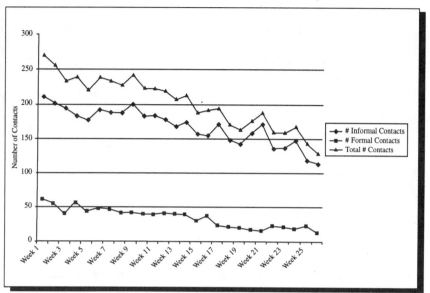

Proximity of People in the Network

Table 6 describes how close families lived to the people in their social networks. It appears from the exit interview that over time families saw members of their informal and formal networks more if they lived very close to them, that is, less than one mile. Contact with the "close" formal networks increased from 36.4 percent at initial interview to 48.5 percent at exit. There was a parallel decline in informal contacts that were farthest away (more than five miles) from 43.4 percent at initial interview to 35.8 percent at exit. Families in the focus group stated that "in the beginning [when the new baby is born] everyone wants to see the new baby and find out how you are." The mothers tended to travel long distances initially for these visits and then contact decreased once the baby got older and the mother got stronger.

Table 6: Proximity to People in Social Networks

Proximity	Initial Interview						Exit Interview					
	Informal Network		Formal Network		Other		Informal Network		Formal Network		Other	
	N	%	N	%	N	%	N	%	N	%	N	%
< 1 mile	45	31.5	20	36.4	0		66	41.5	14	48.3	0	
1–2 miles	13	9.1	6	10.9	1	100	11	6.9	4	13.8	0	
2–5 miles	23	16.1	10	18.2	0		21	13.2	4	13.8	1	100
> 5 miles	62	43.4	6	10.9	0		57	35.8	3	10.3	0	
Visits in the home	0		13	23.6	0		0		4	13.8	0	
Unknown	0		0		0		4	2.5	0		0	
Total	143	100	55	100	1	100	159	100	29	100	1	100

A similar pattern happened with formal contacts. Contact with formal networks that were closest (less than one mile) increased from 36.4 percent at initial interview to 48.3 percent at exit. Contact with formal networks remained unchanged over the length of the study. Focus group participants identified that traveling across the city by bus to get to agencies was difficult particularly in the winter months. With the bus strike they could not access these services at all. The parents reported that often people from the formal network visited the families in their homes and they did not know the distance to the agency. The decline in number of contacts with agencies visiting in the home (13 at initial interview and 4 at exit) reflects the reduced service provided by these agencies to the study families.

Helping Nature of the Networks

Families were asked if people in their networks "helped things a lot," "helped a little," "were neutral," "made things a little worse" or "made them a lot worse" (Table 7). In general, families found formal members of their networks helpful at the initial interview, with only 10.1 percent of the agencies making things a little or a lot worse. At the end of the study there were no formal members that made things a little or a lot worse. There was an increase in the formal networks that helped a bit/a lot from 85.1percent at the initial interview to 96.7 percent at the exit. There was a slight reverse trend with informal members who helped a bit/a lot declining from 75 percent at the initial interview to 70.7 percent at the exit. There was also a slight decline in those informal members who made things a little/lot worse from 13.9 percent at the initial interview to 9.9 percent at the exit. Over time, there was a shift toward more informal members being identified as "neutral" (10.9 percent at initial interview to 19.4 percent at exit). It appears that there is a greater likelihood of people from informal networks "making things worse" compared with people from formal networks.

Table 8 presents data analyzing the perceived overall quality of the relationships with their networks. Families perceived that their formal networks had very positive interactions with them, with this increasing over time (90.7 percent at the initial interview and 96.3 percent at the exit). They were less positive about relationships with their informal network and this declined over time (85.5 percent at initial interview and 78.0 percent at exit).

Table 7: Helping Nature of the Relationship between the Family and their Informal and Formal Networks

| Nature of Relationship | Initial Interview | | | | | | Exit Interview | | | | | |
| | Informal Network | | Formal Network | | Other | | Informal Network | | Formal Network | | Other | |
	N	%	N	%	N	%	N	%	N	%	N	%
Make things a lot worse	7	5.1	7	8.8	0		13	8.1	0		0	
A little worse	12	8.8	1	1.3	0		3	1.9	0		0	
Neutral	15	10.9	4	5	0		31	19.4	1	3.3	0	
Helps things a bit	66	48.2	21	26.3	0		50	31.3	10	33.3	0	
Helps things a lot	37	27	47	58.8	1	100	63	39.4	19	3.3	1	100
Total	137	100	80	100	1	100	160	100	30	100	1	100

Table 8: Families' Perceived Quality of Interaction with their Formal and Informal Networks

Quality of Interaction	Initial Interview						Exit Interview					
	Informal Network		Formal Network		Other		Informal Network		Formal Network		Other	
	N	%	N	%	N	%	N	%	N	%	N	%
Positive	124	85.5	78	90.7	1	100	124	78	26	96.3	1	100
Negative	21	16.9	8	9.3	0		35	22	1	3.7	0	
Total	145	100	86	100	0		159	100	27	100	1	100

Types of Network Support

Many factors shape how people in a network interact. Table 4 describes the level of different types of support that families report getting from their networks. Families were asked whom they could talk to about advice; who would provide material aid such as lending them $25; whom they could talk to about personal feelings; who would provide physical assistance such as going to the store for them; who would provide positive feedback; and with whom they interacted socially. Families had high but accurate expectations from agencies for providing advice (66.3 percent at initial interview and 62.1 percent at exit) but had low expectations of the other five types of support. Families had lower, but also accurate expectations regarding anticipated amounts of advice they would receive from their informal network (21.4 percent at initial interview and 25 percent at exit). They had consistent expectations for the other types of support from their informal networks ranging from 26.5–36.6 percent. They underestimated the amount of positive feedback (26.5 percent at initial interview and 35 percent at exit) and overestimated the amount of support with personal feelings (35.9 percent at initial interview and 24.4 percent at exit) that their informal networks provided. They underestimated the amount of support that agencies provided for personal feelings, positive feedback, and social interaction (range 8–14 percent at initial interview to 24.1–41.4 percent at exit).

Table 9: Families' Expectation and Actual Support Received Regarding their Social Networks

Support from Social Network*	Initial Interview						Exit Interview					
	Informal Network		Formal Network		Other		Informal Network		Formal Network		Other	
	N	%	N	%	N	%	N	%	N	%	N	%
Advice	31	21.4	57	66.3	1	100	40	25	18	62.1	0	
Material aid	51	35.2	4	4.7	0		60	37.5	2	6.9	0	
Personal feelings	52	35.9	7	8	0		44	27.5	7	24.1	1	100
Physical assistance	49	33.8	6	7	0		57	35.6	2	6.9	1	100
Positive feedback	43	26.5	12	14	1	100	56	35	12	41.4	1	100
Social interaction	53	36.6	9	10.5	0		63	39.4	10	34.5	0	
Total	53	36.6	9	10.5	0		63	39.4	10	34.5	0	

Note: *Multiple responses allowed.

Families' Use of Formal Networks: Public, Private and Nonprofit

A subanalysis of the data explores potential difference amongst public, private, and nonprofit organizations that supported the families. The research examined the families' formal networks from the perspective of: frequency of contacts, proximity to the type of organization, helping nature of the relationship, and expectation versus actual support received. There are interesting trends that emerged from this analysis.

The mothers indicated that of the formal organizations in their social networks, public organizations made up 32.9 percent of their contacts, nonprofit organizations 36.5 percent, private organizations 24.7 percent, and other/unknown organizations 5.9 percent. During the initial interview mothers reported that they expected to see people from the formal sector quite often. Despite these high expectations, they still underestimated their actual contact with the public (51.4 percent at initial interview and 71.4 percent at exit) and nonprofit (46.2 percent at initial interview and 60 percent at exit) sectors on a weekly or more often basis. They accurately predicted that most of their contact with private agencies would be once or twice a month (77.3 percent at initial interview and 75 percent at exit). Mothers also thought there were people whom they considered part of their networks that they would not see at all (public 11.4 percent, nonprofit 15.4 percent, and private 4.5 percent). This proved to be correct in only the public sector.

Families maintained contact with private organizations (31.6 percent initially and 62.5 percent at exit) and nonprofits (40 percent initially and 57.1 percent at exit) that were nearer to them, where mothers would have had a greater choice about location of service (e.g., choice of family practitioner, daycare centre). It is clear from Table 10 that organizations from the formal sector tend to help rather than make things worse. While there was some suspicion during the initial interview that public or nonprofit

Table 10: Helping Nature of the Relationship between the Family and Formal Organizations

Nature of the Relationship	Initial Interview								Exit Interview							
	Public		Non-profit		Private		Other		Public		Non-profit		Private		Other	
	N	%	N	%	N	%	N	%	N	%	N	%	N	%	N	%
Makes things a lot worse	3	9.1	4	16.0	0		0		0		0		0		0	
Makes things a little worse	1	3.0	0		0		0		0		0		0		0	
Neutral	3	9.1	0		0		0		1	16.7	0		0		0	
Helps things a bit	7	21.2	8	32.0	6	28.6	1	100	1	16.7	6	40.0	3	37.5	0	
Helps things a lot	19	57.6	13	52.0	15	71.4	0		4	66.7	9	60.0	5	62.5	1	100
Total	33	100	25	100	21	100	21	100	6	100	15	100	8	100	1	100

organizations might make things a lot worse (9.1 percent and 16 percent respectively), this did not appear to be true by the exit interview. Either the mothers found that the organizations tended to help or they abandoned those organizations that made things worse. There was not much difference between the organizations when it came to helping things a bit/a lot. All three types of organizations appeared to help mothers meet the needs of their children and this perceived level of help increased over time for the public (78.8 percent initially to 83.4 percent at exit) and non-profit sectors (84 percent initially and 100 percent at exit). Initial experiences with organizations were very positive (91.7 percent public; 84 percent non-profit; 95.7 percent private). By the end of the study families felt that they had positive relationships with all members in these sectors.

The final level of analysis of the use of the formal networks examined expectation versus actual level of support received (Table 11). Mothers turned most often to public (69.4 percent) and private (82.6 percent) organizations for advice, receiving less help than expected (42.9 percent and

Table 11: Families' Expectation and Actual Support Received from Formal Networks

Nature of the Relationship*	Initial Interview								Exit Interview							
	Public		Non-profit		Private		Other		Public		Non-profit		Private		Other	
	N	%	N	%	N	%	N	%	N	%	N	%	N	%	N	%
Advice	25	69.4	11	44.0	19	82.6	1	100	3	42.9	7	53.8	6	75.0	0	
Material aid	1	2.8	3	12.0	0		0		0		2	15.4	0		0	
Personal feelings	4	11.1	1	4.0	2	8.3	0		2	28.6	3	23.1	1	12.5	0	
Physical assistance	2	5.6	2	8.0	2	8.7	1	100	1	14.3		0	2	25.0	1	100
Positive feedback	6	16.7	3	12.0	3	13.0	0		3	42.9	6	46.2	3	37.5	0	
Social participation	1	2.8	7	28.0	1	4.3	1	100	1	14.3	9	69.2	0		1	100

Note: *Multiple responses allowed.

75 percent respectively). They received more support than anticipated for personal feelings from all organizations and this was most remarkable for public agencies (11.1 percent anticipated versus 28.6 percent actual) and nonprofits (4 percent anticipated versus 23.1 percent actual). Positive feedback was provided more often than anticipated across all organizations (12–16.7 percent anticipated and 37.5–46.2 percent actual). Mothers also received more physical assistance than expected from private (8.7 percent expected versus 25 percent actual) and public agencies (5.6 percent expected versus 14.3 percent actual), however, the numbers were very small. There was a large difference in the amount of social support provided through the nonprofits (28 percent expected versus 69.2 percent actual), emphasizing the important role that local resource or drop-in centres play in mothers' lives. There was a similar but less pronounced difference in the amount of social support provided by public agencies (2.8 percent expected versus 14.3 percent actual). Families correctly had low overall expectations that formal organizations would provide material aid (range 0–12 percent expected versus 0–15.4 percent actual).

The Community Context

The community context was examined in two ways. First, the families were asked to complete the "Perceived Level of Neighbourhood Social Capital Scale" (adapted from Fields and Smith 1998). This scale is designed to assess the parents' perceptions of their community's capacity to meet their needs. We used the information from this scale as part of the contextual data collected to help paint a picture of the communities in which the families lived. Second, we examined five demographic factors that have been identified as putting families and individuals at risk of unwelcome outcomes. These factors include: population growth, lone-parent families, recent immigrants, education level less than grade 9, and child population. We used Statistics Canada data for our study.

The research was interested in the effect the context had on the way families used their social networks. The analysis examined data from the family's postal code areas and indexed this information with the Regional Municipality of Hamilton-Wentworth as a base. The data were then compared to the perceived level of neighbourhood social capital scale completed by the families. By using these two sources of data, we were able to draw a picture of the neighbourhoods in which the families live.

Based on a scale ranging from one to ten, very few mothers identified that "people are a bad influence on the children" in the neighbourhood (mean 1.96) or that there were "dangers in the neighbourhood" (mean 4.05). The availability of "people to help out" was identified as an asset that their neighbourhoods possessed (mean 4.18). However, mothers identified that there were not a lot of "safe places" in the neighbourhoods (mean 6.8). While the number of families in the study was too small to measure significant differences, family members who rated the social capital in their community high, appear to use their social networks less than those who rated social capital low. Based on the risk index, the safer the community the less families use their social networks.

The relationship between the families' perception of their neighbourhood and the quality of their relationships with the people in their social networks also emerged as an important theme from the analysis. It appears that the families who rated their neighbourhoods' social capital as low had poorer quality relationships than those who perceived their neighbourhoods to have higher social capital. There is also a relationship between the community index and the type of social network that families had. It appears that the community in which a family lives plays a role in how the mothers perceive their social network.

Table 12: Social Capital Scale

Characteristics of Families' Neighbourhoods	Mean*	Median
People help each other out	4.18	5
People watch out for each other's children	6.21	7
There are people mothers can count on	5.48	6
There are adults nearby whom mothers trust	5.79	6.5
People are a bad influence on the children	1.96+	1.0+
There are dangers in the neighbourhood	4.05+	4.0+
There are safe places in the neighbourhood	6.8	8

Notes: *Scale of 1 to 10, one being the most positive.
+These two measures are negative statements (so scales are reversed)while the other five are positive.

STUDY LIMITATIONS

The study was designed to focus on particular families who had young children and who had been identified by public health nurses (using a standardized assessment tool) as having at least some degree of risk. We were interested in this population because of their need for community support. Not all families who were identified through the assessment process agreed to be part of the study so we are unable to generalize our findings beyond the study population.

The study began with a sample of 40 families of which 25 completed all of the data collection measures. This is a very modest sample and the differences in the families' experiences with their social networks may be due to unaccounted for variations in the way they live. Our funding only allowed us to follow these families for six months during which time we were able to identify preliminary patterns of support-network utilization. We expect that stronger patterns may emerge over a longer period of time. The use of these tools allowed us to gather far more data than we have had time to analyze and this report presents only our preliminary findings. We believe further analysis will reveal a more detailed picture of how families use their social networks. Families completed the diaries throughout the course of the study. However, there are small sections of missing data as families did not always know the information, such as the proximity of agencies from their home. The missing data do not alter the overall trends in the findings.

Measuring the use of informal networks raises considerable challenges because they do not provide resources in a structured way. Help takes place spontaneously in difficult to identify and difficult to measure situations. The helpful behaviours of family members and friends are idiosyncratic and provide a wide variety of responses. The way mothers use their social networks is multi-focused and diffuse, often changing moment to moment as needs change. We believe that the data collection method of clients recording their contacts in the daily diaries minimizes these methodological challenges.

DISCUSSION

The main focus of this study was to describe patterns and use of social networks in a study population of 25 families who had been identified as having children at risk of poor developmental outcomes. The research focused on informal and formal aspects of the families' support networks and examined the type of support families received.

Families' Use of Informal and Formal Supports

Families use their informal and formal networks to obtain help in meeting their needs. In the initial interview they reported that their networks were made up of 70.4 percent informal relationships, 29.5 percent formal relationships and 0.2 percent other relationships. This had shifted after six months to having 86.2 percent informal relationships and 13.3 percent formal, with 0.5 percent "other." Formal connections decreased rapidly as families connected more with people in their informal networks.

The average size of the family's total network was 22.7 people and ranged from 10 to 51 persons. The average size of the informal network was 15.9 people with a range from 3 to 48. The average size of the formal network was 6.7 people with a range from 1 to 19. Families saw one-third of their social networks once or twice a month, one-third about once a week and one-third about every day. Although the number of contacts families made declined over time, the families saw more of the remaining informal and formal contacts on a regular basis (every day or once a week). During the first week of recording in the diaries, families had an average of 10.8 contacts a week. By the mid-point of the study this declined to 8.3 contacts per week and by the end, was further reduced to an average of 5.2 contacts per week. Formal contacts declined more rapidly than informal contacts. The contact rate appears to be affected by the proximity of the people in the social networks. The further away people lived, the less likely the contact over time. This was true for both formal and informal contacts.

Many factors shape how people in a network interact. Previous research demonstrates that action will depend upon the ability of the family to motivate and mobilize their network, the ability and willingness of the people in the networks to respond, the resources that are available to them to bring to bear on the families' problems, and the fit between the families' needs and the skills, knowledge and resources of people in their network (Vaux 1988). The literature indicates that families with social skills will be able to access their networks more readily than families without these skills (Willmott 1987). Similarly, families who can effectively reward people in their network for assistance are more likely to obtain support in the future.

Families use support and resources in a number of ways and the research examined how they sought help in dealing with personal feelings; seeking material assistance or advice; obtaining positive feedback, or physical assistance, and deciding who would provide social participation. For the most part, the families turned to their informal networks for material and physical assistance and for social participation. They most often turned to their formal networks for advice and they approached both for positive feedback.

In many ways, the findings were as expected. Families with large networks could call on help from their informal networks more often than families with small networks. But all families used their networks to obtain certain types of supports. When they seek help from people in their informal networks they often come up empty-handed because relatives and friends do not have the necessary resources, are under pressure themselves, or do not have the time to provide assistance. It appears that families understand that their informal networks only have limited resources. However, if a parent needs to borrow $25, they will turn to their informal networks, and with a little luck someone will have the money to lend. This does not happen with the formal networks. Parents pointed out that people from their informal networks can respond more quickly than those from the formal network. Formal networks on the other hand, have the resources and the mandate to help the families when they face particular problems. For the most part, when the parents turn to social service agencies or health-care organizations they are able to obtain the help they need.

The ability of agencies to establish long-term relationships with families is an important component of their feeling that formal organizations are supportive and helpful. There is research literature demonstrating that the level of trust established with clients takes time to develop and that mothers living in risk situations benefit from long-term (i.e., more than one-year) home visits by public health nurses (Kitzman *et al.* 2000; Byrd

1997). Public health nurses can facilitate the relationship of the family with the extended family, and encourage the development/use of neighbourhood and community supports. This shifts the reliance on formal organizations to utilizing the assets found in informal networks.

The pattern of network contacts changed over time. While friends and relatives seemed to visit the family to see the new baby for the first week or so, the mothers had more repeat contacts with people from their formal network. Health-care workers, social workers, physicians, and visitors from community agencies all made contact in the first few weeks of the mother being home from the hospital. This changed over time as the parents turned more to their informal networks for assistance. These differences may be explained in two ways. First, during the early part of the study it was very cold and there was a bus strike and this may have kept friends and family from visiting. As the baby got older and the weather warmer, families were able to get out into the community more often to visit with their friends. Second, if the child was in good health and there appeared to be few problems, the agencies would visit less. Agencies and programs are mandated and designed to assist families with identified issues, but if development progresses normally and/or issues resolve, these contacts decrease or stop as the baby gets older. Parents identified this reduction in service as the most significant impact on connections within their network over the six-month period.

The literature indicates that the size of the network has implications for the availability of social support. Larger networks provide greater accessibility, stamina, expertise, information, and perspective than smaller networks (Vaux 1988). The data indicated that the larger the network, the more likely the family was able to find someone to help in times of stress, someone with the type of resources they need, and/or someone with useful information. While there was not a significant pattern, the data indicated that larger networks appear to have less reliance on formal network support. It appears that families with large informal networks turn to the formal networks less often. It is interesting to note that while over time the number of boyfriends and fathers who were reported as being part of the mother's network increased, the frequency of the mothers seeing them on a daily basis remained about the same.

Families report that people from their formal networks help things "a lot" more than people from their informal networks and over time there was a greater likelihood of people from informal networks "making things worse" compared with people from formal networks. In many ways this makes sense. There are many more tensions within families than there are between family members and people from agencies. These tensions affect the way that people within informal networks get along and raise the chances that things can turn out negatively. While family members report that they may not be happy with some of the decisions of the agencies, they do not often believe that the workers actually "make things worse."

Use of Formal Networks: Public, Nonprofit and Private

The mothers were in contact with a wide variety of people from formal organizations. On average, their formal networks were made up of people: 32.9 percent from public organizations, 36.5 percent from nonprofit agencies, and 24.7 percent from private organizations. The mothers thought they would see the people from the formal sector quite regularly and this proved to be the case, although the actual number of individuals they were seeing declined. For the most part the mothers found the people from the formal organizations helpful in providing advice, support with personal feelings, and positive feedback.

The actual levels of support that mothers received were different from what they expected. Mothers underestimated the amount of social support provided through the nonprofits, emphasizing the important role that local resource or drop-in centres play in mothers' lives. While mothers turned most often to public and private agencies for advice, they often received less help than they expected. On the other hand, they received more support from all organizations than anticipated in dealing with personal feelings. This suggests that families do not expect that staff from public sector institutions such as public health to provide support, but when using these services find them very useful. In particular, during the focus group the mothers stated they found the Family Home Visitors (nonprofit sector) very helpful. Positive feedback was provided more often than anticipated across all organizations. Many of the mothers participating in the study had been referred to the HBHC program because issues had been identified by someone in the system and the respondents may have expected some level of "blame" to be bestowed upon them for their particular situation. It was interesting to note that in general mothers had a very positive experience with all organizations.

Influence of Community Context on Support Utilization

The way families use their social networks is influenced by the communities they live in. It appears that parents who view their community positively use their social networks less than those who view their community more negatively. Similarly, the parents who live in a safer community (as measured by the index) appear to use their networks less often than those who live in communities with a higher risk index. This may result from the existence of unspecified resources within the community that the family members could use to help solve problems. As an example, there may be a community park where the mother takes her baby for a walk when the child is upset. The park acts as a resource for the mother who does not have to turn to her social network for help in dealing with the child. There is also a relationship between the families' perceptions of their neighbourhoods and the quality of their relationships. If the family lives in a neighbourhood that has low social capital, the quality of their relationships with family, friends, and agency people are negatively affected. The stress associated with neighbourhoods perceived to be unsafe, where people do not look out for each other and do not share a collective sense of community, has an impact on the manner in which families interact with others. Relationships with families and friends will especially suffer as families struggle to cope in communities that do not offer them feelings of safety and security. Other indicators, such as lone-parent families and education were used to describe high-risk conditions related to poverty. This pattern fits with the notion that the more resources the community has, the less families will have to rely on their social networks.

POLICY RECOMMENDATIONS FOR THE NONPROFIT AND PUBLIC SECTOR BASED ON THIS CAPACITY ASSESSMENT

The service system has been described as a "tangle of roles and responsibilities" (McCain and Mustard 1999, p. 118). Through the findings in this study, we are making four policy recommendations designed to untangle the system, making it more responsive to the needs of families.

> *Recommendation One*
>
> *Agencies need to maintain contact with new mothers and families for longer periods.*

Over half of the families in our study have new babies. They identified that initially they had a large number of supports, however, over time formal contacts decreased sharply. Some of this reduction may be a good thing, demonstrating that the families had become more confident in their own skills and/or were accessing their own informal support networks. However, for some families this meant that the support they needed was no longer available. There is an increasing body of research evidence that demonstrates the effectiveness of long-term (one to two years) public health nurse home visits for pregnant women and families with infants and young children (Ciliska *et al.* 1994; Olds *et al.* 1997; Olds *et al.* 1998). The new HBHC is designed to promote long-term support for families (Office of Integrated Services for Children 1999). This program funds the phoning of all consenting postpartum women by public health nurses within 48 hours of hospital discharge offering a home visit. Families with identified need may continue in the HBHC program, with a focus on assisting families in accessing community supports. The program also assists pregnant women and families with children up to the age of six years. This recommendation is offered with caution in that reliance on professional networks may create dependency and actually undermine the inherent capacities of families and their informal networks. The provision of more services to families identified at risk has the potential to divert attention away from the real issues such as child and family poverty.

> *Recommendation Two*
>
> *Parenting group programs should run for longer periods. These programs should have flexible catchment areas to facilitate families attending with their friends.*

Parents attending the focus groups in our study identified the importance of attending resource centres, prenatal nutrition programs, and
parenting groups, etc. They also identified the need for parenting classes
during pregnancy to help them understand what life is going to be like
with a newborn, as well as parenting classes for dads. However, they also
identified that groups ended sooner than they would have liked, were limited to one-time enrolment, and were very restrictive in their geographic
boundaries. This restriction in catchment area sometimes meant families
could not attend the groups with their friends, further increasing their sense
of isolation. Although many of these programs are run by professional
facilitators, there is an increasing trend in our community toward the use
of peer facilitators. This reduces the cost of providing programs and effectively builds in a shift toward community ownership and sustainability.

Volunteer models to support families may be able to more effectively
engage hard-to-reach populations than formal services/agencies. They are
cost-effective, and will promote the development of community networks
through self-help models (mutual aid offered based on a shared experience). An innovative program in the United Kingdom matches volunteer
mothers with other women in their community using a "befriending" model.
The focus of the support is on "incorporating the strengths of day-to-day
friendships." Mothers participating in this program identified increased
self-esteem and a perceived increased control over their own lives. They
also demonstrated an increased capacity to anticipate their children's needs
(Cox 1993).

Recommendation Three

*Local governments should provide community development programs
in high-risk areas, which will bring people/families together.*

Families in our study were eager to meet other families and expand their
social networks. This was evidenced by the number of requests to the research assistant to organize a social event so that families could meet each
other. A dinner social was held at the end of the study and most of the
families attended. This is but one example of the need for community development programs in high-risk areas as a means of connecting people

who share similar experiences, which in turn builds the capacities of families and neighbourhoods.

Many effective community development programs for vulnerable families have been developed and implemented in specific communities or neighbourhoods (Browne 1995; Schorr 1994). In some parts of Hamilton-Wentworth, early intervention programs (0–6 years) are provided in specific communities (e.g., the Community Action Program for Children). The provision of neighbourhood-based initiatives has the potential to increase the social capacity of families to solve problems and help them become more integrated into the community. Local governments should also be facilitating the development of capacity at the community level by establishing or supporting existing resource/drop-in centres (McCain and Mustard 1999, p.176). Families in the focus group pointed to the need for this service, saying that they often get inconsistent messages from different people and agencies and they "need one person to tell us about everything and how to get it." A community resource centre staffed by community development workers would fit this role nicely. We need to make "communities better places in which to grow," creating a seamless service system that supports families and will promote optimal child development (Pascal 1995).

We recognize that targeted neighbourhood programs will not reach the broad continuum of parents, but they are necessary for vulnerable families living in high-risk areas. Community development programs are essential because they build the social capital within neighbourhoods by increasing "a person's connection to social networks and sources of support" which in turn leads to the accumulation of "trust, goodwill and reciprocity by communities in civil society" (Robinson 1997, p. 8). This benefits everyone.

Recommendation Four

The federal and provincial governments should examine the need for expanding funding to local child-care resource centres.

The results from this study indicate that parents turn to professional networks for advice but not emotional support. They relied on informal networks for emotional support, particularly as agency contact grew more infrequent. There is strong empirical evidence that documents that the past patterns of behaviour and emotional problems within timelines may be replicated and in fact have intergenerational cycles (Zeanah and Zeanah 1989; Hemenway, Solnick and Carter 1994). Child-care resource centres provide a range of support services to caregivers of young children in their care-giving role. Resource centres are funded to provide service to high-risk families within specific neighbourhood communities.[5] The resource centre policy document outlines the kinds of programs that will be funded. They include drop-in programs, community information centres, training, provision of child care, child-care listings, playgroups, lending libraries, and warm-lines for children at home alone. Resource centres are accessible to a variety of families and care-giving situations. At-risk families have been utilizing the many services offered through these drop-in programs. Enhancement of these programs will enable more families and children to be served through the various supports and community linkages helping to break patterns of generational problems.

Recommendation Five

The provincial and municipal governments should address barriers to accessing services.

Some of the families in our study identified feeling isolated because of language, transportation, and winter cold. For families who were new to our country and community, the Family Home Visitor support they received became a lifeline. Without this program, families would have been severely isolated within the community and at much greater risk. Programs such as this are essential and should be looked to as working examples of how one type of social isolation can be alleviated and modified to fit the needs of other families and individuals in our community.

The lack of public transportation is a serious barrier to accessing social services, an important component in the families' social networks. A study on the impact of the bus strike clearly demonstrated that people who access community agencies were directly and negatively affected by the lack of public transportation (Brown 1999*a*).

Both municipal and provincial governments need to address barriers to accessing services through strategies such as providing extra support in the winter, additional travel money when there are bus strikes, incentives to attend programs, interpretation services, and community development programs designed to reduce social isolation. There is a recent positive shift in policy direction at the provincial level emphasizing collaboration and more integration of services for families with young children.

The HBHC program in Hamilton-Wentworth uses a unique model for the Family Home Visiting component in that women from the community are trained and then hired by community agencies so that they can visit women in similar circumstances. Family Home Visitors work with families in their home to provide culturally sensitive peer support, information, and practical tips on parenting. They also help families get connected with other community resources and services. At the time of writing, services were available in 32 different languages.

Recommendation Six

All levels of government should build community capacity and social capital through the provision of universally accessible parenting programs.

There is a basic predisposition in our society to help the innocent rather than those people we deem deficient or "past saving." This focus, although meant to build on social capital, might in fact undermine it. Targeted programs for children signal that support is available for people because they have children in need. The subtext is that adults in this situation are unworthy. This subtly undercuts parents' authority and legitimacy with their children. This targeted approach to programming can also negatively label parents and stigmatize them. The other inherent danger is that most targeted programs rely on some sort of screening to determine eligibility or need. The literature on screening tools suggests that there is a 20–30 percent failure to identify need when it exists.

Because of the inherent problems with screening and the negative consequences associated with targeted programs, Dan Offord espouses the importance of offering universal programs and then implementing targeted interventions (Offord *et al.* 1988). Providing equally for all families bases help on the inherent dignity of every individual rather than the potential worth of children as future "resources" in the economy, thus providing a stronger basis for lines of trust and respect in society — the essence of social capital. Through the new postpartum home visiting component of the HBHC program, all postpartum women may participate in a universal program designed to assist new parents through the provision of information about community programs and in-home parenting support by a public health nurse.

CONCLUSIONS

Often children's services focus on identification of problems rather than on recognizing the strengths and capacities of children and families. Most families with identified needs children receive "professional" services from the for-profit or not-for-profit sectors. Processes that bring families, professionals (service agencies, business), informal supports (family, clergy, friends, co-workers, etc.), and communities together to build on individual and community capacity are likely to have more sustained and positive results.

The results from this study will contribute to an increased understanding of how informal networks and the nonprofit/voluntary sector can support families. Community organizations and agencies and individual members will all benefit from having a systematic analysis of their community assets and the way in which these resources are recognized and used. The information gathered and examined through this research provides a basis for a better understanding of the strengths and weaknesses of the network of community supports and also improves the prospects for addressing gaps in the quilt of organizational responses to problem situations. This analysis and growing community awareness of it, serves as a basis for communities to develop strategies for improved utilization of their capacity.

Each community boasts a unique combination of assets upon which to build its future ... In a community whose assets are being fully recognized and mobilized, these people too will be part of the action, not as clients or recipients of aid, but as full contributors to the community-building process.

Kretzmann and McKnight (1993, p. 6).

The findings from this study can provide direction for community restructuring and service reform. This should increase the government's ability to articulate service outcomes and best practices. The results from this study will also ensure a strong voice for an integrated continuum of early child development and parenting support both at a local and government level.

Notes

Acknowledgements. This research study was supported by grants from the Kahanoff Foundation (School of Social Policy, Queen's University); the Hamilton Community Foundation; and the McMaster School of Social Work/Social Planning and Research Council Partnership Fund. The authors wish to thank our research assistant Marney Cuff for her dedication to this project. We also wish to thank Dr. Kathy L. Brock for her insightful critique of this chapter and formulation of the policy recommendations, the public health nurse who recruited the families, and the Family Home Visitors who assisted with translations for the multicultural families.

[1]The Community Action Program for Children (CAPC), funded through Health Canada supports community groups to establish and deliver services that address the developmental needs of at-risk children (0–6 years). This is a program geared to support specific populations (e.g., children living in low-income families; children living in teenage-parent families; children experiencing developmental delay; children with social, emotional or behavioural problems; abused and neglected children; and/or parents who have, or are likely to have, at-risk young children).

[2]The Healthy Babies, Healthy Children (HBHC) Program is a prevention and early intervention initiative designed to give children a better start in life. This is a voluntary program for expectant women and families with children up to six years of age. Families may refer themselves or be referred by a service provider with their consent. In Hamilton-Wentworth, in-home services are available in over 30 different languages. With the introduction of the new postpartum home-visiting component of the program, HBHC becomes one of the few universal programs available to children in the province of Ontario (Office of Integrated Services for Children, 1998).

[3]These tools are described in Appendices 1, 2, and 3.

[4]This project was approved by the McMaster University President's Committee on Ethics of Research on Human Subjects Committee.

[5]Resource centres are mandated to provide programs that enhance the quality of care provided in unlicensed child-care arrangements; provide information necessary for parents and other caregivers to make informed choices about child-care arrangements and options; and enhance the interaction between children and their parents and other caregivers.

References

AATD Child Care Advisory Committee. 1996. *Child Care Needs Assessment of Hamilton-Wentworth.* Hamilton: Child Care Advisory Committee.

Abelson, J. 1999. "Bridging Academic Disciplines and Policy Sectors: Understanding the Influences on Community Participation," Working Paper No. 99-03. Hamilton: Centre for Health Economics and Policy Analysis, McMaster University.

Baker, E.A. and C. Teaser-Polk. 1998. "Measuring Community Capacity," *Health Education and Behavior,* 25(3):279-83.

Brown, S. 1999a. *The Hidden "Essential Service": The Impact of the Lack of Bus Service on Social Service Agencies and their Clients.* Hamilton: Social Planning and Research Council of Hamilton-Wentworth.

_____ 1999b. *Poverty Profile.* Hamilton: Social Planning and Research Council of Hamilton-Wentworth.

Browne, G. 1995. "So Many children, So Many Problems: What Does Research Tell Us about What Works Best?" *Bulletin of the Sparrow Lake Alliance,* 6(1): 7-14.

Byrd, M.E. 1997. "A Typology of the Potential Outcomes of Maternal-Child Home Visits: A Literature Analysis," *Public Health Nursing,* 14(1):3-11.

Canada. Human Resources Development Canada/Statistics Canada. 1997. "Canadian Children in the 1990's: Selected Findings of the National Longitudinal Survey of Children and Youth," *Canadian Social Trends.* Ottawa: Statistics Canada, Spring.

Canadian Institute of Child Health. 1994. *The Health of Canada's Children.* 2d ed. Ottawa: Canadian Institute of Child Health.

Caplan, G. 1974. *Support Systems in Community Mental Health: Lectures on Concept Development.* New York: Behavioral Publications.

Ciliska, D., S. Hayward, H. Thomas, A. Mitchell, M. Dobbins, J. Underwood, A. Rafael and E. Martin. 1994. "The Effectiveness of Home Visiting as a Delivery Strategy for Public Health Nursing Interventions: A Systematic Overview," Working Paper No. 94-7. Hamilton: Quality of Nursing Worklife Research Unit, University of Toronto and McMaster University.

Community Information Services. 1998. *The Directory of Community Services: Hamilton-Wentworth.* Hamilton: Community Information Services.

Cox, A.D. (1993). "Befriending Young Mothers," *British Journal of Psychiatry,* 163:6-18.

Eng, E. and R. Young. 1992. "Lay Health Advisors as Community Change Agents," *Family and Community Health,* 15(1):24-40.

Fields, J.M. and K.E. Smith. 1998. "Poverty, Family Structure, and Child Well-Being: Indicators from the SIPP," Working Paper No. 23. Washington, DC: Population Division, US Bureau of the Census.

Garmezy, N. 1991. "Resiliency and Vulnerability to Adverse Developmental Outcomes Associated with Poverty," *American Behavioural Scientist,* 34:416-30.

Goodman, R.M., M.A. Speers, K. McLeroy, S. Fawcett, M. Kegler, E. Parker, S.R. Smith and N. Wallerstein. 1998. "Identifying and Defining the Dimensions of Community Capacity to Provide a Basis for Measurement," *Health Education and Behavior,* 25(3):258-78.

Gottlieb, B. 1981. *Social Networks and Social Support.* London: Sage Publications.

Hamilton. Social and Public Health Services Division. 1999. *Health Issues Report: 1999.* Hamilton: City of Hamilton and Region of Hamilton-Wentworth.

Hamilton, N. and T. Bhatti. 1996. *Population Health Promotion: An Integrated Model of Population Health and Health Promotion.* Ottawa: Health Promotion and Development Division.

Hemenway, D., S. Solnick and J. Carter. 1994. "Child-Rearing Violence," *Child Abuse and Neglect,* 18(12):1011-20.

Henry, T. 1997. *Risk and Capacity Profile: Hamilton-Wentworth.* Hamilton: Ministry of Community and Social Services, Hamilton Area Office.

Hertzman, C. 1995. "Child Development and Long-Term Outcomes: A Population Development and Population Health Perspective and Summary of Successful Interventions: CIAR Programs in Human Development and Population Health," Working Paper No. 1. Toronto: The Canadian Institute for Advanced Research.

Israel, B. A. 1985. "Social Networks and Social Support: Implications for Natural Helper and Community Level Interventions," *Health Education Quarterly,* 12(1):65-80.

Kelly, K. 1995. "Visible Minorities: A Diverse Group," *Canadian Social Trends.* Ottawa: Statistics Canada.

Kitzman, H., D.L. Olds, K. Sidora, C.R. Henderson Jr., C. Hanks, R. Cole, D.W. Luckey, J. Bondy, K. Cole and J. Glazner. 2000. "Enduring Effects of Nurse Home Visitation on Maternal Life Course: A 3-Year Follow-Up of a Randomized Trial," *Journal of the American Medical Association,* 283(15):1983-89.

Kretzmann J.P. and J.L. McKnight. 1993. *Building Communities from the Inside Out: A Path Toward Finding and Mobilizing a Community's Assets.* Evanston, IL: Center for Urban Affairs and Policy Research.

Lee, K.S., I.N. Luginaah, T.J. Abernathy, D. Sheehan and G. Webster. 1999. "Variations in Perinatal Mortality, Low Birth Weight: The Contribution of

Socioeconomic Risk Factors to Outcomes," *Canadian Journal of Public Health,* 90(6):377-81.

MacMillan, H.L., J.H. MacMillan and D.R. Offord. 1993. "Periodic Health Examination, 1993 Update: Primary Prevention of Child Maltreatment," *Canadian Medical Association Journal,* 148(2):152-63.

Marini, M. and B. Shelton. 1993. "Measuring Household Work: Recent Experience in the United States," *Social Science Research,* 22:361-82.

Matthews, K., K. Webber, E. McKim, S. Banoub-Badour and M. Laryea. 1998. "Maternal Infant-Feeding Decisions: Reasons and Influences," *Canadian Journal of Nursing Research,* 30(2):177-98.

Maykut, P. and R. Morehouse. 1994. *Beginning Qualitative Research: A Philosophic and Practical Guide.* London: The Falmer Press.

McCain, M. and F. Mustard. 1999. *The Early Years Study: Final Report.* Toronto: The Canadian Institute for Advanced Research.

Mechanic, D. 1989. "Medical Sociology: Some Tensions among Theory, Method, and Substance," *Journal of Health and Social Behavior,* 30(June):147-60.

Nash, J.M. 1997. "Fertile Minds," *Time Magazine,* 149(23):46-55.

National Council of Welfare. 1997. *Healthy Parents, Healthy Babies.* Ottawa: National Council of Welfare.

_____ 1999. *Healthy Babies, Healthy Parents.* Ottawa: National Council of Welfare.

Oakley, A. 1992. "Measuring the Effectiveness of Psychosocial Interventions in Pregnancy," *International Journal of Technology Assessment in Health Care,* 8(Suppl. 1):129-38.

Office of Integrated Services for Children. 1999. *Implementation Guidelines: Phase 2 for the Healthy Babies, Healthy Children Program.* Toronto: Queen's Printer for Ontario.

Offord, D.R., H.C. Kraemer, A.E. Kazdin, P.S. Jensen and R. Harrington. 1998. "Lowering the Burden of Suffering from Child Psychiatric Disorder: Trade-offs among Clinical, Targeted, and Universal Interventions," *Journal of the American Academy of Child and Adolescent Psychiatry,* 37(7):686-94.

Olds, D., C. Henderson, R. Cole, J. Eckenrode, H. Kitzman, D. Luckey, L. Pettitt, K. Sidora, P. Morris and J. Powers. 1998. "Long-Term Effects of Nurse Home Visitation on Children's Criminal and Antisocial Behavior," *Journal of American Medical Association,* 260(14):1238-44.

Olds, D., J. Eckenrode, C. Henderson, H. Kitzman, J. Powers, R. Cole, K. Sidora, P. Morris, L. Pettitt and D. Luckey. 1997. "Long-Term Effects of Home Visitation on Maternal Life Course and Child Abuse and Neglect: Fifteen-Year

Follow-up of a Randomized Trial," *Journal of American Medical Association,* 278(8):637-43.

Pascal, C. 1995. "Moving Ahead in Hard Times: Cuts and Creativity," *Bulletin of the Sparrow Lake Alliance,* 6(2):15-16.

Rice, J.J. 1990. "Volunteering to Build a Stronger Community," *Perception,* 14(9):14.

Roberge, R., J. Berthelot and M. Wolfson. 1995. "Health and Socio-Economic Inequalities," *Canadian Social Trends.* Ottawa: Statistics Canada.

Schorr, L.B. 1994. "Making the Most of What We Already Know: An Academic Talks with CEOs about Tracking Success and Improving the Odds for Children and Families," *Public Welfare,* 52 (Spring):22-26.

Robinson, D., ed. 1997. *Social Capital and Policy Development.* Wellington, NZ: Institute of Policy Studies, Victoria University.

Salamon, L.M. and H.K. Anheier. 1992. "In Search of the Non-Profit Sector II: The Problem of Classification," *Voluntas,* 3(3):267-309.

Social Planning and Research Council of Hamilton-Wentworth. 1999. *Community Trends in Hamilton-Wentworth: Information Sheet Poverty Profile.* Hamilton: Social Planning and Research Council.

Statistics Canada. 1996a. *The National Longitudinal Survey of Children and Youth.* Ottawa: Supply and Services Canada.

_____ 1996b. *Updated Postcensal, 1995.* Ottawa: Supply and Services Canada.

Thomas, H., B. Burcher, D. Ciliska, L. Feldman and K. Wade. 1997. *Systematic Review of Literature Related to Parent-Child and Other Factors Influencing Child Health.* Hamilton: Quality of Nursing Worklife Research Unit, McMaster University.

Turner, J. R., C. F. Grindstaff and N. Phillips. 1990. "Social Support and Teenage Pregnancy," *Journal of Health and Social Behaviour,* 31:43-57.

Vaux, A. 1988. *Social Support: Theory, Research and Intervention.* New York: Praeger.

Wheeler, L. and H. Reis. 1991. "Self-Recording of Everyday Life Events: Origins, Types, and Uses," *Journal of Personality,* 59(3):1-30.

Willmott, P. 1987. *Friendship Networks and Social Support.* London: Policy Studies Institute.

Zeanah, C.H. and P.D. Zeanah. 1989. "Intergenerational Transmission of Maltreatment: Insights from Attachment Theory and Research," *Psychiatry,* 52(2):177-96.

Appendices

APPENDIX 1

Social Network Inventory

This tool — adapted from the Arizona Social Support Interview Schedule — (Gottlieb 1981) examines the structure of the parent's social network. This style of inventory was used because it is relatively easy for respondents to understand and for researchers to administer. The questions are read to the participants who respond by identifying people in their network who meet the conditions described in each question. The design of the inventory encourages the families to separate their support networks from their larger social networks by asking them to identify the way people provide specific support.

The inventory examines the number of people in the informal and formal parts of the families' networks; the resources and support the family receives from their networks; how often they meet with the people in their networks; how close people live to them; and whether the people in the networks normally help make things better or worse. The inventory assesses six modes of support: material aid, physical assistance, intimate interaction, guidance, feedback, and social participation. The research assistant interviewed the families in their homes. The interviews took approximately two hours. During the session the research assistant and the families got to know each other and a rapport was developed. She explained to the families how much time the data-gathering would take and the type of information that would be needed. Families were encouraged to ask questions about the social network inventory, the diaries, and the social capital scale. Each family was given a $10 voucher for being part of the study.

The social network inventory was used again during the closing interview. A final $10 voucher was given to each family.

APPENDIX 2

Diaries

The diaries were designed to gather data about the daily contact of the mothers as well as the nature of the relationship between the family and the support they received. The diaries provided families with a way of recording not only "who" but also "how," "how often," and the "quality" of each contact. Two problems had to be overcome in the design of the diaries: they had to be easy to fill out so that they did not discourage the respondents and they had to overcome the reading problems of some of the respondents (Mechanic 1989; Wheeler and Reis 1991). With these problems in mind, a diary was developed which used symbols (such as smiling face or a sad face) as indicators of social involvement, had a list of the respondent's social networks (with space for new contacts) and used a check-off system of recording. The individual completing the diary had to tick off options about who had made the contact, how it was made, and whether it was helpful or not. The respondent was expected to fill out the diary three times a week. The pattern, based on Wheeler and Reis (1991), included the following: Wednesday, Friday, Sunday; or Tuesday, Thursday, Saturday; or Monday, Wednesday, Friday. The assigned days were consistent throughout the data-collection period in order to help maintain a high incidence of reporting. Marini and Shelton (1993) suggested that Monday to Thursday can be viewed as similar enough to be considered the same day. However, Friday, Saturday, and Sunday are each viewed as unique. For this study an attempt was made for each family to have at least one unique day included in the diary pattern.

The diary also asked the mother to identify when she visited the various organizations. It asked where she went, who made the contact, how the contact was made, and whether it was positive, negative or in-between. The diaries also asked the mothers about any support they wanted but could not find and the supports they *wished* they had.

APPENDIX 3

Perceived Level of Neighbourhood Social Capital Scale

This tool (adapted from Fields and Smith 1998) is designed to assess how parents perceive the capacity of the neighbourhood in which they live. The scale is comprised of seven questions which ask parents to rate their community. Five questions reflect potential positive aspects related to the safety and support for their children (e.g., other people to count on).

The other two questions reflect potential "negative aspects" of their community (e.g., perceived danger for their children). For scoring purposes, the scales for the two negative questions are reversed.

APPENDIX 4

Community Risk Indicators

There are many demographic and social factors which have been identified as putting families and individuals at risk of unwelcome outcomes (Canadian Institute of Child Health 1994). Although one of the most meaningful indicators of health and well-being is income, we were unable to use this as part of our index. We constructed the index based on postal codes as Statistics Canada does not provide income data by postal code. Instead we chose five other indicators of risk which were selected and indexed against the benchmark of the Hamilton-Wentworth region. The indicators were: population change, lone-parent families, recent immigrants, education level below Grade 9, and children aged 0–14 years.

The first indicator of risk was the percentage of change in population in selected postal codes between 1991 and 1996. Population change is an important risk factor as high growth areas are generally a sign of social and economic health, which translates into better job stability, higher employment, and less reliance on social services. Conversely, low growth or declining growth areas indicate an increase in unwelcome outcomes, specifically high rates of poverty, mental illness, crime, and low social status (AATD Child Care Advisory Committee 1996).

The second indicator of risk was the number of lone-parent families in the community. Lone-parent families face a number of challenges which place families at risk of unwelcome outcomes; 85 percent of lone-parent families are headed by women, whose income falls below that of their male counterparts and far below the income of two-parent families (Brown 1999b). Nationally, a single mother with two children under seven years of age had a poverty rate of 80.7 percent in 1996 (Canada. HRDC/Statistics Canada 1997). The negative impacts of poverty on children and families is well documented (National Council of Welfare 1999). As well, children in single-parent families are also at higher risk for emotional or behavioural problems, and academic and social difficulties, than children in two-parent families (Canada. HRDC/Statistics Canada 1997).

The third indicator was the number of people with an education level under Grade 9. Education levels also help to determine socio-economic status as it is tied to employment, income, and lower health levels (Roberge, Berthelot and Wolfson 1995). The lower the average level of education in a community, the higher the risk factors related to unemployment, low income, and poor health (Brown 1999b).

The number of recent immigrants was chosen as the fourth indicator. The greater the number of recent immigrants in a neighbourhood, the higher the risk factor due to both discrimination and racism; but also because language creates a barrier to participating in community life as 50 percent of recent immigrants speak neither English nor French. Some newcomers may have no family and friends to help them through this difficult transition, which further isolates them to the margins of society and prevents them from active involvement in community life, including employment (Henry 1997; Kelly 1995).

The number of children aged 0–14 years was the last indicator of risk. A large child population is associated with healthy economic conditions, while a small child population indicates poor economic conditions. Exposure to just one risk factor does not place a family or child more "at risk" than another family or child who have not been exposed to the same risk factor. However, exposure to two risk factors makes a child four times more likely to develop unwelcome outcomes, and exposure to four or five factors makes a child ten times as likely to develop unwelcome outcomes (Kelly 1995).

The five socio-demographic indicators of risk were indexed using the regional municipality of Hamilton-Wentworth as the benchmark. The region was chosen as the benchmark so that the neighbourhoods (as given by postal code), in which the families live could be compared to all other neighbourhoods that combine to make up the region. The region is not intended to represent the ideal level of health for communities, but rather is used as a relative point of reference.

The five indicators were given a value determined by the percentage amount they deviated from the base value of 100, which represents the regional percentage for that indicator. Values were then summed to give one value (or index) for that particular neighbourhood. Negative index numbers indicate that the neighbourhood is more at risk compared to the region, while positive index numbers show neighbourhoods that are healthier than the region.

5

Building Capacity or Straining Resources? The Changing Role of the Nonprofit Sector in Threatened Coastal Economies

Darcy Mitchell, Justin Longo and Kelly Vodden

As senior governments simultaneously reduce direct service provision and expand the range and intensity of community-based consultative processes, there is a tendency for new local and regional groups and associations to be formed (Fukuyama 1995). These organizations may come into existence in order to advance particular interests (in the consultative processes) or to maintain service provision (in the face of public sector retrenchment), or both. For non-governmental organizations in sectors such as health, social services, and education, many of the challenges they face stem from governments' redefinition of their role in service provision (Phillips and Graham 2000).

Organizations concerned with economic development, natural resource management and the environment — especially those in rural, resource-dependent communities — are also affected by changes in their relationships with governments and in the way governments manage resources in their area, as well as by changes in local and global markets and in the structure and activities of companies that have traditionally been the primary employers in their communities. Such organizations are faced with a gap that is extending in both directions: from government and from the private sector, as governments retreat and corporations abandon communities for the global marketplace. Under these circumstances, new local organizations may form or existing organizations and agencies may assume new roles and responsibilities, often without adequate preparation or resources, or both.

On the one hand, this expansion of local activity could represent and contribute to increased social cohesion and organizational capacity at the community level. On the other hand, however, this tendency might lead to a dilution of effort, an increased strain on community financial and human resources, and a reduction of overall effectiveness of the local and regional nonprofit sector. A proliferation of local organizations raises questions for governments in trying to determine how various interests might be legitimately represented and consequently how funding and resources should be allocated.

Accompanying the proliferation of groups with more limited or narrow purposes has been an expansion of collaborative or coordinating bodies, in the form of federations, coalitions, councils, and so forth. This study sought to identify both the reasons for the formation of new community groups, particularly coordinating bodies and collaborative initiatives, and the benefits that may be generated by cooperative action, such as reduced transaction costs and more efficient, effective, and legitimate decision outcomes at local and regional levels. As well, the implications of coordinating organizations for senior governments were examined by asking the following questions:

- To what extent do such bodies affect how senior governments collaborate with local communities/regions, in particular how they determine what represents legitimate representation of various interests and how services and programs are developed and delivered?

- Does such collaboration influence effectiveness (including local and regional satisfaction) and efficiency of publicly delivered or funded services and programs?

These specific research questions led us in some intriguing directions. It seems clear that nonprofit organizations are playing an increasingly important role in addressing economic stress, and related social, cultural and ecological issues, in the communities in the study. Further, there has been an increase in the number of collaborative organizations or "organizations of organizations" in the region under study (Northern Vancouver Island, British Columbia) and in the influence they hold over both local development and relations with senior governments and other agencies outside the region. Yet the implications of these changes have not been carefully examined. Our results indicate that there is a need for nonprofit organizations to re-evaluate the roles they play in relationship to governments, the private sector, and each other, and for governments to give serious consideration to the implications of "partnerships" in economic and resource development with nonprofit organizations, including the place of these institutional representatives of civil society in governance.

NONPROFIT ORGANIZATIONS AND GOVERNMENTS

Salamon describes the growth of nonprofit organizations around the world as a global "associational revolution," which may be "permanently altering the relationships between states and citizens, with an impact extending far beyond the material services they provide" (1994, p. 109). Although the number of nonprofit organizations in Canada is unknown, the number of registered charities has been growing by about 3 percent a year for the past ten years (Hall and Banting 2000). A similar, or perhaps even greater rate of growth, can be assumed for other types of legally incorporated organizations and grass-roots associations.

What accounts for the existence and, secondly, the proliferation, of nonprofit organizations? Economic theory attributes the existence of the voluntary sector to either market failure or government failure or both, that is, to "inherent limitations in both the private market and government as providers of 'collective goods'" or to the failure of markets as providers of goods where ordinary consumer choice or information is limited (Salamon 1995, pp. 39-40). Both Salamon (1995) and Phillips (1995) question this residual approach to explaining the role of the nonprofit sector (which both prefer to describe as the voluntary sector). Phillips (1995, pp. 3-4) states that the "voluntary sector needs to be understood as a force in society and in public policy in its own right," having three roles distinct from those performed by government or business: representation, citizen engagement and service delivery. Salamon (1995) proposes that we view the voluntary sector as the primary mechanism of response to market failure, with government becoming mobilized where voluntary action fails. In this view, government and the nonprofit sector complement each other, with government supplying resources, establishing priorities based on democratic principles, ensuring widespread access to services, and instituting quality control standards for the provision of services, and with nonprofits acting as a third-party government — the principal delivery mechanism for collective goods.

Ware's discussion of market failure (1989) introduces another segment within the nonprofit sector: "mutual benefit organizations" (such as clubs, business and trade associations, trade unions, co-operatives, clubs). Ware's analysis is particularly pertinent to the types of organizations that are the subject of this paper and to the field of community economic development. In real-world capitalist economies, three kinds of market failure account for the rise of mutual benefit organizations. First, there are areas of economic activity that are marginal, that is, where for-profit entrepreneurs cannot realize a normal rate of return on their investment. When deemed important for objectives other than financial return, a group of people may work together to generate this type of activity by mobilizing resources not available to for-profit organizations (such as volunteer labour). Second, the market may be too insensitive or lack incentives to provide consumers with exactly what they need (e.g., information on product lifecycle leading to consumer advocacy groups). Finally, mutuals such as consumer co-operatives and credit unions may form when consumers are faced with a firm which is in a "position of natural monopoly or otherwise faces very limited competition" (Hansmann, cited in Ware 1989, p. 39).

However, mutual benefit organizations serve not only the needs of their members, although this may be their primary intent, but the needs of whole communities and can, in fact, respond to failures of the market and the state at this broader level. Here, Salamon's and Ware's analyses converge. This is particularly true in a time when economic development and resource management are deemed to be in a state of crisis, with impacts that are not only economic and isolated to certain individuals or economic sectors, but community-wide with social, ecological, and cultural dimensions.

CED Organizations: An Important Element of the Nonprofit Sector

Like other segments of the nonprofit sector, community economic development (CED)[1] organizations are diverse, including co-operatives and credit unions, registered societies, informal community groups, roundtables, and development corporations run by community boards (Smith 1999). Some are for-profit. Many are not. Established to meet community rather than individual or corporate needs, CED organizations represent a component of the nonprofit sector that is becoming increasingly important as trends such as globalization, deindustrialization, and devolution transform and weaken local communities and their economies (Blakely 1994).

CED organizations are directly concerned with addressing the repercussions of market failure and of corporate decisions made in the best interests of owners and shareholders rather than the communities where they operate. However, when a community decides to pursue development within a given sector, their interests may then converge with those of the private sector. CED recognizes the important role a vibrant private sector plays in community well-being.[2] Thus, partnerships with the private sector and the employment of market-based tools and strategies are common.

Similarly, CED organizations both respond to failures of public policy, such as unsustainable resource-management practices, and tend to be dependent on and/or partners with governments in pursuing their mandates. Thus, they sit on an uneasy fence between their roles as both critics and beneficiaries of these sectors of society.

The Changing Relationship Between Nonprofits and Governments

In Canada, as elsewhere, the rise of the nonprofit sector and its contemporary challenges are widely attributed to the rise of the "welfare state" (creating new opportunities for public funding for nonprofit agencies) and its subsequent retrenchment (often leaving a void which nonprofits are expected to fill). Ware suggests that nonprofit organizations emerge in tandem with the expansion of state activity: "private welfare agencies do not tend to cluster in areas where state provision is weakest. Rather they tend to be found where state activity is already strong" (1989, p. 238).

Governments are the major source of revenues for voluntary organizations in most countries (Phillips 1995). In recent years, government support has declined, and the form of support has shifted more heavily to project grants rather than sustaining funds. Under the "New Public Management," with its emphasis on reducing the size and scope of governance, governments have seen advantages to increasing the use of nonprofits as service delivery agencies: "lower labour costs, greater flexibility when subsequently cutting back programmes and altering policy priorities, and reducing direct client pressure on the state when programmes are eliminated or reduced" (Ware 1989, p. 235). As a result, states Phillips (1995), nonprofits are faced with both rising demands and falling budgets; as pressure for service delivery rises, the capacity of nonprofits to perform their roles of representation and citizen engagement is stretched thin. At the same time, however, governments are placing increasing demands on nonprofits to identify and articulate public views on every conceivable public policy issue. As will be discussed in later sections of this paper, British Columbia witnessed an explosion of public participation processes in the early 1990s related to land and resource planning, economic development, and the environment. These processes can place enormous demands on the limited resources of nonprofits (as well as First Nations and local governments), but if they do not participate, they risk being left out of the game.

Government also plays a large role in encouraging (or demanding) that nonprofits form partnerships as a way of rationalizing the nonprofit sector, and also of attracting new sources of funding to offset government cuts. Phillips and Graham have identified a continuum of organizational collaboration, ranging from "insular" (no collaboration) to "merger." The first level of collaboration beyond insular is described as "collabitation," in which

> (organizations) ... may be collaborating for some purposes, but are still in head-to-head competition for many of their fundamental organizational needs, such as program resources. Most of this type of collaboration takes place as joint ventures around specific programs, projects or events and generally is quite informal. Because the underlying competitive stance of the collaborators is not conducive to laying down a firm foundation of trust, collabitation arrangements are inherently unstable and transient, usually disbanded after the project has been completed, and sometimes falling apart before that (Phillips and Graham 2000, p. 157).

We may speculate that many government induced relationships among organizations are more in the nature of collabitation than true partnerships.

Governments and Community Economic Development

When examining government involvement in CED organizations one must distinguish between two types of government: those accountable directly to local communities (e.g., First Nations, regional districts, and munici-palities) and those accountable to a larger society (e.g., provincial, federal). The Task Force on Community Economic Development in Newfoundland and Labrador (1995) pointed out that local governments are playing an increasingly important role in CED in Atlantic Canada, in part through active participation in CED organizations. This pattern has been repeated in other provinces, including British Columbia where a provincial pro-gram for providing regional economic development officers was cancelled in 1996, leaving, once again, a gap to be filled at the local level. Small communities tend to pool their resources for CED at the regional level as they do not have the resources to hire their own development officer or conduct significant development activities (ibid.). This characteristic was also demonstrated in the case study region.

While it is clear that local governments have an interest in the well-being, economic and otherwise, of the communities they serve, the role of federal and provincial governments in CED is less than clear. Savoie points out that "Canada's constitution does not assign to either level of govern-ment explicit responsibility or powers for economic development or for combating regional economic disparities" (1992, p. 14). However, he adds, "Provincial governments have a major function in economic development because they own natural resources and control most determinants of hu-man resources and land use. The federal government has created for itself a major role, essentially on the basis of its spending power."

A 1994 study (Douglas Smith and Associates 1994) found that all Cana-dian provinces and the federal government have taken measures to encourage local community economic development efforts. The key ques-tion is: How do they encourage these efforts and what impact does this have on CED outcomes and on the nonprofit sector? In some cases gov-ernments have been directly involved in the establishment of new CED organizations (e.g., the federal Community Futures program). In others they have provided financial, legislative, administrative, or technical as-sistance (access to public sector expertise) (Decter and Kowall 1989; Roseland 1994).

Increasingly, these government contributions are viewed as "partnership" arrangements to be of mutual benefit to all parties involved. While partnerships can be mutually beneficial providing, for example, resources and expertise to community groups and assisting governments through their ability to "consolidate interests in economic development and reduce competing demands for attention" (MacNeil 1994, p. 178), authors in the field caution that partnerships with governments and other outside agencies are difficult to build and maintain and can lead to dependency and the risk of program/organizational failure when government agencies "pull out" (Blakely 1994; Vodden 1997). MacNeil categorizes communities' historical expectations of government support and leadership as a "state of learned helplessness." Co-optation is also a concern. Jesierski observes that community groups, the "weak partner" in collaborative arrangements with government, tend to "become less adversarial and increasingly technical and bureaucratic in order to participate" (1990, p. 237). Additional concerns relating to government-organized NGOs (GONGOs) raised in this research are discussed below.

While governments do provide significant support for CED organizations and activities, it is also recognized that governments can, and do, also serve as a significant barrier to CED. To effectively facilitate community development, a more coordinated and flexible approach within government is required (Savoie 1992; MacNeil 1994). MacNeil suggests that vertical partnerships (e.g., partnerships between one level or department of government and one community organization) are ineffective without corresponding arrangements that are more complex and horizontally integrated, involving broad-based community coalitions and cooperation between various levels and government departments in intergovernment-intercommunity relationships.

Finally, MacNeil points out that "neither outside leadership (primarily political) nor outside capital encourages a population to engage in social learning and assume responsibility for economic change" (1994, p.179). The key conclusion reached in the CED literature with respect to provincial and federal government involvement in CED is that governments should act as facilitators or enablers rather than initiators of CED efforts, leaving the chief responsibility for development in local hands. However, much more must be done by governments, researchers, and communities to understand how they can better fulfil that facilitation role.

Representation and Accountability

Changing roles of nonprofit organizations are accompanied by a continuing debate about issues of representation and accountability. To whom are these agencies accountable, and for what? Is it clear whom they represent and how they acquire their mandates? The Panel on Accountability and Governance in the Voluntary Sector (1999) has defined three basic elements of accountability: (i) taking into consideration the public trust in the exercise of responsibilities; (ii) informing and explaining by providing detailed information about how responsibilities have been carried out; and (iii) accepting the consequences for problems created, not avoided or not corrected.

These requirements are particularly challenging for collaborative organizations, in part because of potentially conflicting responsibilities to the constituent organizations *and* to the partnership itself (Phillips and Graham 2000). Issues of representation and representativeness become increasingly significant as nonprofit organizations move beyond policy advocacy and advice, or service delivery under contract, to roles which involve resource allocation among competing interests in the community and representation of divergent community views as the "official" view in a decision-making process. As Schechter notes:

> NGOs cannot be considered representative in the usual political sense. They tend to be self-constituted, and the public has no means for selecting among competing NGOs at any level. Internationally, these characteristics have provided a ready rationale for limiting the role of NGOs even as their presence helps to legitimize the decisions of multi-lateral bodies (1999, p. 247).

NORTHERN VANCOUVER ISLAND: COMMUNITIES, ORGANIZATIONS AND ECONOMIC CHANGE

The region of interest for this study is the "North Island" (the common local term for British Columbia's Northern Vancouver Island region. The North Island is a rural, resource-dependent area where fish, lumber, and minerals have traditionally been the backbone of the region's economy. Today, as a result of restructuring in each of these industries, the local economy is under considerable stress. Apparent outcomes of this stress include: an increasing number of nonprofit organizations active in the areas of resource management, community and economic development, increased pressure on governments for access to scarce resources and restructuring assistance, and increased tension and conflict at the local level. The simultaneous retrenchment in government services due to budget cutbacks has made this pressure more acute. As nonprofit organizations assume an increasingly prominent role in the efforts of communities to deal with economic and social changes, identifying and supporting successful approaches to maintaining and enhancing their contribution to community well-being is particularly timely and important for both the communities themselves and for governments at all levels.

The Region and Its Communities

The Mount Waddington Regional District includes the top third of Vancouver Island (i.e., the North Island region), the adjacent mainland area ranging from Seymour Inlet to the upper Klinaklini Valley, and the islands in between. Only seven of the more than 20 communities in the region are incorporated as municipalities: Alert Bay, Port Alice, Port McNeill, Port Hardy, Sayward, Zeballos and, recently, Woss. Other smaller, unincorporated communities include Sointula, Coal Harbour, Echo Bay, Fort Rupert, Gwayasdums (Gilford Island), Holberg, Hyde Creek, and others. Most are home to fewer than 300 individuals, and are diverse in their cultural, economic, physical, social, and demographic characteristics.

Since the mid-1980s, the population of the regional district has remained at roughly 15,000, spread over a 21,500 square kilometre area, creating a population density of approximately 0.7 people per square kilometre according to 1996 census figures. The North Island lies in the midst of the Kwakwaka'waka (Kwakiutl) traditional territory. Of the region's residents, an estimated 12 percent are of First Nations ancestry and live on-reserve (Statistics Canada 1996). As on-reserve estimates are undercounted, many off-reserve residents are of First Nations ancestry, and several reserves in the region did not participate in the census survey, the actual percentage is significantly higher.

Regional Identity

Regional development patterns and regional initiatives relating to economic development and resource management are extremely important on the North Island. Regional identity is defined not only by geography (e.g., Vancouver Island north of Campbell River) but by political, administrative, and cultural boundaries. The adjacent inlets of mainland BC and the islands between are valued in economic and cultural terms to the people of the North Island and, therefore, are also a part of the North Island regional identity.

Communities within the region tend to identify with one another and to work on collaborative initiatives. An exception to this common regional identity appears in the communities on the west coast of Vancouver Island, particularly those in the southwestern part of the region, which are isolated from those on the east (e.g., by limited road access). Other divisions sometimes drawn within the region are those between larger and smaller settlements, fishing versus forestry towns, and Aboriginal and non-Aboriginal communities.

Land-Use Planning and Resource Policy

Land use is a significant determinant in the sustainability of ecosystems and communities within a region. Profound changes in land-use practices took place in BC in the early 1990s, including implementation of the Protected Areas Strategy and a series of comprehensive land-use planning processes. The processes were designed in recognition of the importance of land-use to sustainable development, and the conflicts that had arisen over the allocation of land and resources (Wilson 1998). The BC provincial government has launched two major land-use planning processes in the Mount Waddington Regional District/Kwakwaka'waka territory since 1990. Management of the lands and waters of the region has been significantly affected by these processes. The first was the Vancouver Island Commission on Resources and Environment (CORE) Regional Land Use Planning process, and the second was the Central Coast Land and Coastal Resource Management Plan (LCRMP) process. The Vancouver Island CORE process was highly divisive, resulting in protests by loggers and their families and, in 1994, the removal of 900 hectares (0.5 percent) from the timber harvesting land base. The Central Coast LCRMP process, launched in 1996, is still underway but is expected to be equally challenging given the remoteness of the area, international interest, community and ecological sensitivity, ongoing treaty negotiations, and other issues. Timber harvesting has been deferred within nearly 10,000 hectares due to the LCRMP process (British Columbia. Ministry of Forests 1996).

Also contributing to economic change and uncertainty in the region has been a host of resource management policies brought in by both provincial and federal governments in the 1990s. Substantial changes were made in forest management in the province due to a number of factors which culminated in the "war in the woods" waged between environmental and industry interests in the 1980s and early 1990s.[3] The Forest Practices Code, effective June 1995, was put into place to broaden forest development planning to include considerations such as visual quality, biodiversity, wilderness use and protection, and cultural heritage resources (Marchak in Markey 1999). In 1996 a timber supply review was conducted in the North Island region, resulting in a 16 percent harvest reduction in the timber supply area and a warning that "a large immediate decline in the allowable annual cut is required in order to avoid future disruptions" in resource supply (Fitzgibbon & Associates 1995, p. iii).

Perhaps even more significant in terms of employment loss in the region was the 1996 Pacific Salmon Revitalization Strategy (the Mifflin Plan), implemented by the federal Department of Fisheries and Oceans to reduce the number of salmon fishing vessels in British Columbia by 50 percent. The North Island region was among the hardest hit by the policy, with 585 jobs lost — at least 217 of them permanent — in 1996 alone (Gislason, Lam and Mohan 1996). Hundreds more would be lost in subsequent rounds of licence buybacks. Coupled with stock declines and low prices the fishing industry was left in a state of crisis.

The Treaty Process

Unlike Aboriginal peoples in most of Canada, very few of the First Nations in the area that is now British Columbia signed treaties with the Crown at the time of European settlement. In 1974, the federal government (following the Calder Case) agreed to negotiate what were then called "comprehensive land claims." The Government of British Columbia reversed its long-standing and adamant refusal to do so in 1990. Since then, most BC First Nations have entered the so-called "treaty process," a six-stage approach to concluding the most extensive and intensive series of agreements between governments and First Nations in Canadian history.[4] Within the study area, all of the First Nations have reached stage three of the treaty process (Preparation for Negotiations) as part of either the Winalagalalas Treaty Group or the Kwakiutl Liach-Kwil-Tach Council of Chiefs. The treaty process and associated issues surrounding Aboriginal rights and titles are highly contentious matters in BC, heavily influencing all policy and planning concerning land use, resources and economic development. Treaty settlements and court cases such as the landmark Delgamu'ukw decision present both a challenge and a need for cooperative relationships between neighbouring First Nations and non-First Nations communities in British Columbia as they adjust to new and forthcoming realities in the legal and political landscape.

A Time of Economic Change

Forestry, fishing, tourism, and the public sector are major sectors in the North Island economy. The forest industry is still the region's principal employer. However, a dramatic shift is taking place — a shift to an economy less reliant on the primary extraction of timber, fish, and minerals. The importance of primary industries in the region dropped from 35 percent of employment (by industry division) in 1986 to 19 percent in 1996 (Statistics Canada 1986, 1996). While the majority of the region's natural resources are still exported in raw form, manufacturing employment in the region rose from 10 percent in 1986 to 13 percent in 1996. Manufacturing is now the second largest employer. Retail trade followed as the third in 1996, accommodation, food, and beverage fourth and education services fifth.[5]

At 11 percent the unemployment rate for the region is only slightly higher than that for the province of British Columbia as a whole (10 percent in 1996) and has, in fact, dropped from its 14 percent in 1986. The region's labour force participation rate is significantly higher than the remainder of the province, a reflection of the region's younger, working age population

(Statistics Canada 1996). Due in large part to high wages in the forest sector, average incomes in the Mount Waddington Regional District are consistently higher than those for BC.

Regulatory, technological, and market changes have all contributed to reductions in resource-related employment. Efforts to adapt are underway, however, and new sectors have taken the place of some of the primary industry jobs lost. Each community has felt the impact of change to varying degrees and, similarly, has responded in their own unique way with varying levels of success. Port Hardy, for example, has undergone a shift from copper mining to other industries and has not seen dramatic declines in average economic well-being despite a major mine closure. Dependency on the forest sector in Port McNeill declined significantly over the past decade (1986 to 1996), with the percentage of occupations unique to primary industry falling from 30 percent to 13 percent. At the same time, however, real average income rose and unemployment rates fell (Statistics Canada 1986, 1996).

Vodden (1999) points out that in one North Island community, Alert Bay, fields such as resource management, silviculture, watershed restoration, and aquaculture, along with employment by First Nations governments, have provided work for some of those who have been displaced from the fishing sector. In this community, resource dependence has shifted to a significant extent to dependence on government services, along with the sales and service industry. However, these sectors have not fully made up for declines in the fishing industry, with income and employment rates in the community, particularly on-reserve, falling well below regional and provincial levels. Unemployment reached 27 percent in the summer of 1996 and is reported to be higher than 80 percent in winter months.

Other noteworthy shifts in the regional economy include increasing reliance on self-employment and female workers. While male labour force participation rates in the region fell from 1986 to 1996, female participation rates jumped from 39 percent to 71 percent. Women are playing a key role in the changing North Island economy.

Despite the apparent ability of North Island communities to adapt to economic change, assisted by the volunteer sector and all levels of government, research results demonstrate that the impacts of these changes have been felt at the individual, family, and community level and that the scale and speed of the transition required has been difficult.

The Case Study Organizations

As noted earlier, the focus of our research is the emergence of collaborative organizations. Three such organizations have emerged on Northern Vancouver Island within the past few years. The primary study organization is the Inner Coast Natural Resource Centre (ICNRC), based in Alert Bay. The ICNRC was formed in 1997 and consists of more than 25 member agencies and organizations concerned with economic, ecological, cultural, and social development in the region.

Two other organizations examined were the Vancouver Island North Visitor's Association (VINVA) and North Island Fisheries Centre (NIFC). These groups were selected in order to provide additional information with which to answer the research questions, beyond that which could be provided through the single ICNRC case. VINVA and NIFC are also collaborative, regional groups concerned with community economic development and community-based resource management in the tourism and fisheries sectors respectively. Information was gathered using a variety of methods, including document review, observation, and interviews. A total of 21 interviews were conducted with volunteers (primarily board members) and the staff of the three study organizations. An additional 13 interviews were conducted with provincial and federal government officials familiar with their activities.

The Inner Coast Natural Resource Centre

> The mission of ICNRC is to provide a forum for North Island communities that recognizes, enhances and sustains social, cultural, economic and environmental values by sharing the wisdom of the elders and the historical perspectives of the residents with the research and academic communities in order to promote, encourage and support responsible and accountable decisions in partnership with communities, First Nations and other governments, local organizations, business and industry (ICNRC 1998).

North Islanders have long realized that knowledge and information are key requirements of development. Yet, often, studies about the region are conducted by outside agencies who come in, conduct research, and then take the results and knowledge gained with them. In 1995 a group of Alert Bay residents decided to launch an initiative that would help address this issue. A three-person steering committee was formed through the Alert

Bay Economic Development Commission to work toward implementing what was to become the Inner Coast Natural Resource Centre, a locally-driven research and education centre. The centre was established to offer services such as the collection and dissemination of data and information pertaining to the natural resources and communities of the region (a central, information clearing house); facilitation and administration of research and development projects; and assistance with community involvement in land and resource-management planning.

After the completion of a viability study, partnership development process and business plan initiated by the Village of Alert Bay and funded by the provincial agency Forest Renewal BC, the centre, located in an abandoned school, officially opened its doors in June 1997. Start-up funding was provided by the Regional District of Mount Waddington and the Vancouver Foundation. Other partners made in-kind contributions such as equipment and furniture.

Since that time its projects have included: research on social capital, selective fisheries, and non-timber forest products; production of a manual for training "shorekeepers" to collect data on shoreline health and biodiversity; and public workshops, conferences, and planning sessions on topics such as the development of a sustainable non-timber forest products industry,[6] regional fisheries management, shellfish aquaculture, value-added seafood production, and "Linking Science with Traditional and Ecological Knowledge." Information gathering and dissemination have been emphasized with the development of a Web site (www.icnrc.org) and a public library of resources pertaining to the region. Approximately 37 percent of the centre's project funding has come from provincial and federal government sources (ICNRC 1999).[7]

Finally, the ICNRC is seen as a vehicle for the development of "educational tourism," bringing researchers and other visitors to the community who not only bring money to the island but also provide other benefits (e.g., knowledge, skills, information-sharing). The academic community also benefits from the "on-the-ground" experience of working in a remote coastal community, integrating academic with local knowledge.

The ICNRC is directed by a coalition of 15 partnering organizations from the region, including local and First Nations governments, community organizations, educational institutions, and labour and business groups.

These "internal partner" organizations are represented on the centre's board of directors, which is co-chaired by representatives of the Alert Bay Marine Research Society and the 'Namgis First Nation.

Partnerships with organizations and institutions outside the region also play an integral role in the centre's operations. "External partners" such as Simon Fraser University, University of Victoria, Ecotrust Canada, and the BC Ministry of Forests Research Branch provide benefits to the centre and its local partners such as financial support and technical and scientific expertise. In turn, external agencies have an avenue for gathering and exchanging information concerning the region.

Many of the centre's activities have involved partnerships with senior governments. For example, the ICNRC facilitated a meeting in October 1998 that brought 11 organizations, including First Nations, local and regional governments and fishing industry organizations, together to discuss proposed partnering provisions for the *Fisheries Act*.[8] Further examples include the roles that staff of BC Ministry of Forests Research Branch and the federal Department of Fisheries and Oceans have played as advisors in the centre's non-timber forest products and stream habitat work. The ICNRC has also served as a public viewing area for materials produced through the provincially-driven Land and Coastal Resource Management Planning process currently underway.

Vancouver Island North Visitors' Association (VINVA)

> VISION: The North Island will be a four season Destination Playground. It will be in connection with Nature-Culture-Industry and Social acceptance of the Communities.

> MISSION STATEMENT: The North Island Tourism Industry will deliver cultural and leisure experience year round. We will partner with Community Tourism Committees-TAVI-Tourism Victoria and all forms of government to give our visitors the experience that only North Island can do (VINVA Web site).

VINVA's roots can be traced back to the provincial Community Tourism Action Program. Approximately ten years ago, a Tourism Action Committee (TAC) for the North Island was formed under this program and, by 1993, a Community Tourism Action Plan (CTAP) was developed (Ministry of Small Business, Tourism and Culture 1993). These provincial programs did not last long, however. In fact, one VINVA representative claims that "they dropped us and we didn't even know about it until two years later" (Gault 1998). Businesses in the region, however, "recognized the need for a unified and cohesive approach to sell the North Island area" (Addison Travel Marketing 1999, p. 43). So in 1995 they formed the Vancouver Island North Visitors Association (VINVA). Says Director Donna Gault: "we were started out of the ruins of a government project" (1998).

Since then, the association has grown to an organization of over 85 members, including tourism operators, community tourism associations, local governments, and other community organizations. VINVA's accomplishments include: promotion of the region through trade shows in British Columbia and the United States as well as a VINVA Web site; hosting annual conferences as a venue for regional dialogue on tourism issues; development of a tourism Code of Ethics, tourism marketing plan, and partnerships with the forest sector.

North Island Fisheries Centre

The North Island Fisheries Centre (NIFC) is a community-driven organization whose mission is to assist individuals and fishing communities who have been adversely affected by economic changes, through rebuilding a productive, self-sufficient and renewable fishery resource, and through supporting diversification within fishing communities (NIFC 1998).

In 1997 the Government of Canada, through Western Economic Diversification, allocated funds to Community Futures Development Corporation of Mt. Waddington, also a government-initiated economic development NGO governed by a local community board, to hire a fisheries coordinator. An advisory committee or board representative of all subsectors of the fishery was required to advise the Community Futures staff and board of directors on ways to assist residents of the region who were dependent on the fishing sector. This new fisheries board was appointed in January 1998 and has now been incorporated as an independent society (CFDC 1998).

The North Island Fisheries Centre's strategy includes: assessment (of habitat problem areas and restoration priorities); project planning (for fish production); and fishery resource management (assisting in the formation of regional aquatic-management boards). NIFC has, to date, focused much of its attention on its role as a funding delivery agent for agencies such as

Fisheries Renewal BC, Human Resources Development Canada, and the federal Community Economic Adjustment Initiative.

Offices of NIFC have been established in the communities of Port Hardy, Alert Bay, and Sointula. Fisheries adjustment coordinators assist with delivery of short-term projects intended to lead to long-term employment, including wage subsidies and on-the-job training programs. The centre's presence has also helped provide improved access for residents with an affiliation to the fishing industry to business development services and financing offered through Community Futures.

Finally, the centre has played a role in facilitating discussions on regional/community-based fisheries management on the North Island. In November 1998 the centre co-sponsored a workshop on community partnering. In part, the workshop was intended to provide input to the federal government, which had recently initiated a number of seriously flawed consultation processes on topics such as changes to the *Fisheries Act* and a program for Habitat Conservation and Stewardship (NIFC 1998). An agenda for the workshop explained "to date there has been no systematic process for input by First Nations, fishers or communities." A second objective was to discuss the development of regional/community-based fisheries management on the North Island among those who were likely to be involved and affected.

THE EMERGENCE AND CONSEQUENCES OF NORTH ISLAND COLLABORATIVE ORGANIZATIONS

The brief theoretical discussion offered earlier in this paper sheds some light on the emergence of organizations such as the ICNRC, VINVA, and the NIFC. From the perspective of North Island communities, markets have indeed failed to provide many desired goods, including employment in desired occupations that will allow Islanders to remain on the North Island. Government is seen to have failed in responding to economic changes, and to have sacrificed local communities to "big business," and to the demands of urban-based environmental interests.

Each of the study organizations is responding to these failures by attempting in various degrees to articulate local views, engage citizens in public service, and provide direct services to their members and others. They are more akin to mutual benefit associations than to conventional service providers: their clients are primarily themselves or others like themselves. None of these organizations would have been created without the infusion of public funds, and their effectiveness (indeed their existence) remains contingent on funding from the public sector.

The organizational purpose and function of each of the three organizations is, however, quite different. ICNRC was created in response to a failure of both the market and the public sector (primarily educational and research institutions) to provide the kind of information that North Island individuals, businesses, and communities felt they needed to make better economic, environmental, and social decisions at the local level, and to participate more effectively in public decisions that affected their interests. VINVA is a fairly conventional trade association, formed to assist an industry of growing importance in the new North Island economy. The NIFC is the direct creation of a nonprofit with the chief purpose of delivering a service for government (resource allocation) and is, therefore, supported almost exclusively by government.

The Genesis of New Organizations

The research team explored reasons for the evolution of not only collaborative organizations but a suite of nonprofit agencies dealing primarily with economic development, training, research, natural resource management, community planning, and infrastructure. This broader overview helped explain the context in which the coordinating bodies have evolved and the nature of the relationships among the network of (broadly) related NGOs.

A survey of North Island organizations found more than 40 institutions dealing with economic development and resource management. Of the 35 organizations for which starting dates were obtained, only two were established before 1970 and 12 since 1995 (see Table 1).

More than half of the organizations surveyed were not in existence before 1991; about a third have been created within the past four years. These results appear to confirm the perceptions of both community and government respondents that there has been an increase — one might almost say an explosion — in the NGO sector broadly concerned with economic

Table 1: Formation of New Organizations

Date of Establishment	Number of Organizations
Before 1970	2
1971–80	5
1981–90	8
1991–95	8
1996–99	12

development and resource management on the North Island. Collaborative/regional organizations have also become more common. Such conclusions must be made with caution, however, as limited data were obtained on the number of organizations of this nature which began and failed during the same period.

According to interview respondents, the increasing number of organizations is a response to three key factors: (i) economic downturns in the traditional resource sectors; (ii) government policies (access limitations, budget cutbacks, public consultation processes, funding programs); and (iii) public demand for more involvement in decision making (in part a response to both of the latter factors). Lands claims and other First Nations issues are also thought to have played a role.

Our survey of organizations found that more than 300 North Island residents volunteer their time as members of boards of directors in this segment of the NGO sector. These numbers do not include individuals who participate in more informal ways in the various activities undertaken by the agencies.

The Consequences: Building Capacity?

One result of the formation of collaborative organizations has been the creation of networks between groups with more specific purposes. One way of assessing the nature and extent of these networks is to determine the degree of cross-membership of boards of directors. We found that many of the organizations surveyed are heavily interconnected through the memberships of their boards of directors, that is, by the same individuals sitting on the boards of several organizations. Some groups show particularly rich connections with others. As would be expected, two of these groups are the ICNRC (15 links) and the North Island Fisheries Centre (12 links) as each is an "organization of organizations." Our third target organization, VINVA, has fewer linkages with other nonprofit groups included in the survey as its membership is primarily individual tourism operators, although it is linked to ICNRC and several individual communities through their local tourism organizations (see Table 2).

Table 2: Other Organizations with More than Five Linkages

Organization	Number of Linkages to Other Organizations	Number of Individual Board Members who Create Linkages
Alert Bay Boat Harbour Committee	6	2
Alert Bay Marine Research Society	7	3
Mt. Waddington Community Futures Development Corporation*	11	6
Cormorant Island Economic Development Society	10	9 (3 from one organization)
Mt. Waddington Community Resource Board	13	11
Mt. Waddington Regional Economic Development Commission	12	11 (4 from one other organization; 6 from another and overlaps among these two groups)

Note: *Including committees with separate boards.

Most of the organizations with heavy cross-memberships are regional in their scope: i.e., ICNRC, NIFC, and the Mt. Waddington Community Futures Corporation, Mt. Waddington Community Resource Board, and Mt. Waddington Regional Economic Development Commission. Interestingly, the other three organizations listed above are all based in Alert Bay, reflecting perhaps the level of social integration, or the level of perceived crisis, in this community.

There are comparatively few cross-memberships between the boards of directors of Aboriginal and non-Aboriginal organizations. The exceptions to this general rule include the North Island Fisheries Centre, ICNRC, the Nimpkish Resource Management Board, the Alert Bay Tourism Strategy Team, and the Cormorant Island Economic Development Society. Again, all but one are headquartered in the community of Alert Bay.

As Table 2 clearly indicates, the linkages represented by cross-memberships are carried by a relatively small number of individuals. Two individuals are each board members of seven of the organizations surveyed. Five others are members of four or more boards. These individuals are key to the organizational network of the region.

When asked to assess common attributes of social capital — trust, social cohesiveness, etc. — most respondents described the level of social capital on the North Island, both within organizations and in the region as a whole, as moderate to high (and growing). In support of this belief, respondents pointed to the core group of dedicated and hard-working volunteers and to clear evidence that communities have responded to the need for community action in the arena of economic development through, for example, the creation of new and expanded agencies.

Respondents believe that the North Island has made progress toward partnership-building and regional cooperation among sectors, communities, and organizations. They believe further that collaborative agencies such as the ICNRC and the NIFC have contributed to this outcome, and that results can be seen in the increasing number of cooperative projects, joint funding proposals, and sharing of information, space, expertise, and other organizational resources. Provincial and federal respondents also pointed to evidence of social capital creation on the North Island in terms of joint projects and proposals and the creation of forums for discussion of local issues that appear to avoid political scrums.

Building Bridges between Aboriginal and Non-Aboriginal Communities

I think we have to get really more involved now and really start working together. Somehow, a reconciliation as the governments like to call it. Because the local communities and the First Nation people aren't going anywhere ('Namgis representative, quoted in Vodden 1999).

Aboriginal/non-Aboriginal relationships were not a primary focus for this study. Issues surrounding these relationships are, however, of key importance to questions of social cohesion and cooperation in the North Island region and indeed throughout British Columbia, particularly where land and resource allocation and management are concerned.

Regional cooperation has generally been between non-First Nations communities and between First Nations, not both. Interview respondents noted that First Nations were underrepresented in regional economic development organizations and suggested that it was important to correct this imbalance. This requires a greater understanding of Aboriginal/non-Aboriginal relationships in the region, barriers to Aboriginal participation in the past, and suggestions for improvement in the future (e.g., greater understanding of protocol, up-front involvement).

The issue of Native/non-Native cooperation, however, is not one that will be resolved quickly or easily. "Trust and acceptance is very difficult" (workshop participant in Vodden 1999). One external consultant observed, "the Native and non-Native communities, while sharing many values, obviously have deep and historical cultural differences" (John Ronald and Associates 1990, p. 8). Time constraints, particularly for First Nations representatives, appear to be a significant problem: "It is difficult to get First Nations to the table. There's just too much on the go" (Representative of Mt. Waddington Regional District, quoted in Vodden 1999).

Vodden (1999) also examines cases of Native/non-Native collaboration taking place on a regional basis, including two of the three organizations included in this study. First Nations' representatives make up 50 percent of the board of directors of the North Island Fisheries Centre initiative, an unprecedented level of shared decision making in a regional organization. First Nations have also collaborated to a limited degree with private industry, particularly the forest industry. Finally, the 'Namgis First Nation has played an important role in the development of the ICNRC.

Other Outcomes and Benefits

All three of our target organizations are concerned with economic diversification and better management of natural resources, leading to a more stable economy and employment base. Many of the other institutions surveyed for this study have similar objectives. Perspectives on the impact of these organizations are mixed. Community respondents tend to feel that although local/regional resource-management organizations are primarily advisory, they have resulted in improved resource management on the North Island, including healthier ecosystems and resources. There was some disagreement about whether or not more employment had resulted. Most agreed that a more stable, sustainable well-being had not yet been achieved but that initiatives undertaken by the ICNRC, NIFC, and VINVA have contributed significantly to training, education, public awareness of diversification and resource-management opportunities, and outside recognition of local efforts.

Several community respondents commented on the hazards of: (i) too much reliance on government and (ii) too great a local role in the allocation of scarce resources. One First Nations respondent pointed out to Vodden some of the results of having a community organization allocate a limited number of fishing licences among its members, for example:

> Yeah, we don't trust each other. One person gets one license more than the other person — internal fighting. Again it goes back to the government. It's that the government is giving them up, it's like we're a bunch of dogs and they throw little chunks of meat in the middle and we have to fight over it. That, that has to change — there's no meaning to them giving us fourteen gillnet licenses when you're talkin' about seven thousand people. What good is fourteen gillnets. All it does is create a fight (Vodden 1999).

Yet, community respondents also contend that community effectiveness is limited because so many processes are advisory only and give community organizations little real power over local resource decisions. Limited success of community activities was sometimes attributed to the specific government processes through which community interests are involved. For example, some respondents contended that CORE was a failure and expressed uncertainty about the processes and usefulness of the Central Coast LRMP.

Most provincial and federal respondents felt unable to comment on the impact of collaborative agencies on resource management or other specific outcomes at this stage. One federal respondent observed that while "there is potential for local groups to improve resource management, relationships are too new [and] there has not yet been much impact."

Straining Resources?

A clear message from both community and government respondents is that the successes achieved by collaborative agencies on the North Island, and their potential impact, are balanced on a fragile base of overtaxed volunteers, inadequate funding, and insufficient clarity about the roles and mandates of community organizations and government agencies.

Respondents noted that the success of the institutions studied relies on strong local support, links to outside support and, "keen people running them." With respect to the ICNRC, a federal respondent observed that the key is "leadership — the right people with great commitment to the ICNRC." Organizations are vulnerable to a base of human and financial resources that is too narrow. Reliance on a small group of dedicated people is both their strength and their weakness. Collaborating bodies place considerable pressure on "linking" members who sit on both the original organization and the coordinating body.

Provincial respondents observed that all the target agencies (and others on the North Island) face problems of avoiding volunteer burnout and getting local citizens to buy-in to mandates and efforts of the organizations. Distance between the communities makes communication and maintenance of partnerships and regional focus particularly challenging, with board members having to travel long distances to attend meetings.

All organizations also face the hazard of "biting off more than they can chew." As Addison Travel Marketing noted, for example, VINVA's goals and objectives "provide a solid foundation to build upon, [but] are ambitious, even unrealistic, unless funding for a paid staff member can be obtained" (1999). Funding limitations represent a serious constraint, with financial resources for core staff, administration, communications and travel support noted as particularly important but hard to find.

One way that organizations have reacted to the challenge of limited resources and a seemingly unlimited workload is through planning and prioritization. Efforts in these areas, however, could be improved.

COLLABORATIVE ORGANIZATIONS AND GOVERNMENTS

From the perspective of senior governments and the public policy implications of encouraging and supporting such groups two key questions were asked: Whether the presence of a group like the ICNRC help governments develop fairer, more stable, efficient and effective outcomes; and if such organizations make it easier or more difficult for government to determine representativeness and legitimacy of representation in their consultations and work with communities? A third, related question raised was, from the broadest societal perspective, whether such groups serve to establish what Rawls (1987) describes as an "overlapping consensus," that is, "a consensus affirmed by opposing theoretical, religious, philosophical and moral doctrines" that provides a basis upon which, "public policy is more likely to thrive over generations?" Thirteen provincial and federal representatives who have worked with the study organizations in some capacity lent their insight into these questions.

Reconciling Divergent Viewpoints

All government respondents perceived benefits *for governments* from the existence of collaborative groups. Community groups bring local perspectives, and provide coordinated input and community-based advice to government (e.g., through the Community Resource Boards, or the Land and Coastal Resource Management Planning process). They provide a focal point for government consultation and help agencies decide how resources should be prioritized and distributed. Provincial respondents noted that community organizations can be effective in developing local solutions to problems which might otherwise require senior government attention, they can mobilize volunteers, and animate community action in a way that government cannot.

One respondent observed that "local organizations may not be as efficient as centralized governments could be. They are not experienced power players and thus have difficulty negotiating political channels [but] they are best able to act as boosters for local interests, making sure that local concerns are heard in political arenas."

Federal respondents recommended that local organizations "should stay out of politics." Their focus should be on consolidating local views around issues and "articulating united views with recognition of diversity." Respondents recognized that coordinating organizations help to create greater understanding among various interests of their individual positions/ perspectives, and sometimes common goals and objectives that may not have been apparent. At least to some degree they are seen to consolidate individual interests into common regional goals/interests. Collaborative organizations should therefore be able to contribute to establishing local and regional priorities and developing strategies for achieving them. In addition, government representatives admitted they may "sometimes be appropriately involved in implementation."

The message in these comments seems to be that collaborative organizations best serve government requirements by remaining outside the political arena, by debating, consolidating, and articulating local views, and by thus assisting government in providing: a focus for local consultation and help in making resource-allocation decisions.

All three of the study organizations have fulfilled the former role, NIFC in particular, the latter. The NIFC is a clear example of collaborative or "umbrella" groups helping government make (or avoid having to make) resource-allocation decisions. A block of funds is allocated for a fairly broad purpose, and the community agency makes the decisions about which particular projects and which organizations will receive funding.

Our research suggests that the relationships between government and non-governmental institutions on the North Island have changed significantly in several respects. First, the number of NGOs dealing with economic development and resource management has increased dramatically in the 1990s. Collaborative/regional organizations have also become more common. As they increase in number, NGOs, especially coordinating or collaborative organizations are taking on roles more akin to those of government agencies than those of more traditional philanthropic or special interest organizations. They are assuming an ever greater role in eliciting, mediating, and articulating public concern and priorities across a rather wide range of community interests. These new roles are symptomatic of the assumption of quasi-governmental roles by non-governmental organizations and raise questions about representativeness, accountability, and organizational capacity.

Representativeness, Legitimacy and Accountability

Although local respondents felt they were both legitimate and accountable, government representatives raised some concerns about these issues, particularly about whether representatives of individual organizations report back decisions made in collaborative groups.

The membership of NGOs such as those discussed in this report are self-selected — participation is voluntary and may be on an invitation basis. There are no clear rules that determine which agencies or individuals are represented in the organizations, and no clear rules as to the manner in which constituent organizations are themselves representative of, and accountable to, their own members, although a number of them are elected local governments. The result is a degree of fluidity and fuzziness in organizational mandates and legitimacy that impairs the ability of NGOs to move beyond consultative processes and one-off projects.

Some provincial respondents also identified negative implications of increased community activity, local identification and organizational development, including potential for community isolationism and exclusion of outside interests. For instance, concerns were expressed that a group of communities could engage in bidding wars for new industry, or lobby for the exclusion of undesirable activities such as waste treatment facilities from their specific area, with little or no thought as to the larger public good (or ill) from strategies that focus only on the good of the region. As another example, community-based resource-management arrangements such as community fisheries may exclude legitimate beneficiaries, simply because these beneficiaries are not local residents. Nevertheless government agencies would prefer to work with collaborative groups. Efficiencies in communication and information-sharing created by these groups were referred to by both local and government representatives.

It was interesting to note that most respondents consider "community organizations" to include local governments and their agencies, as well as NGOs, and believe that most North Islanders have more confidence in local government than in senior governments. This observation suggests a range of possible new arrangements among local governments and NGOs that might capitalize on the strengths of elected permanent governments in increasing local capacity and control over local and regional resource and economic development. The Regional Aquatic Management Society (a resource-management body on the west coast of Vancouver Island whose core membership is made up of elected officials from local and First Nations government) is often cited as an example of strength and legitimacy derived from a board of directors composed of elected First Nations and municipal officials.[9] At the same time some respondents view the evolution of NGOs as resulting, at least in part, from dissatisfaction with the manner in which local governments have dealt with growing economic and other problems on the North Island, and consider the NGOs to be a necessary counterweight to the undue influence of local municipal councils.

Strengthening the NGO Sector

Community and government respondents suggested a number of ways in which NGOs could become more efficient and effective, and a number of ways in which governments could assist in this process. Community respondents recommended that organizations address the following priorities:

- prioritize, plan, and ensure mandates and purposes are clear;
- seek efficiencies in the use of time and resources;
- seek ways to overcome barriers of geography (e.g., use of video conferencing technology for meetings);
- seek ways to compensate efforts of key people (e.g., provide honoraria for executive positions, other forms of volunteer appreciation and recognition);
- provide training for volunteers and board members to maximize effectiveness;
- be aggressive in seeking funding from a range of sources (corporate, foundation, government, and revenue-generating activities);
- continue to explore opportunities for sharing resources, information, and service with other organizations;
- keep lines of communication open with the public and other organizations;
- educate others about the benefits of cooperation (e.g., articles in local newspaper about successful partnerships); and

- welcome and encourage involvement of new volunteers, especially from underrepresented groups.

Community respondents recommended that government support the NGO sector by providing core funding and advisory support for organizations that assist in delivering services which fall within the mandate of senior governments; continuing to encourage cooperation among community organizations; supporting efforts to make better use of limited resources (e.g., contribute to initiatives that help sustain volunteers); assisting in the sharing of information among NGOs, including those from different areas; and streamlining programs meant to provide assistance to community agencies and entrepreneurs.

Government respondents recommended that NGOs work toward regional priority-setting and a regional focus for economic development, continue to build networks and contacts, and provide capacity-building and leadership training. To be more effective, NGOs need to have a better understanding of "the system" (i.e., the political and administrative structures and process of government) and how to gain access to decisionmakers.

Government respondents felt that they were hampered in their ability to work effectively with NGOs by program rules and rigidities, by a lack of experience and understanding in how governments can and should deal with community groups, and by the absence of long-term frameworks for government-NGO collaboration. "There needs to be less politics — governments should not focus on immediate political returns from working with community groups." "Public servants working on the ground need to be able to facilitate solutions and to be more flexible in how resources are used."

CONCLUSIONS AND UNANSWERED QUESTIONS

Governments, NGOs and Community Capacity

Our research suggests that governments have been very significant in the evolution of collaborative organizations, most directly in the case of NIFC, but also in the development of VINVA from the "ruins of a government program" and in providing the resources to support the creation and projects of the ICNRC. The NIFC might in fact be described as a government organized non-governmental organization.

The role of government is so pervasive in resource management and economic development generally that it is difficult to underestimate the possible impact of government programs in encouraging cooperation (e.g., by rewarding partnerships and community contributions in resource-allocation decisions) or discouraging it (by fragmented programming or "divide and conquer" techniques). Most of the NGOs surveyed are strongly oriented toward the public sector and look to government for funding, information, and other resources. None of the three targeted organizations have similarly strong relationships with either the private sector or the domain of private foundations and charitable trusts.

One of the apparent reasons underlying the creation of collaborative organizations is the need for an intermediary between community and government. As global forces negatively impact local communities (e.g., falling salmon prices, market collapses in the forest sector), demand for more local control and a greater say in matters where provincial and national governments can have an impact. Collaborative, regional organizations, it appears, may be able to help governments to meet this demand, providing information to communities and back to government, for example. Broad-based groups may, therefore, also be more influential in policy making than individual organizations, particularly as relationships are established. In the process of creating collaborative relationships, however, some interests may be excluded, and some groups may become even more marginalized; as the "in-group" becomes more established, the "out-groups" may lose whatever influence they may once have had.

Results from our review of the literature and comments by interview respondents suggest that government actions may have the effect of skewing community attention and energy in some directions rather than others. For example, the procedural requirements for funding applications and the objectives which these applications must (at least purport to) achieve may well cause government priorities to dominate an agency's agenda. Especially in the absence of sustaining core funding, the need to chase projects to fund administration can exhaust an organization's resources and distract from its own stated purposes. Bureaucratic requirements for reporting and accountability are often onerous for local agencies and, again, tend to focus concerns about accountability for funding and performance on the funding source, rather than the community of those whom the organization is trying to serve. It appears, as well, that government-initiated processes like CORE and the Central Coast LRMP may not foster local initiative or build trust to the same degree as grass-roots initiatives, and may even split people into camps by interest and sector as government seeks to achieve a balanced representation at the planning table.

There is clearly a great deal of consideration yet to be given to the appropriate role of community organizations, especially collaborative organizations, vis-à-vis both senior and local governments.

Collaborative Organizations and Economic Development

The changing nature of North Island economies has created a need for services that would not have been required if a few large corporations and prosperous fishing and forestry industries had continued to provide employment and a tax base for the region. Many of the services that the ICNRC and VINVA provide are supplied internally by large companies: research, product development, marketing, communications, employee development and training, and identification of sources of financing. Small, often marginal, businesses, however, cannot supply these services for themselves, nor can they afford to hire consultants to do it for them. Other organizations, such as the Community Futures Development Corporation also provide business support services to those who cannot access them in the market.

The ICNRC, the NIFC, and other community organizations are also instrumental in taking on activities that invest in the *supply* of common pool resources (Ostrom 1990) that allow businesses to be created for their extraction: watershed restoration, research on selective fisheries, and sustainable non-timber forest products development, are examples. The ICNRC is unusual in its role, perhaps, because it attempts to intervene at an even earlier, more basic stage in the transformation of a conventional resource-dependent community by taking on research and communication roles that would more normally be provided by postsecondary institutions and/or government extension agents *and* by providing a forum within which economic, social, and environmental interests can be debated in the overall interests of sustainable employment and business creation. For the ICNRC in particular, reliance on project funding is especially problematic as many of its results are in the form of community knowledge and awareness: results not easily conducive to evaluation as project outcomes.

Clarification and Coordination of Roles

Coordination and collaboration have proved to be an effective response to some of the pressures of increasingly limited resources. It has also helped with regional priority-setting and planning. It is generally agreed that better decisions also result from collaborative bodies representing a range of perspectives from the region. Establishing collaborative organizations and facilitating communication and cooperation between communities and sectors are in themselves seen to be significant achievements of these organizations.

While the creation of a few larger institutions that subsume several smaller ones seems an attractive solution to the rather untidy current situation of multitudes of organizations with related if not similar objectives, it contains hazards of its own. There is an identified need for "coordinating the coordinators" as the number of coordinating bodies themselves have begun to multiply and confusion has developed as to the structure of these agencies and their respective roles and mandates. This process can result in conflict with other groups (e.g., in competition for resources) and negate benefits to senior governments.

As funding and volunteer resources are seen to be scarce, organizations must continuously calculate whether they have a better chance of obtaining funds (and enhancing organizational recognition, prestige, and survival) through cooperative funding proposals or "going it alone," which is likely to be a quicker and less contentious approach. Where the benefits of cooperation are unclear, participation by individual interests is less likely. Larger communities with greater resources, such as Port Hardy, for example, have opted out of some regional processes, favouring instead to undertake their own independent development efforts.

In a time of change and uncertainty, it may be very useful to encourage the degree of innovation and diversity represented by many smaller organizations. "Institutionalization" can occur too early, and tend to fossilize processes and structures before they are proven to be effective. Loose federations may permit groups with both common and conflicting interests to cooperate where they see the benefits of cooperation without being forced to deal with all of their differences simultaneously. From the perspective of senior governments, monolithic community organizations may limit government's ability to encourage innovation or to maintain a broad base of community support (including dissenters).

Based on our survey of North Island NGOs, however, it appears that some *de facto* consolidation/coordination of responsibilities is occurring, largely through the dense network of overlapping board memberships. A relatively small group of individuals are (informally) serving as a sort of *de facto* "super board" for institutions concerned with economic development and resource management.

In an ideal world, individual organizations on the North Island, collaborative and otherwise, would have a clear and widely understood role (or set of responsibilities) with respect to economic development in the region; a sort of organizational structure for the economic-development and resource-management activities of the region. Elected governments, representing the interests of their constituents politically, it could be argued have the rightful role as overseer of this structure. Other organizations are interested only in one particular economic sector and/or community. Still others play a specific functional role in the economic-development process (e.g., providing funding, research or technical assistance). Each of the roles is extremely important. No one organization on the North Island can fulfill all of them. However, since each role is important in the overall process, each agency must be aware of how it fits with the others in order for the parts or the whole to be most effective (e.g., point their clients or constituents in the right direction for other kinds of help they may need). Despite increasing levels of communication and cooperation this organizational structure has not yet been fully developed in the region; thus, some ambiguity remains as to who is responsible for what.

Recommendations for Further Research

In scratching the surface of research on nonprofit organizations on the North Island, we have inevitably uncovered more questions than answers. First, more study is needed on relationships between senior governments and

NGOs, and senior and local governments. Government actions have an impact on social capital and economic development in ways that are not fully understood; the trade-offs between "government support" and "government domination" are hinted at in this study, but not fully explored.

Government respondents recognize that this relationship is poorly understood, yet understanding is becoming particularly important as local communities respond to global forces and look to senior governments for their assistance. It is clearly important to look at the functions that agencies perform in their communities and vis-à-vis both the state and the market to determine the appropriate role of public sector support and involvement.

Second, this research has highlighted the importance of key actors in volunteer organizations and raised questions about how these key volunteers can be better supported. There appears to be a growing need to recognize and compensate individuals who supply ongoing professional and managerial services to institutions, particularly where those organizations are not supported to hire core staff. Honoraria and/or modest stipends could go a long way toward encouraging new volunteers (such as the active retired or semi-retired professional) and recognizing the contributions of current individuals who are managers in all but name. Technological solutions such as teleconferencing may also have potential for reducing the time and cost involved in NGO activity, particularly in sparsely populated areas.

Third, the linkages between local voluntary organizations and local elected governments, often reflected in a panoply of advisory groups and committees, also deserve greater study. In particular, we might speculate that an expanded role for local governments may be one route to addressing the issues of representativeness, accountability, and organizational stability that plague many NGOs as they increasingly take on "quasi-governmental" functions. In British Columbia, this area of study is of particular interest in light of increased levels of self-government being assumed by First Nations through the treaty settlement process. Perhaps these new forms of local and regional government offer some clues as to more effective community governance in non-Aboriginal communities, also.

Finally, this chapter has touched on the role of collaborative nonprofit organizations in facilitating cooperative relationships between Aboriginal and non-Aboriginal communities within a region. This is a topic of critical importance in British Columbia and across the country and is therefore worthy of more in-depth investigation.

Notes

This chapter is the result of a collaborative research project involving the Centre for Public Sector Studies, University of Victoria; the Community Economic Development Centre, Simon Fraser University; and the Inner Coast Natural Resource Centre, Alert Bay, British Columbia. A detailed report is available at <http://web.uvic.ca/cpss/npsri>. The project team thanks the Kahanoff Foundation for its generous grant which made this project possible. Thanks also to the British Columbia Ministry of Fisheries for a supplemental grant which allowed us to extend the scope of our inquiry. Most importantly, we thank the numerous individuals who made themselves available for interviews and focus groups and thus provided us with the insights that were revealed through this study.

[1]CED is defined here as "a process by which communities can initiate and generate their own solutions to their common economic problems and thereby build long-term community capacity and foster the integration of economic, social and environmental objectives" (Ross and McRobie 1989).

[2]Although some communities prefer the co-operative and/or community-run business model to a purely private entreprise model of economic development, all participate in the market economy. Reed and Gill (1997) point out that such activities lie on a continuum between two types of development, referred to as CED and LED (local economic development), depending on the degree of importance given to narrow economic/private sector objectives — the emphasis of LED programs and organizations.

[3]These factors included an increasing environmental sensitivity among BC residents, demand for "non-consumptive" uses of the forest land base such as tourism and recreation, a realization that current forestry practices simply were not sustainable and the shortage of once-abundant old-growth timber.

[4]The first modern treaty was concluded with the Nisga'a in 1999 and received Royal Assent in Ottawa on 13 April 2000.

[5]Retail trade accounted for 10 percent of 1996 employment, accommodation, food and beverage at 8 percent and education services at 7 percent.

[6]The commercial and non-commercial harvest of non-timber forest products (NTFPs) is not new, yet economic development practitioners in BC have only recently started to consider its role in economic development and community diversification. NTFPs — including wild mushrooms, berries and other wild foods, plants used in the floral and craft industry, and medicinal plants — have a long

history of use among indigenous peoples and have become an important source of annual or supplemental income for both First Nations and non-native communities.

[7]This excludes dollars received from provincial Crown corporations Fisheries Renewal BC and BC Hydro, which, if included, would raise the government contribution to 67 percent.

[8]The members of the Panel Studying Partnering failed to arrive in the community because of weather conditions, but a statement from local agencies was drafted. This meeting led to a second workshop, organized by the North Island Fisheries Centre on models of regional fisheries management for the North Island.

[9]These observations reflect similar comments about the role of local governments in Newfoundland and Labrador:

Local electoral accountability makes municipal governments bottom-up organizations. They not only see the community as a client; they are the organizational vehicle for people to meet their needs at the local level. The local accountability of municipalities is a fundamental element of community economic development, overlooked until recently in Newfoundland and Labrador. No other local development organization has the direct electoral accountability and accompanying authority of municipal governments (Task Force on Community Economic Development in Newfoundland and Labrador 1995, pp. 106-07).

References

Addison Travel Marketing. 1999. *North Island Tourism Strategy*. Vancouver: Addison Travel Marketing.

Blakely, E. 1994. *Planning Local Economic Development: Theory and Practice*, 2d ed. Thousand Oaks: Sage Publications.

British Columbia. Ministry of Forests. 1996. *Timber Supply Review*. Victoria: Government of British Columbia.

_____ Ministry of Small Business, Tourism and Culture. 1993. *Community Tourism Action Plan*. Victoria: Government of British Columbia.

British Columbia. Mount Waddington Community Futures Development Corporation (CFDC). 1998. "Synopsis of Annual Report." Port McNeill, BC. CFDC.

Bruyn, S.T. 1987. "Beyond the Market and the State," in *Beyond the Market and the State*, ed. S.T. Bruyn and J. Meehan. Philadelphia: Temple University Press.

Decter, M. and J. Kowall. 1989. *Yukon 2000: Comprehensive Planning for Diversification*. Local Development Paper No. 13. Ottawa: Economic Council of Canada.

Douglas Smith and Associates. 1994. *A Brief Survey of Structures for Municipal Participation in Community Economic Development in Canada.* St. John's: Economic Recovery Commission

Fitzgibbon & Associates. 1995. *Kingcome Timber Supply Area Socio-Economic Analysis.* Victoria: Economics and Trade Branch, British Columbia Ministry of Forests.

Fukuyama, F. 1995. "Social Capital and the Global Economy," *Foreign Affairs,* 74 (5):89-103.

Gault, D. 1998. Personal communication.

Gislason, G., L. Lam and M. Mohan. 1996. *Fishing for Answers: Coastal Communities and the BC Salmon Fishery.* Victoria: ARA Consulting Group Inc. for the BC Job Protection Commission.

Hall, M. and K.G. Banting. 2000. "The Nonprofit Sector in Canada: An Introduction," in *The Nonprofit Sector in Canada: Roles and Relationships,* ed. K.G. Banting. Kingston and Montreal: School of Policy Studies, Queen's University and McGill-Queen's University Press.

Inner Coast Natural Resource Centre (ICNRC) Website: <www.icnrc.org>.

_____ 1998. *ICNRC Newsletter*, Fall.

_____ 1999. "Proposal for Development." Alert Bay: ICNRC.

Jezierski, L. 1990. "Neighbourhoods and Public-Private Partnerships in Pittsburgh," *Urban Affairs Quarterly,* 26(2):27-49.

John Ronald and Associates. 1990. *Village of Alert Bay Proposed Economic Development Strategy.* Victoria: John Ronald and Associates.

Longo, J. 1999. "What Exactly Do You Mean 'Social Capital'? Multiple Meanings and a Myriad of Terms in the Space Between the Market and the State." CPSS Working Paper. Victoria: Centre for Public Sector Studies.

MacIntyre, G.A., ed. 1998. *Perspectives on Communities: A Community Economic Development Roundtable.* Sydney, NS: UCCB Press.

MacNeil, T. 1994. "Governments as Partners in Community Economic Development in Galaway," in *Community Economic Development: Perspectives on Research and Policy,* ed. B. Galway and J. Hudson. Toronto: Thompson Educational Publishing.

Marchak, P. 1999. *Falldown: Forest Policy in British Columbia.* Vancouver: The David Suzuki Foundation and Ecotrust Canada.

Markey, S. 1999. "Structural versus Symbolic Change in Canadian Forest Policy: The Case of British Columbia." Unpublished paper.

NIFC (North Island Fisheries Centre). 1998. Brochure.

Ostrom, E. 1990. *Governing the Commons.* New York: Cambridge University Press.

Panel on Accountability and Governance in the Voluntary Sector (PAGVS). 1999. *Building on Strength:Improving Governance and Accountability in Canada's Voluntary Sector.* Ottawa: PAGVS.

Phillips, S.D. 1995. "Redefining Government Relationships with the Voluntary Sector: On Great Expectations and Sense and Sensibility." URL: <http://www.web.net/vsr-trsb/publications/phillips-e.html>.

Phillips, S.D. and K.A. Graham. 2000. "Hand-in-Hand: When Accountability Meets Collaboration in the Voluntary Sector," in *The Nonprofit Sector in Canada: Roles and Relationships*, ed. K.G. Banting. Kingston and Montreal: School of Policy Studies, Queen's University and McGill-Queen's University Press.

Rawls, J. 1987. "The Idea of an Overlapping Consensus," *Oxford Journal of Legal Studies,* 7(1):1-25.

Reed, M. and A. Gill. 1997. "Community Economic Development in a Rapid Growth Setting: A Case Study of Squamish, B.C.," in *Troubles in the Rainforest: British Columbia's Forest Economy in Transition*, ed. T. Barnes and R. Hayter. Victoria: Western Geographical Press.

Roseland, M. 1994. *Bottom-up Initiative, Top-down Leadership in National Round Table Review.* Ottawa: National Round Table on the Environment and the Economy.

Ross, D. and G. McRobie. 1989. "A Feasibility Study for a Centre for Community Economic Development at Simon Fraser University." Vancouver: Simon Fraser University. At <http://www.sfu.ca/cedc/resources/online/cedconline/mcrobie.htm>.

Salamon, L. 1994. "The Rise of the Nonprofit Sector," *Foreign Affairs* 73(4):109-22.

_____ 1995. *Partners in Public Service: Government-Nonprofit Relations in the Modern Welfare State.* Baltimore: Johns Hopkins University Press.

Savoie, D. 1992. *Regional Economic Development: Canada's Search for Solutions*, 2d ed. Toronto: University of Toronto Press.

Sawhill, J. 1999. *Mission Impossible? Measuring Success in Nonprofit Organizations.* The Nature Conservancy.

Smith, R. 1999. "Strategies, Initiatives and Models for CED." CED for Forest Communities Project Working Paper. Vancouver: Simon Fraser University Community Economic Development Centre.

Stanton, K. 1999. "Promoting Civil Society: Reflections on Concepts and Practice," in *The Revival of Civil Society*, ed. M.G. Schechter. New York: St. Martin's Press.

Statistics Canada. 1986. Census data. Ottawa: Statistics Canada.

_____ 1996. Census data. Ottawa: Statistics Canada.

Task Force on Community Economic Development in Newfoundland and Labrador. 1995. *Community Matters: The New Regional Economic Development — Report of the Task Force on Community Economic Development in Newfoundland and Labrador*. St. John's, Newfoundland.

Vancouver Island North Visitors' Association (VINVA). Web site: <www.vinva.bc.ca>.

Vodden, K. 1997. "Working Together for a Green Economy," in *Eco-City Dimensions: Healthy Communities, Healthy Planet*, ed. M. Roseland. Gabriola Island, BC: New Society Publishers.

_____ 1999. '*Nanwakola: Co-management and Sustainable Community Economic Development in a BC Fishing Village*. Vancouver: Simon Fraser University.

Ware, A. 1989. *Between Profit and State: Intermediate Organizations in Britain and the United States*. Oxford: Polity Press.

Wilson, J. 1998. *Talk and Log: Wilderness Politics in British Columbia*. Vancouver: UBC Press.

6

VON "doing commercial": The Experience of Executive Directors with Related Business Development

Joseph A. Tindale and Erin MacLachlan

INTRODUCTION

In 1995, the national office of the Victorian Order of Nurses (VON Canada) began promoting opportunities for its branches across the country to partner with it in developing related business activity, as a means of generating new revenues. As the then Business Development Officer, Richard Marritt, explained:

> We are a charitable organization providing health care to all Canadians regardless of their situation. In today's climate of fiscal restraint, we've had to seek additional sources of funding to continue to offer our services to the community. One way of doing this has been related business ventures (VON Canada 1997, p. 1).

The national office initiated a joint venture with Berlex Canada in 1995 to have VON nurses deliver in-home education to patients using the Berlex multiple sclerosis medication Betaseron. This was followed in 1997 by a shared initiative with a national department store chain to have VON nurses offer monthly wellness clinics in their stores. These program initiatives from the national office legitimated these commercial activities and provided financial support for branches facing an income reduction from declining donations and more limited opportunities to obtain provincial government contracts for visiting nursing. Concurrently, a number of branches across the country began to develop local related business ventures. Although the funds generated in this way have been directed to supporting branch benevolent programs, some self-reflection is required any time a nonprofit agency engages in activity designed to turn a profit. It is not surprising then that the title of the article from which Marritt was quoted is "New Business Ventures Support VON's Charitable Role."

Developing commercial activities requires more of branch executive directors than had been asked of them previously. At the same time, directors have had to work with volunteer boards, staff, and community stakeholders while many of their organizations were experiencing revenue shortfalls from traditional sources. This study profiles three VON branch executive directors from three different provinces whose organizations developed commercial activities as a means of offsetting the declines in revenues from publicly funded contracts.

The executive directors in the study are Joan Gamble from the Fredericton, New Brunswick branch; Sandra Hanmer from the Wellington-Waterloo-Dufferin branch in Ontario; and Joan Wagner with the VON branch in Edmonton, Alberta. The executive directors collaborated in this research with the dual intention of learning from a comparative study of their branch experiences with business activities and VON Canada, and contributing to the literature on nonprofit Canadian health-care firms engaged in developing related businesses. Thus, this research explores their experiences within a national VON context where many branches are trying to survive in similar circumstances. As such, they are akin to other nonprofit organizations challenged by more competition for both donor dollars and publicly funded contracts to deliver health-care services (Banting 2000; Dart and Zimmerman 2000).

Why are these executive directors moving their branches in this direction? Are they managing to be successful? Are there implications for their charitable mission? The initial assumption in this research was that such a vast sea change in the branch health-care climate implied a volatile situation. This assumption has proved accurate. However, the loss of government contracts to deliver visiting nursing services does not signal the imminent demise of the VON or the branches. The story is still unfolding, but the experiences of the three branch cases explored here suggest an ongoing vitality.

The VON, across Canada, is a nonprofit charitable organization. The three VON branches in the different provinces share this characteristic. As registered VON branches they each adhere to principles of governance set by the national organization that include the national mission statement. The Edmonton branch even uses this statement in its branch *Fact Sheet* outlining its services. In 1998, the national mission statement was: "VON Canada provides leadership across Canada in the developing of health and social policy, the delivery of innovative community based nursing, and other health care and support services, based on the principles of primary health care" (VON Canada 1998, p. 13).

In the fall of 1998, VON Canada issued a strategic planning document that proposed revising the mission statement to highlight the organization as a charity and the role of local branches in delivering community-based care. That proposal was accepted in 1999 and reads: "VON Canada, a charity, guided by the principles of primary healthcare, works in partnership with Canadians for a healthier society through: 1. Leadership in community-based care. 2. Delivery of innovative, comprehensive health and social services. 3. Influence in the development of health and social policy." The statement signifies the desire of VON Canada and its branches to emphasize their charitable nature and their role as community-based care providers when they are entering business-related activities. They are reaffirming their identity while embracing the goals to "preserve and increase market share of government funded health and social service programs ... and compete on quality, price and service in the for-profit marketplace" (VON Canada 1998, pp. 26-27).

The mission statement of the Waterloo-Wellington-Dufferin (WWD) branch in Ontario reflects the same tone. It states:

VON WWD *cares for life* through the provision of a diverse range of client focused, community-based health care and support services. Staff and volunteers are committed to:

- excellence
- quality of care

- cost-effective service delivery
- collaboration with partners
- response to needs, and
- equitable access for everyone

VON WWD, a not-for-profit charity, is a leader in the development and provision of community health programs in Waterloo Region and Wellington and Dufferin Counties (WWD VON 1998).

The mission statements suggest the ideal that everyone in the branch is expected to follow.

THEORY AND LITERATURE

Research into the nonprofit sector has often been neglected by social scientists and by welfare state theorists (Gronbjerg 1997; Johnson 1997). There is a limited amount of American research on this domain and even less Canadian information (MacLachlan 1999). There are signs, however, that this is slowly changing. Zimmerman and Dart (1998) surveyed issues among Canadian charitable organizations engaged in commercial ventures. Subsequently, the report of the Panel on Accountability and Governance in the Voluntary Sector (PAGVS 1999) sought to explore what was needed in terms of governance and accountability among organizations that rely, at least in part, on charitable fundraising to support benevolent programs. More recently, a program sponsored by the Kahanoff Foundation and administered by the School of Policy Studies at Queen's University initiated a series of publications that looks at roles and relationships in the nonprofit sector (Banting 2000).

A common thread running through these publications is that nonprofit agencies have encountered serious financial challenges throughout the late 1980s and the 1990s (Johnson 1997; Mellor 1997; WWD 1998; Zimmerman and Dart 1998). In particular, all levels of government have been focusing on what is sometimes referred to as a crisis of the welfare state (Jenson and Phillips 2000), and they have dealt with this crisis by promoting deficit reduction through constricting public expenditures (Mellor 1997,1998; WWD 1998; Johnson 1997). The retraction of the state in turn, has had a major impact on the funding for charitable organizations (Zimmerman and Dart 1998). Historically, nonprofit organizations have relied on approximately two-thirds of their total revenue from government sources (ibid.). This revenue source is in serious decline, particularly in the health sector. For example, between 1974 and 1994, the federal government reduced its share of total health expenditure from approximately 30 to 25 percent, thereby transferring responsibility for this proportion of costs to the provinces (Canada. Health Canada 1996). In 1994, provincial governments covered 44 percent of health-care funding, with the rest being made up by private funds (28 percent) and municipalities (1.2 percent). As of 1994, the rate of increase in health-care spending by the federal government had slowed down to 1 percent, a considerable decline from 2.5 percent in 1993 and 5.6 percent in 1992.

More recently, the February 2000 federal budget increased Canadian Health and Social Transfers to the provinces by $2.5 billion, but not enough to offset the more than $4 billion withdrawn from such transfers since 1995 when the federal government moved to eliminate its deficit and begin to pay down the national debt (*National Post* 2000). The provinces have protested against these cuts in transfers and are now engaged in an ongoing debate with the federal government over the payment structure. Some provinces, facing a shortfall in surplus, have turned to other sources. Alberta, for example has introduced Bill 11 to expand the opportunities for privatized health care in the hopes of replacing the missing federal dollars.

In the face of this reduction in government revenues, nonprofit organizations are confronting intense competition for donated funds and an associated state of donor fatigue (Hall 1998; PAGVS 1999; WWD 1998). An escalating number of charities are competing for the same shrinking pool of donor funds (Mellor 1997).

The literature has identified two choices that nonprofit organizations have for coping with these numerous challenges (Hutton 1999; MacLachlan 1999). They can reduce the programs they provide, or find ways to increase revenue from non-governmental sources (Weisbrod 1997). Indeed, numerous nonprofit organizations have investigated alternative revenue possibilities, the most prominent being commercialization (Dees 1998; Hodgkinson 1989; Weisbrod 1997; Zimmerman and Dart 1998).

Nonprofit organizations are turning to commercial funding in the belief that market-based revenue will be easier to obtain and is potentially unrestricted (Dees 1998). This move to diversification is thought by these organizations to be the optimal financial strategy since this process decreases their dependence on a single or narrow source of funding, and provides them with a cushion should that funding diminish (Dees 1998; Zimmerman and Dart 1998).

Dees suggests analyzing nonprofits by identifying their place on a continuum from purely philanthropic to purely commercial. He suggests that "few social enterprises can or should be purely commercial: most should combine commercial and philanthropic elements in a productive balance" (1998, p. 60). Furthermore, it is only rarely, and in very specific circumstances, that commercial ventures by nonprofit organizations generate revenue that represents a substantial proportion of total revenue. In most circumstances, revenue from commercial ventures supplement the core funding obtained elsewhere (Zimmerman and Dart 1998).

This shift to commercialization may lead nonprofits to emulate for-profit firms (Hodgkinson 1989), resulting in a "clash of organizational values" (Larson 1992). By engaging in more commercial and profit-making activities, nonprofit organizations are entering a realm not ordinarily identified with the benevolence of their organizations, and thus potentially undermining their philanthropic goal (Johnson 1997; Weisbrod 1989).

If nonprofit organizations emulate for-profit firms, then public confidence in the organizations may decline (Lawrence 1997). The public may suspect that these new approaches detract from the organizations' original intent of providing care to needy beneficiaries (Hutton 1999). As a result, this tarnished reputation has the potential to change the character of a nonprofit relationship with its beneficiaries, clients, donors, funders, volunteers, and staff (Zimmerman and Dart 1998).

Nonprofit organizations pursuing for-profit activities also face both operational and cultural challenges (Dees 1998). Commercialization requires skills, knowledge, and expertise more commonly found in the for-profit sector. Nonprofit organizations require both social and commercial entrepreneurial skills in order to engage successfully in for-profit activities and not all are confident that this dual capacity can exist in charitable organizations (Zimmerman and Dart 1998). Moreover, obtaining these skills can prove to be costly and difficult for nonprofit agencies. In addition, this move to commercialization can result in a dramatic change in the culture of these organizations and can cause conflict with nonprofit agency staff (Dees 1998).

While much of the literature emphasizes the deleterious effects of nonprofit agencies engaging in commercial ventures, some literature encourages such organizations to investigate commercial sources of revenue. Philanthropic fundraising can be time-consuming and uncertain, and some analysts suggest that diversified funding can improve their efficiency and effectiveness by decreasing the need for donated funds, forcing nonprofit organizations to be more client-focused, and refocusing the organization energy on its mission (Dees 1998; Zimmerman and Dart 1998).

The work of Dart and Zimmerman makes a different contribution. In a study of nonprofits functioning within a mixed economy model, they found that commercial activities among these agencies can help sustain benevolent programs without being used to prop up under-nourished core programs. Further, they emphasize the important distinction between an organization engaging in commercial activity and the commercialization of a charitable agency. This, they argue, is a distinction that needs to be sharpened (Dart and Zimmerman 2000, p. 145).

Without a doubt, the challenges of reduced access to government contracts, more competition for charitable dollars and the development of commercial programs has great implications for VON Canada. VON has been operating as a nonprofit organization in Canada since 1897 (VON Canada 1998) and faces the same challenges as other nonprofit agencies (Hutton 1999). Our study explores the experience of three executive directors of VON branches in New Brunswick, Ontario, and Alberta. These branches have increasingly developed business activities to compensate for the loss of government-contracted services such as visiting nurses and homemaking, and to reduce reliance on government contracts as a source of revenue. As such, the research was guided by the following questions:

- What meanings have the executive directors given to their experience with developing related businesses?

- Is the development of related business activity an exercise in commercial programming or a commercialization of the organization?

- What insights and recommendations associated with developing related businesses can be drawn from comparing the experiences of the three executive directors?

METHODOLOGY

This research employs a comparative case design (Patton 1990; Neumann 1997) in order to analyze the experiences of executive directors in three different settings. We sought interpretive validity (Altheide and Johnson 1998) through our understandings of how these persons defined, constructed, and gave meaning to the social world that led them to engage in the development of related businesses. The initial case was the Waterloo-Wellington-Dufferin (WWD) branch. With the collaboration and support of VON Canada, two other branches — VON Fredericton and the VON Edmonton — were selected for study. Like the WWD branch, Edmonton lost a considerable amount of market share to government and subsequently to for-profit rivals. In the end, VON Edmonton decided it would be too expensive to compete in these areas. VON Fredericton has been developing for-profit programs where they have the resources to cover start-up costs. They have extended this approach since losing their visiting nursing contract when the province decided to deliver this program itself in the mid-1990s.

We first gathered data through archival material, primary documents, annual reports, and brochures of the three VON branches. Such information included annual reports and brochures on selected services. The branch material provided a basis for a comparative assessment of past activities of the branches, their services, and their engagement in commercial activities. The documents and archival data were used, along with the research literature, to develop a questionnaire which was mailed to the three branch executive directors. Their responses provided an initial assessment of the issues surrounding the use of for-profit activities by these three branches. Next, a key informant interview methodology was utilized (Patton 1990; Neumann 1997; Huberman and Miles 1998). Separate interview schedules with each executive director enabled us to focus on information specific to their branch and to inquire into possible reasons for the similarities and differences between them.

The instrument was semi-structured with closed questions seeking descriptive information about agency programs, finances, and marketing, and a number of open-ended questions. The open-ended questions were used in an attempt to evoke the executive directors' own understandings (Fontana and Frey 1998). Specifically, these questions were designed to elicit the negotiation process around the development and expansion of for-profit ventures, as well as the executive directors' views on where their organizations lay on the Social Enterprise Spectrum, if that positioning was satisfactory along with their reasoning. During the interviews, the executive directors mentioned the opinions of board members, staff, clients, and various stakeholders. While we were still focused on their experiences, their sense of other people's views in their organizations added richness to their own observations.

Content and narrative analysis are techniques for analyzing data. If we were to place them in a larger context, it would be fair to say our approach was one of grounded theory. Our understanding of this process is one where "grounded theory is a *general methodology* for developing theory that is grounded in data systematically gathered and analysed in an ongoing interaction between data collection and analysis. This feature has led to grounded theory also being known as the constant comparative method" (Strauss and Corbin 1998, pp. 158-59). In this study, there was an ongoing interaction as we first sought collaboration from VON branches on what we wished to examine, initially reviewed documentary evidence, and then analyzed it to provide the basis for the mail-out questionnaire. The questionnaire, once analyzed, gave rise to the interactive interviews.

THE CASE STUDIES

The three branches are all multi-service organizations, but have lost all or some of their government contracts to deliver visiting nursing and/or home-making services over the past ten years or so. The branches are dissimilar in size and scope of operations. The Waterloo-Wellington-Dufferin branch is substantially larger than either of the other two. It serves a population of 575,000 and has approximately 550 paid staff (many of whom are part-time) and 300 volunteers. Presently, its annual budget is around $10 million.

Fredericton, by comparison, has a budget of about $500,000 annually. The Edmonton budget is larger than that of Fredericton but it is not as large as that of the WWD VON.

Waterloo-Wellington-Dufferin VON (Ontario)

Sandra Hanmer is the executive director of a relatively new branch, resulting from the 1997 amalgamation of the Guelph-Wellington-Dufferin branch with the Waterloo branch. These two branches merged as a means of addressing the same issues that led all three branches to develop related businesses. Merging was a way to cut fixed costs and facilitate access to expanded markets for the range of complementary services they each provided. The merger was accomplished in the middle of the transition in Ontario to "managed competition," which took place between 1995–96 and 1999–2000. During this period, the VON market share for visiting nursing and homemaking in the Guelph area dropped from approximately 95 percent to roughly 50 percent.

Fredericton VON (New Brunswick)

The Fredericton branch was one of three city branches that together delivered the Extra Mural Hospital (EMH) visiting nursing contract. (VON government-contract for visiting nursing in other parts of the province had been lost years earlier.) Moncton and St. John were the other two left. In Fredericton the process was a little different. At the outset of the 1990s, VON New Brunswick was contracted by the Extra Mural Hospital, a division of the provincial government which had held the mandate to provide for the delivery of long-term care since 1990. Before that, long-term care had been the responsibility of Public Health. In 1993, the provincial government published a *Long Term Care Strategy*. Its guiding principles were that informal caregiving should be recognized, and that services be accessible, appropriate, client-focused, effective, and efficient, and that services should be assessed for quality (New Brunswick 1993a, pp. 3-4). Then, in 1993–94 the government undertook a review of the EMH program and its contractual relationship with VON New Brunswick in order to find the "most cost effective method of delivering home care services" (New Brunswick, 1993b, pp. 1, 7-8). The result was a decision by the government to cancel VON contracts and deliver the service in-house. The provincial view was that in so doing, there would be savings in one-site record-keeping, and an elimination of the almost quarter-million dollar administration fee paid to VON. The government argued that, because the EMH agreement limited the private services VON could offer while under contract for visiting nursing, cancelling the contract gave VON the opportunity to develop additional related businesses. VON New Brunswick did not see the decision as such good news! They would lose their contract and the $200,000+ operational fixed-cost payment. As well, in VON's view, the government would have to pick up commensurate administrative costs in taking over the service. This change in government policy meant that Fredericton VON entered the last five years of the millennium with significantly reduced resources and had to embark on a reorganization and rebuilding process.

Edmonton VON (Alberta)

In Edmonton, there was again a process of provincial "take-away" that had the objective of "efficient and effective service delivery." In 1987, a decision was made by the provincial government to give local boards of health the mandate to contract home-care nursing services. The process was not smooth, took until 1995 to resolve completely and, in Joan Wagner's view, featured lower efficiency and increased expenditures. VON contract volumes fell to a point where it was no longer fiscally responsible to continue and the branch began to seriously seek out related business opportunities.

Similarities and Dissimilarities in Service Complement

There are several programs that are common to each of the three branches (see Branch Program Profile). Visiting nursing is offered by all three sites as a charitable service, on a commercial basis, and — in the case of WWD VON — under government contract. Similarly, homemaking is provided by all three as a commercial service. WWD and Edmonton also provide it on a benevolent basis, and Fredericton and WWD have some government contract work in this area. While these two services are offered by each as private services, they are the traditional services that VON had for many years delivered as core programming and under contract to government.

Wellness, foot care, flu vaccination clinics, and adult day programs are also offered by all three branches. Here we see programs that reflect the development of related businesses. Foot-care clinics have often been at least partly charitable for many VON branches, and that remains the case for WWD and Fredericton. However, all three offer the service as a commercial service. The experience of WWD has been that foot-care clinics are difficult to make profitable and are used more as a marketing tool. The clinics enhance VON visibility and give the staff an opportunity to offer assessment and promotion of other branch services.

The wellness programs were initially VON Canada initiatives in partnership with related business development. This relationship continues for the branches and has been further developed in some cases. WWD, for example, also offers these clinics on a charitable basis.

Flu immunization clinics are principally a commercial activity, although WWD also provides this service on a charitable basis. These clinics typically provide a good return on investment and bring money into the branch. The service can be delivered quickly and involves corporate or institutional clients who offer it as a staff benefit.

Adult day programs may be designed for clients who are elderly and frail or have dementia. Fredericton, WWD, and Edmonton branches offer one or other of these services under government contract, but this too may change. There are rumours in Ontario that day programs, like visiting nursing and homemaking services, may be offered under the umbrella of "managed competition." If this occurs, WWD VON will need to bid on a contract to offer the service.

Other services, such as occupational health services, or home helpers, are common services among VON branches in Canada but not to all three of these particular branches. Edmonton and WWD each offer these services and do so principally on a commercial basis with some allowance for charitable cases for the home-helper program.

Overall, only WWD still provides the traditional VON services of visiting nursing and homemaking as core, government-funded contract work. Like Edmonton and Fredericton, WWD also offers these services as a commercial activity. Edmonton has only the adult day centre as government contract work. Fredericton has a similarly funded adult day program as well as contracts to do some homemaking and some foot-care clinics. These programs are not large enough to justify shifting staff back onto a five-day week, as we see below. Although the branches vary in size, they are each involved to a significant degree in a mixed economy model offering nine to ten commercial programs. The experience of the executive directors in maintaining and developing what they see as a workable mixture of nonprofit, for-profit, and charitable work is explored in what follows.

DISCUSSION OF FINDINGS

Why Be Entrepreneurial?

All three executive directors stated that their principal reasons for introducing commercial ventures into the organization were a combination of increasing the money available to support charity work and an independence from a single and declining funding source — government contracts. Fredericton's John Gamble added "continuity of employment opportunities for nurses" while Edmonton's Joan Wagner noted that fee-for-service is sometimes just cost recovery and sometimes generates profit. Cost-recovery operations provide employment, referrals for other services and sometimes a base for revenue generation. Sandra Hanmer, executive director of the WWD branch, stated that managed competition in Ontario "has forced us to diversify our revenue streams to try and regain/maintain stability." WWD's first ventures into for-profit activity came earlier in the 1990s when it felt distinctly vulnerable after the New Democratic Party government imposed what was termed a "social contract," an enforced roll-back of wages over three years. Hanmer noted that charitable donations were also down and there was an awareness of the need to generate revenue. Joan Gamble, of the Fredericton branch, observed that "the loss of the Long-Term Care programs to the Extra-Mural Hospital forced the branch to seriously evaluate what possibilities existed that could help maintain the branch." She felt government contracts could not be relied upon. Edmonton VON too picked up the commercial pace in the 1990s but, consistent with the "old novelty" concept, their first entrepreneurial efforts date back to the 1970s. Other VON branches also have been engaged in activities such as private duty nursing for many years.

All three executive directors believe that business ventures will improve the long-term sustainability of the health-care system. Sandra Hanmer stated that for-profit programs will provide nonprofit firms with an "opportunity to better 'ride the wave' of increased/decreased volume from government contracts." This refers not only to recent lost contracts and reduced volumes but also to the business instability inherent in WWD being dependent for much of their revenue on government. Beyond firm viability, WWD and Fredericton executive directors also stated that commercial activities were intended to support charitable work. For Joan Gamble, for-profit business was a way to "maintain employment for staff formerly fulfilling government contracted nonprofit work."

The work that all three branches continue to do for government has changed in character and organization from the end of the 1980s. Ontario, New Brunswick, and Alberta have all decentralized and in some cases "down-loaded" community health-care responsibilities to municipal or regional levels. The Edmonton branch almost lost its adult day program when the regional health authorities took over from the province. The Fredericton branch lost all of its visiting nursing, and now has a couple of small contracts granted by a Regional Hospital Corporation. Joan Gamble stated that:

> The Saint John branch has been contracted by their health region to visit these [postpartum] patients. They are the only branch [in New Brunswick] to benefit. Public Health services have become targeted to high-risk families, which account for only 20–30 percent of births. The remainder do not receive home visits or Public Health services unless they access Immunization Clinics. No branch is addressing this unmet need. The provincial Seniors Health Insurance, administered by Blue Cross, significantly reduced the amount reimbursed for nursing care in the home, and at foot clinics. This has resulted in a loss of private fee paying patients. [In New Brunswick patients can contract themselves, when eligible, for services and be reimbursed by the provincial government.]

In late 1995, the Ontario government began shifting responsibility to municipal/regional authorities in the form of Community Care Access Centres (CCACs). (See Jenson and Phillips 2000; Williams *et al.* 1999.) Over a three-year transition period they moved from uncontested contracts (primarily for visiting nursing and homemaking) to what they term "managed competition," government-regulated competition among nonprofit and for-profit firms. While the 1999–2000 fiscal year is the first year of full competition, not all CCACs have issued Requests For Proposals (RFPs) for full competition to date. In the interim, some VON branches in Ontario have lost all their nursing contracts. Others, such as WWD, now have half the market share they had in 1995.

Thus, in all three branches, VON now does less and, in some cases, almost no government business. The business they have retained has been won in competition at the regional as opposed to provincial level. When these VON branches were facing significant declines in government business, they were also encountering shifts in provincial organization of community health care. How did these twin phenomena affect the organizational structure of the VON branches themselves?

Organizational Consequences

The VON was forced to reorganize because their volumes were reduced and there was less revenue to pay fixed costs of rent and salaries. How, in this environment, did they muster the organizational expertise to mount for-profit ventures? The Fredericton and Edmonton branches are quite small, and their executive directors took on the responsibility of generating new business. In contrast, the WWD branch reallocated existing resources while simultaneously using in-service educational activities to reorient the skills of some of their staff. Joan Gamble reported that Fredericton only had three full-time support staff, 5.4 full-time nurses, 38 full-time personal support workers and the executive director is a 0.8 full-time equivalent position. WWD, on the other hand, has 55–60 managerial and support staff, 220 part- and full-time nurses, and 155–160 part- and full-time workers employed as homemakers. The WWD branch has more flexibility in reallocating and retraining existing staff to address the needs of start-up and maintenance of for-profit business.

The Edmonton branch has been downsized for over ten years now. It has one significant charitable activity, providing primary care at seven crisis shelters for women, youth, and children, a government-funded adult day program and a variety of for-profit services. Interestingly, the adult day program is a nonprofit government-funded program and the branch has partnered with a for-profit long-term care facility to get free space for the program. These kinds of innovations can enable a small branch to run a program at a very competitive cost. At the same time, it must be remembered that the legislation that created regional health authorities ten years ago was only one piece in an ongoing social policy history. The Alberta government is considering Bill 11, legislation that opens up more health-care services to private operators. The evolution of mixed economy health care will continue to create a climate of change for community health-care providers.

Although Fredericton lost their visiting nursing to the provincial government in 1995, layoffs occurred. In light of Joan Gamble's concern about providing employment continuity, staff, including the executive director, agreed to a plan of work-sharing, essentially going to a four-day week. Since then they have taken on for-profit business, continue to deliver some charitable services and have taken over a small homemaking business, this is all generating more work than existing staff can handle. However, the executive director does not feel that demand is sufficient to cover the fixed overhead costs that would be associated with expanding the numbers of front-line staff to meet the demand.

All three branches seek niches for new programming opportunities. They are hampered in this by the lack of resources for extensive marketing that could, in turn, generate new business. The branches are short on expertise in this area and limited in their ability to buy consultant help. An additional organizational handicap is that the greater the volume, the lower the per unit fixed cost. However, some fixed cost staff and resources have to be in place to enable the volumes to grow to the point where those overhead costs begin to fall.

The WWD branch demonstrated effective leadership in merging two branches. The new branch was able to lower fixed costs by reducing the number of management and support staff and to expand their accessible market territories, especially for for-profit activities, but also in bidding on government contracts.

Culture Change: Commercial Activity or Commercialization?

These kinds of organizational pressures and changes have an impact on organizational culture. The three VON branches are part of a national governance structure. VON Canada has initiated some national for-profit ventures, such as the wellness clinics where appropriate, and local branches have been expected to participate. The three branches have done so. However, each branch expressed concern about a lack of sensitivity to cultural context. Joan Wagner believes that the national office was not sufficiently helpful in tailoring programs to meet local conditions. For example, Edmonton conducts occupational health and safety assessments for Canadian National workers, but VON Canada wanted to accept payment substantially below Edmonton rates. All three branches support their association with VON Canada, but also feel that the help they have received in engaging in for-profit activity has not been sufficiently attuned to local branch circumstances.

The most important cultural issue for these three executive directors concerns the open solicitation of for-profit business. Staff are not always comfortable doing for-profit business when they had always thought of themselves as a charitable agency. Some Edmonton staff did not want to determine eligibility on the basis of ability to pay. Wagner replied that for-profit activities were now an important means of funding charitable activities but that no one is refused service because of financial hardship. Joan Gamble also noted that board members felt commercial enterprises might have a negative impact on fundraising. However, the boards of the other two branches did not share this concern, and the Fredericton board's fears proved unfounded. Nevertheless, all branches have become conscious of how they publicize and report their for-profit work in the context of their nonprofit and charitable status, all three have experienced some problems with public misunderstanding their charitable/nonprofit status.

Once commercial venues have been accepted as a concept, Sandra Hanmer noted the challenge was "thinking like a business, and adopting marketing strategies." According to Joan Wagner, Edmonton, "staff had to learn to work on an 'as needed' basis. They no longer simply worked a 7.5 hour day. Staff also developed a strong awareness of the cost of their time and the need to be cost-effective." In WWD, a principal way of checking costs was time per visit (TPV). Staff needed to develop an appreciation that an extra minute per visit, on average, could mean $50,000 per year in added costs for the branch. In part, according to Sandra Hanmer, WWD dealt with these challenges by "hiring individuals with the skills to lead the change and also develop and implement for-profit programs."

Do these adjustment difficulties experienced by some staff and the executive director's revised expectations lead to commercialization of the organization? Certainly they are engaged in commercial activity and have experienced changes in their internal cultures. But are the changes sufficient to suggest a shift from charitable, nonprofit agencies to a for-profit format?

Mixed Economies and Reflections on the VON Mission

The three branches were sensitive about how they distinguished their different lines of work. All branches were able to report for-profit revenues separately from nonprofit revenues, but programs cannot be distinguished simply. For example, visiting nursing can be a for-profit, nonprofit or charitable service depending on the client and the source of payment. Even so, the branch always knows what category each and every service delivery falls into, and the branches make clear to nurses that the fee structure is identical for for- and nonprofit client visits.

How a nonprofit charitable firm perceives itself, how it constructs a corporate culture, and how it balances for-profit and nonprofit enterprises, all affect whether the firm has stayed true to its charitable mission and where it fits on the business spectrum. As noted earlier, Dees (1998) describes a "social enterprise spectrum" running from free enterprise to nonprofits. Not too surprisingly, all three of the VON branches placed themselves somewhere in the middle, as mixed enterprise firms. Sandra Hanmer described their branch as a "charity run like a business." However, these descriptions more closely approximated the ideals rather than the reality. For Joan Gamble, the charitable side is not as developed as she would like. Joan Wagner states that her branch looks to increased for-profit volumes to better enable them to deliver their desired charitable programming. And WWD currently sees itself as being 80 percent reliant on nonprofit government contracts for branch revenues. Sandra Hanmer states that she "would like to change our reliance on CCAC contracts from an 80/20 split to probably a 60/40 split." To reduce to 60 percent would entail not giving up nonprofit contracts, but expanding for-profit ventures and other nonprofit revenue sources that are not tied to the local CCAC.

We asked each branch about emergent outcomes from the inception of their for-profit activities. The Edmonton branch felt that the level of financial risk that the branch experienced increased by requiring the employment of a business manager, but the executive director argued that "diversification kept the branch alive." Both the WWD and Fredericton branches perceived their financial risk level to have fallen because the risk had been diffused over a greater number of sources so that now there were "fewer eggs in the same basket." And while Fredericton found their risk to have fallen, they also felt hard-pressed to cover development costs such as purchasing equipment, training staff, and achieving a marginal rate of profit. The outcomes were mixed, especially when the discussion was financial risk. In the short term costs may have risen but in the longer term there was a sense the financial risk had lessened.

On another front, Edmonton and Fredericton perceived that the for-profit firms considered them to be unfair competition. Where this sense of unfairness exists, it seems to be related to differences in regulations for the respective types of firms regarding fundraising and taxes. Another dimension of this is the "social capital" to which VON can lay claim. Joan Gamble noted that for-profit agencies felt that the public image of VON provided it with an unfair advantage since it did not have to advertize. Sandra Hanmer did not share this perception and instead argued that "in many cases, our reputation as a charitable organization is 'getting us in the door' for our for-profit activities," but not providing an edge. This question of whether there is unfair competition and what it means to be a charitable firm taking part in for-profit ventures is a subject dealt with by the Panel on Accountability and Governance in the Voluntary Sector (1999). These firms were asked their views on the panel's final report. However, the report obviously has not yet touched them "on the ground," and they are not actively involved in explicitly addressing any of its recommendations.

Financial outcomes have also been mixed. Fredericton branch executive director, Joan Gamble, found most of their for-profit activities, such as community wellness clinics and flu vaccination programs, to be worth the development work. The exception was the MS therapy program, where volumes have been low and the work process complicated and confusing. Edmonton executive director, Joan Wagner, reported that they had done better with local for-profit initiatives than they had with VON national enterprises. In comparison, the WWD Branch has not seen the revenues it had hoped for in for-profit ventures. Sandra Hanmer stated that "it has taken three years to really be able to say for-profit activities are making a noticeable contribution to the branch." The WWD branch is taking a closer look at which programs truly have the potential to bring in revenue and/or raise the profile of the branch sufficiently in the community to attract business elsewhere. The branch has strong expectations for collaboration with for-profits around issues like hiring. There is a severe nursing shortage and the firms need to find ways to make the most of the available staff to serve clients in ways best suited to their needs.

When the executive directors were asked how they measured success for their for-profit activities, Joan Wagner of Edmonton was most instructive: "Is the charitable mission sustained? Were the for-profit ventures making a profit? Did these activities improve the organization's community profile?" The branches are also looking to performance benchmarks. In this respect, WWD has been very assertive in lobbying local CCACs to employ standardized performance evaluations as part of the assessing RFP submissions for government contracts. WWD also applied for Canadian Council on Health Services Accreditation. Their accreditation was awarded mid-year 2000. That assessment was for a nonprofit charitable firm with a governance structure and range of activities to match.

In such various ways then, these executive directors are working to manage mixed economy branches. They think related business activities add diversity, a small but critical level of additional revenue and some independence from the uncertainty of government-funded contracts. They adhere to the VON Canada mission which stresses charity while underscoring the desire to pursue related business opportunities. In our view, they are and wish to continue to engage in commercial activity. In order to be successful, they need to adopt some practices, such as cost effectiveness, of the for-profit sector. However, the term "commercialization" does not seem to fit insofar as the charitable part of their mixed economy remains a constant touchstone against which they judge themselves and offer themselves to others for evaluation.

CONCLUSION

Joan Wagner, Sandra Hanmer, and Joan Gamble have taken leadership roles in moving their organizations into the development of related businesses as a diversification strategy. In each case, the provincial government reduced public sector health-care funding as a means of meeting a government goal of eliminating deficit budgets. This process made nonprofit organizations more dependent on fundraising; and, as demand went up, the supply of charitable dollars available to any particular organization was liable to go down. Developing commercial or related business activity was a diversification strategy with objectives to: (i) replace lost revenues from government-funded contracts and fierce competition for fund- raised dollars, (ii) lessen branch financial reliance on government-funded contracts, and (iii) support employment continuity for health-care staff.

The particular mix of commercial, nonprofit contract, and charitable service programs which has been developed in each branch reflects the programs they traditionally provided, the impact of government cutbacks, and the niche opportunities they could pursue. As a result, the visiting nursing program, which was a founding program for VON, is now offered by all three branches as a commercial and charitable activity, but only in the case of WWD does the service command a viable market share as a nonprofit government-contracted service. Each branch offers about ten related business programs and while all three have partnered with VON Canada in running wellness clinics, their other business activities often differ.

There have been organizational consequences for all three branches as they struggle to restructure. New services have been developed, and existing services have been offered as commercial ones. But only Sandra Hanmer at WWD pilots a big enough organization to have a business development officer on staff. Joan Wagner in Edmonton and Joan Gamble in Fredericton each think the financial risk of adding such a person outweighs the potential benefits. Instead, they have had to add these responsibilities to their existing job descriptions.

All of the executive directors have experienced changes in organizational cultures. Joan Wagner reported that some staff had difficulty adjusting to the need for being more cost effective. She had to create a culture in which staff focused on getting tasks done instead of thinking as wage employees tied to a set number of work hours each day. Sandra Hanmer found that she had to put management people in place who could "think like a business." Joan Gamble was less inclined to push this kind of motivation and works more to maintain stability for staff. She did this, in negotiation with staff, by work-sharing through a four-day week instead of laying people off or aggressively pursuing related business ventures. The Fredericton branch has as many commercial programs as do WWD or Edmonton, but the branch has less sense of having to adopt a business ethic. It is unclear to what extent this difference reflects a community culture or organizational culture expressed in the executive director's leadership. Nevertheless, there are differences in approach among the three directors with WWD and Edmonton sharing more similarities with each other than they do, on this point, with Fredericton.

This raises the question of whether the development of related business activity is a story of charitable nonprofit organizations being commercialized in an effort to survive a tough business climate, or whether it is a diversification of activity to create a mixed economy organization that does not challenge their charitable mission. The evidence found in the experience of these three directors suggests the charitable mission has been reinforced, not diminished, and that branch participation in commercial activities will grow.

Change in the mix of branch services is an ongoing story. These branches have always offered some commercial service, often in the form of fee-for-service visiting nursing. However, the active pursuit of related business opportunities is generally less than ten years old and has been associated with declines in government funding. If, as time and circumstances change, the commercial activity in the branches were to begin to define the operation at the expense of the charitable mission, then a commercialization phenomenon might be underway. Such a process could occur in particular branches of the VON Canada umbrella organization. Were it only branches, then those individual branches might find themselves in conflict with the national organization and have to defend their charitable status. If VON Canada were to commercialize, then it would face the same charitable status challenge and its individual branches would have to decide if they wanted to remain a health-care agency under the VON banner.

To underscore our point, the evidence at this time suggests a strong charitable mission in the context of emerging commercial activity. We are clearly moving to a new understanding of what it means to be a charitable nonprofit organization. The changes experienced by the executive directors in Fredericton, Edmonton, and WWD *have* transformed important elements of the branches. They offer different services now, they offer some traditional services on a different basis, their organizations have been re-structured, and the benchmarks for performance are being measured more closely now than ever before. However, there is no going back. The only direction is forward, the challenge for each of these executive directors is to transform their VON branches into new forms of nonprofit charitable organizations.

Note

We wish to acknowledge that this research was made possible by a grant from the Kahanoff Foundation administered by the School of Policy Studies, Queen's University and to thank Brenda Zimmerman for the constructive feedback she provided on an earlier draft.

References

Altheide, D. and J. Johnson. 1998. "Criteria for Assessing Interpretive Validity in Qualitative Research," in *Collecting and Interpreting Qualitative Materials*, ed. Denzin and Lincoln.

Banting, K.G., ed. 2000. *The Nonprofit Sector in Canada: Roles and Relationships*. Kingston and Montreal: School of Policy Studies, Queen's University and McGill-Queen's University Press.

Canada. Health Canada. 1996. *National Health Expenditures in Canada 1975-1994*. Ottawa: Supply and Services Canada.

Dart, R. and B. Zimmerman. 2000. "After Government Cuts: Insights from Two Ontario 'Enterprising Nonprofits,'" in *The Nonprofit Sector in Canada: Roles and Relationships*, ed. Banting.

Dees, J. Gregory. 1998. "Enterprising Nonprofits," *Harvard Business Review*, (January/February):53-67.

Denzin, N. and Y. Lincoln. 1998. "Introduction: Entering the Field of Qualitative Research," in *Collecting and Interpreting Qualitative Materials*, ed. N.K. Denzin and Y.S. Lincoln. Thousand Oaks, CA: Sage Publications.

Fontana, A. and J.H. Frey. 1998. "Interviewing: The Art of Science," in *Collecting and Interpreting Qualitative Materials*, ed. Denzin and Lincoln.

Gronbjerg, K.A. 1997. Book review of L.M. Salamon. 1995. *Partners in Public Service: Government-Nonprofit Relations in the Modern Welfare State*, in *Social Service Review*, 71:321-23.

Hall, M. 1998. "A Knowledge Base for Voluntary Organizations." Paper presented at the conference, "Spotlight on Nonprofit Organizations: Current Challenges and Future Directions," Ryerson University, Toronto.

Hodgkinson, V. 1989. "Key Challenges Facing the Nonprofit Sector," in *The Future of the Nonprofit Sector*, ed. V. Hodgkinson and R. Yman. San Francisco: Jossey Bass Inc.

Huberman, M. and M. Miles. 1998. "Data Management and Analysis Methods," in *Collecting and Interpreting Qualitative Materials*, ed. Denzin and Lincoln.

Hutton, L.L. 1999. "The Impacts of Governmental Activities on Non-Profit Organizations: A Case Study Involving VON Canada." Unpublished undergraduate thesis. Guelph: University of Guelph.

Jenson, J. and S. Phillips. 2000. "Distinctive Trajectories: Homecare and the Voluntary Sector in Quebec and Ontario," in *The Nonprofit Sector in Canada: Roles and Relationships*, ed. Banting.

Johnson, N. 1997. Book review of L.M. Salamon and K. Helmut. 1997. *Defining the Nonprofit Sector: A Cross-National Analysis,* in *Journal of Social Policy,* 26:559-62.

Kuttner, R. 1997. *Everything for Sale: The Virtues and Limits of Markets*. New York: Alfred A. Knopf.

Larsen, P. 1997. "Public and Private Values at Odds: Can Private Sector Values Be Transplanted into Public Sector Institutions?" *Public Administration and Development,* 17:131-39.

Lawrence, D. 1997. "Why We Want to Remain a Nonprofit Health Care Organization," *Health Affairs,* 16:118-20.

MacLachlan, E. 1999. "The Commercialization of Non-Profit Organizations: A Study of the VON Waterloo-Wellington-Dufferin." Unpublished undergraduate thesis. Guelph: University of Guelph.

Mellor, R. 1997. "The Shift to the Community: A Home Care Dilemma." Unpublished Discussion Paper.

_____ 1998. *V.O.N. Canada Caregiver Symposium: Final Report*. Ottawa: VON Canada.

National Post. 2000. "Budget Highlights 2000," 29 February, p. A2.

Neumann, W.L. 1997. *Social Research Methods: Qualitative and Quantitative Approaches*, 3d ed.. Toronto: Allyn & Bacon.

New Brunswick. 1993a. *Long Term Care Strategy*. Fredericton: Government of New Brunswick.

_____ 1993b. *New Brunswick Extra Mural Hospital and Victorian Order of Nurses review: Phase 1 Long Term Care (DRAFT)*. Fredericton: Government of New Brunswick.

Panel on Accountability and Governance in the Voluntary Sector (PAGVS). 1999. *Building on Strength: Improving Governance and Accountability in Canada's Voluntary Sector.* Final Report. Ottawa: PAGVS.

Patton, M.Q. 1990. *Qualitative Evaluation and Research Methods,* 2d ed. Newbury Park, CA: Sage.

Strauss, A. and J. Corbin. 1998. "Grounded Theory Methodology: An Overview," in *Strategies of Qualitative Inquiry,* ed. N.K. Denzin and Y.S. Lincoln. Thousand Oaks, CA: Sage Publications.

Tindale, J.A. 1993. "Participant Observation as a Method for Evaluating a Mental Health Promotion Program with Older Persons," *Canadian Journal on Aging,* 12:200-15.

_____ 1997. "Becoming Competitive while Maintaining Quality Care: Case Study of a Community LTC Agency." Paper presented at the Canadian Association on Gerontology (CAG/Acg) meetings in Calgary.

Victorial Order of Nurses (VON Canada). 1997. *VON Canada Report.* Ottawa: VON Canada.

_____ 1998. *Strategy 2000: A Strategic Partnership for VON's Second Century.* Ottawa: VON Canada.

Waterloo-Wellington-Dufferin (WWD) VON Branch. 1998. "Response to *Helping Canadians, Help Canadians.*" Waterloo: WWD.

Weisbrod, B.A. 1997. "The Future of the Nonprofit Sector: Its Entwining with Private Enterprise and Government," *Journal of Policy Analysis and Management,* 16:541-55.

Williams, P., J. Barnsley, S. Leggat, R. Deber and P. Baranek. 1999. "Long-Term Care Goes to Market: Managed Competition and Ontario's Reform of Community Based Services," *Canadian Journal on Aging,* 18:125-53.

Zimmerman, B. and R. Dart. 1998. *Charities Doing Commercial Ventures: Societal and Organizational Implications.* Ottawa: Canadian Policy Research Networks Inc. and the Trillium Foundation.

7

At the Loose End of the Continuum: Two Nonprofit Organizations Delivering Preventive Homecare Services in Saskatchewan

Luc Thériault and Sandra Salhani

INTRODUCTION

Remarkably little is known about the contribution of organizations from the social economy (or third sector) to health-related services in Canada. The social economy is generally understood as the world of formally-constituted, self-governing, democratically-structured organizations established for the public benefit of the collectivity or the mutual benefit of its members. As such, social economy overlaps with concepts such as third sector, voluntary sector, cooperative sector, nonprofit sector, and civil society. Many experts believe the social economy will be a significant player in health and social services delivery over the coming decades. Yet, there have been relatively few comprehensive studies of third sector organizations in Canada. In the absence of accurate knowledge about the social economy's scope, resources and potential, policymakers are hampered in determining how governments could best encourage service delivery by that sector.

This study is intended to help close this knowledge gap by looking at two Saskatchewan-based nonprofit organizations involved in what can be termed *non-medical* or *preventive* homecare services. It triangulates information from different sources in order to obtain a fuller view of these organizations and meet the following five research objectives:

- To document the activities of two nonprofit organizations (NPOs) involved in the delivery of non-medical homecare services in Saskatchewan's two largest cities;

- To evaluate the clients' satisfaction with the quality, quantity, range, and accessibility of the services received from these nonprofit organizations, and identify the needs of the clients that remain unmet;

- To provide information on service delivery from the perspective of the service providers, with particular emphasis on their assessment of their working conditions;

- To assess the current level of services including their place in the continuum of care and prospects for improvement; and

- To identify key gaps which exist between the public sector services and those provided by these nonprofit organizations, and recommend needed services, including under what conditions and at what cost they might be provided.

The first section of this chapter lays the groundwork for the rest of the paper by outlining a theoretical framework for the place and role of third sector organizations in the delivery of human services, and by introducing the reader to the terminology of preventive homecare. This first section ends with a brief historical note on the homecare activities of nonprofit organizations in the province of Saskatchewan. The second section provides a profile of the two organizations chosen for this study and offers some details about the characteristics of their clients. The third and fourth sections are at the heart of the exposé. Section three presents a qualitative thematic analysis of the views of managers and service providers on the work performed by the chosen organizations. The next section analyzes the perspective of the clients with regard to the services they received. The conclusion synthesizes the findings, revisits the original objectives of the study, and offers a brief discussion linking the results to the question of the social economy.

THEORETICAL FRAMEWORK:
THE THIRD SECTOR AND HUMAN SERVICES[1]

A good part of the public debates about human services[2] delivery is centred on the strengths and weaknesses of the privatization option versus the maintenance and/or further development of public services. The view we adopt here is that it is time to look pass this binary alternative. In this perspective, we refuse to choose only between state-controlled or privatized services, to look instead at what we call the third sector (or social economy) delivery option.

Our analysis of human services delivery builds on insights provided by French economists during the late 1980s.[3] They point out that during the *Fordist* era — approximately 1945 to 1975 — salaried workers had greater access to unionization and collective agreements; at the same time, the protection afforded by social policies was expanded. As a result, the purchasing power of workers improved significantly. However, this golden age of the welfare state was not characterized by a democratization of workplaces. Both private and public sector workplaces remained, in fact, very hierarchical and Taylorist. Similarly, the citizen-consumers had access to human services, but had little say about how they were managed and delivered. In other words, human services delivery suffered from a "double deficit of democracy."

One exciting possibility which presents itself with the third sector delivery option is the reduction of the Taylorist work organization. This form of management, which prevailed in the health and social services systems in previous decades, could now be replaced by an organizational culture that is characterized by a "double empowerment," which affects both service providers and service users. The empowerment of service users presents an interesting basis to counter the neo-liberal attempts to oppose the interests of users (clients) and producers in order to attack the union movements. At the same time, the double empowerment question is a challenge to the traditional labour arguments that claim that what is good for the workers is also automatically good for the users and for society as a whole.

The desire for a more democratic workplace and for a double empowerment has led us to view favourably the transformation of human services systems that promote a preventive approach to health care. This can be done by decentralizing resources and redirecting them toward the lighter end of the continuum of care, like community clinics[4] and community-based, nonprofit organizations. This general position is based on the belief that an over-emphasis was placed on hospital-centred services and medicalization in public sector services during the welfare state period.

Along with other analysts, we seek a new model of state intervention in social policy that is less centralized, more participatory, more flexible, and closer to local needs (Boucher and Favreau 1997; Burrows and Loader 1994). As welfare pluralists,[5] we favour the establishment of new partnerships between social actors from the private, public, and community sectors (Vaillancourt and Jetté 1997; Favreau and Lévesque 1996; Cloutier and Hamel 1991).

The Four Sectors in the Delivery of Human Services: A Typology

To better understand where nonprofit organizations fit in the delivery of human services, it is useful to view them as part of one of the four sectors involved in the mixed economy of welfare (see Figure 1).

The *first sector* is the public sector, which principally includes government departments and regional health boards. These are responsible for services in their respective territories. In this first sector, most service providers are union members. The *second sector* is the private market, which comprises competing private, for-profit businesses such as private homecare agencies. In this second sector, unionization is less frequent.

The *third sector* refers to private, but nonprofit, organizations of the community (including co-operatives) that belong to neither the first nor the second sector. The organizations in this sector tend to make use of both salaried workers and volunteers. The two organizations under study in this research belong to this third sector. Finally, we can distinguish a *fourth sector* which can be called the informal sector.[6] The main characteristic of this fourth sector has to do with the fact that those who provide services do so on a voluntary basis and without remuneration. The service providers of this sector are usually family members, friends or neighbours, and more often than not, they are women. The informal sector is therefore not to be confused with the third sector.

The third sector encompasses the large portion of the economy that is neither in the private sector nor is it government-owned; however, this is a rather descriptive definition (Quarter 1992). In fact, the third sector refers

Figure 1: The Four Sectors in the Delivery of Human Services

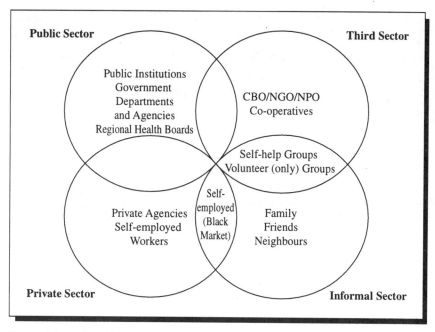

Source: Adapted from Vaillancourt and Jetté (1999, p. 4).

to independent, formal organizations which are created to provide a service to either the public or to a defined membership. Third sector organizations tend to meet the needs of people within their communities; thus, many of these agencies or enterprises have a local character.

While Americans use the term "nonprofit sector" rather than third sector, placing the emphasis on a legal definition; the British, on the other hand, prefer speaking of a charity or voluntary sector. This can be confusing, as the third sector makes use of volunteers as well as paid employees. In France and Quebec, the term social economy (*économie sociale*) is the one most often used to refer to formal association-based economic initiatives that are founded on autonomy, solidarity, and citizenship. The term social economy is a little more prescriptive than is that of the third sector, as democratic management and priority to services over profits are among the principles promoted (but not always achieved) by organizations belonging to the social economy.[7]

A New Sharing of Responsibilities

As we said, in this period of relative decline of state intervention in human services delivery, much of the public policy analyses are focused on the issue of privatization.[8] This is an important issue, but it is not the only process social policy analysts should be thinking about. Returning to Figure 1, we can identify at least two other noteworthy phenomena. If privatization can be conceptualized as a transfer from the public to the private sector, then something called *communitarization* could be conceptualized as a transfer going from the public sector to the third sector (or social economy). Hence, in communitarization, existing or new services are delegated to the community-based organizations of the third sector. This process can take place in different ways, under various conditions, and with positive or negative outcomes. The other process, which could be called *informalization*, would involve the transfer (some would say the abandonment) of responsibility from the state directly to the caring families and friends (informal sector). We find this scenario much less appealing and hope, in fact, that an emphasis on communitarization could help to prevent it and perhaps reduce as well the use of the privatization option. To assess whether communitarization could be a viable alternative to privatization and informalization in the future, we must now learn more about what nonprofit organizations are doing, and how. This chapter intends to contribute to building this knowledge base by focusing on two organizations which deliver preventive homecare services.

Preventive Homecare in Canada: Terminology and Issues

Homecare has a relatively short official history in Canada. As such, it lacks the wealth of comprehensive data that more traditional aspects of the Canadian health-care systems enjoy.[9] The paucity of data is even more pronounced with regard to non-medical or preventive homecare; "the least studied and most taken for granted" (Picard 1999).

The definition and the place of homecare in the health-care continuum are problematic. Formal homecare may be delivered under numerous organizational structures in the public, private, and/or nonprofit sectors, and within these structures, homecare activities can vary widely. It may refer to home-based services that address needs specifically associated with medical interventions, such as intravenous antibiotic treatments or home oxygen therapy; alternatively, it may refer to non-medical services that provide support for daily living activities, such as housekeeping and food preparation. The common link among these services is that they meet the needs of people who previously or potentially might have required "light" institutional care, thereby enabling them to maintain their independence and remain in the community.

Homecare services are often included in the category of "continuing care," which is generally devoted to non-acute needs, and in particular, to the need for personal assistance among people with activity limitations (Federal/Provincial/Territorial Subcommittee on Continuing Care 1992). There are two categories of daily activities which are frequently identified in the literature: the activities of daily living (ADL), and the instrumental activities of daily living (IADL). If an individual has limitations with ADL, help may be needed with personal care or assistance with moving about the house (this is more often associated with medical homecare). If an individual has limitations with IADL, the needed assistance would be with non-medical activities — grocery shopping, housekeeping, or running errands — that are crucial for independence. While nearly all persons requiring assistance with ADL also require assistance with IADL, the reverse is often not the case (Chen and Wilkins 1998). These two categories of need give way to the term "instrumental homecare," which is often used to describe non-medical homecare. Non-medical homecare refers primarily to low-level homemaking and meal services (HSURC 1998a). Maintenance and/or preventive homecare are synonymous terms with instrumental or non-medical homecare, and it is these types of homecare services that are provided by the two organizations studied in this chapter.

In recent years, there has been some recognition of the importance of non-medical or preventive homecare (Canadian Home Care Association 1998). Yet, most of this care is typically provided by informal caregivers such as family, friends, and neighbours (Rimer 1998). In fact, most seniors who are in need of non-medical homecare receive none, aside from informal sources (Marshall 1989). Health authorities are, at best, only slowly allocating funding to maintenance and preventive homecare (MPHC) as the cost-effectiveness of such programs is still being debated (HSURC 2000). Hence, non-medical homecare services have always been, and continue to be, underfunded by the public purse.

Some analysts are concerned that homecare services (both medical and preventive) could be privatized in the near future.[10] To prevent this, they suggest that homecare might be more effectively provided by nonprofit, third sector agencies. For instance, Lesemann and Nahmiash (1993) have proposed that nonprofit, private resources be used as a complement to the public health systems. Despite the relative lack of literature on nonprofit homecare delivery, it was documented that organizations from this sector "allocated more funds for direct patient service and had larger staff-patient ratios" (Elwell 1984). It is difficult, however, to form a conclusion as there have been too few formal evaluations of nonprofit homecare programs.

Whether homecare services are provided by the public, private or nonprofit sectors, one problem that remains is the relative exploitation of the low-paid homemakers. The primary role of the homemaker is to ensure that the household is maintained as a functioning unit. This generally includes performing such tasks as household cleaning and laundry, as well as meal preparation; however, the scope of the homemaker is not limited to these activities: homecare often involves outdoor maintenance (such as snow removal), help with financial matters, and grocery shopping. In essence, a homemaker does many things that are necessary to help the client remain independent in his or her home. For their efforts, however, these homecare service providers are among the most poorly compensated workers. This gives rise to concerns that there will not be an adequate workforce in place to keep pace with the increased demand for homecare services.

Third Sector Homecare in Saskatchewan: A Brief History

The third sector has been active in the delivery of homecare services in Saskatchewan since its inception. Lawson and Thériault (1999a) have analyzed this involvement through five historical periods. Third sector participation in the homecare field began with the provision of home-based nursing services by the Victorian Order of Nurses in the early 1900s. A second period began in 1962 with the development of the first state-funded, comprehensive homecare programs, with services and administration still provided by third sector organizations. These homecare schemes were funded as pilot projects by the provincial and federal governments and can be considered the predecessors of the first state-sponsored, province-wide homecare plan implemented in the late 1970s and early 1980s. During the third period from 1970 to 1978, a large number of non-medical homecare schemes were developed by third sector organizations with National Health grants and provincial financing from the Saskatchewan Department of Social Services. This era was the pinnacle of the social economy presence in the homecare services field.

Transition and decline for the non-governmental organizations characterized the fourth period. From 1978 until 1983, funding responsibility for the delivery of homecare services was transferred from the Departments of Health and Social Services to 45 Home Care District Boards which could either contract with existing homecare agencies or provide services directly. This period saw the transfer of third sector programs and personnel to the homecare boards and the disbanding of the vast majority of homecare third sector organizations. The services of others were drastically curtailed. This contraction of the social economy in the homecare field continued into the 1990s as a result of the restructuring of the healthcare system.

The fifth and current phase of homecare delivery in Saskatchewan began in 1993 with the termination of the homecare boards and the transfer of their mandates to 32 District Health Boards. Each board is responsible for the delivery and administration of health-care services in its district. Under this regime no contracting out of services is permitted, resulting in the further disbanding of third sector homecare agencies. The third sector organizations that do remain active provide non-medical homecare support that the health districts are unable or unwilling to develop. In fact, the recent (1996–97) elimination of home maintenance from the list of mandated public services might expand, once again, the role played by third sector organizations in homecare delivery. These organizations offer services to citizens who are not eligible for publicly-funded homecare or to those who want to supplement the public services they receive. This is where third sector organizations are now helping to fill the gap.

With 140,700 individuals 65 years old and over, Saskatchewan is the province with the highest proportion of seniors (14.4 percent) in Canada. Saskatchewan Health reports that in 1999, 22,800 Saskatchewan seniors (16 percent) were receiving homecare (personal communication). The District Health Boards currently deliver publicly-funded homecare services (including some homemaking services). However, the client must contact or be referred to the health board and undergo an individual assessment (usually taking place in the client's own home). It is the board (not the client) who decides whether and what services are to be received. The first ten hours of services per month are delivered free of charge. Additional hours can be provided, but a user-fee is then charged. This user-fee is structured on a sliding scale and ranges between $5.60 and $6.06 per hour, depending on the client's income. A client wanting to obtain homemaking services but who cannot (or does not want to) receive them from the health board, is then left with the option of purchasing the services from a private for-profit business or from a nonprofit agency. There is no sliding scale fee structure in private businesses. In Regina and Saskatoon, an hour of services can be purchased at anywhere between $13 to $15, depending on the company. More details on the fee and services of the nonprofit organizations studied here will be provided in the next section.

PROFILE OF THE ORGANIZATIONS AND THEIR CLIENTS

This section briefly examines the two organizations studied here including their objectives, history, structure, personnel, financial state, and services provided. It concludes with a short profile of their clients, including their health status and social support network. The two organizations were chosen because they are the largest and most important nonprofit agencies involved in this type of preventive homecare activities in the province. Their mandates are similar: to provide senior citizens (and people with physical challenges) with affordable, reliable, and accessible home assistance services to enable them to live independently and safely in their homes as an alternative to institutionalization.

The *Regina Senior Citizens Centre* is a nonprofit charity with two locations in Regina. Its home services are coordinated out of the office located on Winnipeg Street. The organization began in 1971, with a view to upgrading the living conditions and physical and emotional well-being of seniors who still lived in their own homes. It began as a home-maintenance and housekeeping service, but over the years these services were expanded in response to the expressed needs of seniors. Newer volunteer services included window installation, snow shoveling, an adoptive grandparent program, transportation services, a garden produce-sharing program, a service to telephone-isolated seniors, and a home-visit program.

In 1990 serious financial difficulties were experienced and it was necessary to cut back services in order to focus on fundraising activities. By 1991, the organization was forced to close its doors temporarily, due to a lack of funds. It reopened two years later with financial and professional assistance from the provincial Seniors Secretariat, the City of Regina, the United Way, and Health Canada's New Horizons Project. Over the next few years, the organization began to receive more regular funding, enabling it to deliver housekeeping and home-maintenance services to the seniors of Regina. As of 1998, approximately 900 clients were assisted in the Regina area.

Saskatoon Services for Seniors, also a registered charity, began its nonprofit operation in 1988. In the previous year, Saskatoon Home Care (the local Home Care District Board) found itself inundated with requests for snow removal and grass-cutting, which it considered outside its mandate. In response, Saskatoon Home Care gave administrative and financial support (a $20,000 grant) to Action Now. This seniors' advocacy group was to start a service to meet the needs of the elderly in the areas of grass-cutting, snow removal, and housekeeping.

Due to low fees, the client base and service offerings of Saskatoon Services for Seniors grew very quickly. The organization developed a handyman crew to help with minor home repairs, a full-time housecleaning crew, and a yard work crew to perform necessary seasonal yard work such as gardening, tree trimming, and snow removal. Saskatoon Services for Seniors now serves approximately 600 clients each year.

Service Provision

The Regina Senior Citizens Centre currently offers a diverse range of services such as wellness clinics, reflexology, and a noon meal program. However, its primary service is a home help program that provides yard maintenance, home maintenance, and housekeeping.[11] In 1997, approximately 8,000 hours of housekeeping and home maintenance services were provided by the centre. Fees for the services are based on a three-tier payment system. The standard rate for service is $12/hour for seniors who do not receive income supplements. Clients who receive the Guaranteed Income Supplement (GIS) pay $10 per hour. For those clients who receive the GIS and the Saskatchewan Income Plan (SIP), the rate for service is $8 per hour.[12]

Similarly, Saskatoon Services for Seniors currently offers three main categories of paid service: home-helpers, home maintenance, and outside services.[13] Saskatoon Services for Seniors will try to ensure that a client is served by the same employee whenever possible. The standard rate for service is $12 per hour; however, clients who receive GIS pay $10 per hour. There is a one-hour minimum charge for services, and clients are charged twice the normal rate for situations requiring intensive labour. The client is expected to provide the necessary tools, equipment, and cleaning products for the work inside the home, and is charged a fee of $2 if he/she fails to do so; additionally, there is a $2 annual membership fee for all clients. Like the Regina Senior Citizens Centre, Sasktoon Services for Seniors also responds to many telephone requests for information and referrals. This is an unpaid service provided as a courtesy.

Organizational Structure

In terms of organizational structure, an executive director and a volunteer-based board of directors governs the Regina Senior Citizens Centre. Three-quarters of the board's 16 members must be senior citizens. The board oversees four standing committees responsible for operations, finance, human resources, and programs.[14] The executive director of the Regina Senior Citizens Centre earns $36,000 annually. Her primary responsibility is to raise adequate funds and ensure the effective management and administration of the centre, as well as the provision of non-medical homecare services. She supervises five senior staff, one of which is the service coordinator. She also serves on the board committees, and advises the board with regard to policies that need to be developed. About 20 percent of her work is directed toward the administration of the homecare services. These services are managed by a service coordinator who earns $18,000 annually. Five casual housekeepers, five full-time and 30 casual home-maintenance workers provide the services. Most casual service providers earn $7 per hour, slightly more than the minimum wage in Saskatchewan.

Saskatoon Services for Seniors is also governed by a volunteer board of directors. Sixty percent of its 12 members must be senior citizens. An executive director and a full-time office manager carry out the daily activities of the organization. The executive director earned $28,800 in 1998.

His responsibilities are to ensure the viability of the organization through effective management, promotion, and fundraising. The office manager earns $18,000 annually, and is primarily involved with the service providers, as she schedules their appointments and dispatches them to jobs. The number of casual field employees varies seasonally, reaching its peak of over 20 employees in the summer season. Board policy dictates that all employees must undergo a security check and all employees are bonded. Casual service providers earn the minimum wage, or slightly more.[15]

Financial State

The Regina Senior Citizens Centre generates much of its own income but, as with many nonprofit organizations, it also relies on grants and donations. Member activities (such as bingo, afternoon dances, and noon meals) generated $232,345 in 1998. That is the majority of non-grant revenue, and approximately 47 percent of the organization's total income ($495,781). Comparatively, the revenue generated by the centre's housekeeping and home-maintenance services amounted to $52,854 or 11 percent of total income. The Regina Senior Citizen Centre relied on grants for 38 percent of its income in 1998. The grant from the City of Regina ($154,900) provided 31 percent of total income. In 1998, the organization's receipts were $14,110 over expenses, thereby enabling it to reduce its accumulated debt to $36,391. Employee salaries and benefits ($266,323) accounted for 55 percent of total expenditures ($481,671). The next highest expense (member activities) accounted for 26 percent of total expenditures. The Regina Senior Citizens Centre leases two buildings from the City of Regina at a cost of $1 for a one-year renegotiable lease.

Similarly, Saskatoon Services for Seniors has always required grants and donations to supplement its service income; it could not otherwise finance its services. In 1998, the organization received $16,901 in the form of grants. This was approximately 14 percent of its total income ($120,136). The majority of these funds were from the City of Saskatoon, the Saskatoon Charities Bingo Association, the United Way, and government-funded summer student programs. Saskatoon Services for Seniors also receives support from the Saskatoon Housing Authority, primarily in the form of office space and administrative support. Since it is registered with the Charities Division of Revenue Canada, Saskatoon Services for Seniors is able to receive some tax-deductible donations from individuals, corporations, and service clubs. In the 1998 fiscal year, the organization generated $86,887 in service revenue. The majority of this income was derived from its home-helper division, which accounted for 45 percent of the organization's total revenue. This was followed by the snow removal/grass-cutting service, which generated 22 percent of the total revenue. The yard work and home-maintenance divisions together generated less than 7 percent of the organization's income. The majority of the expenses are in the form of employee wages, which account for nearly 85 percent of total expenditures.

Clients

A survey of clients of the two organizations revealed that they are mostly women (80 percent), generally in their late 70s, and just over half of them are widowed.[16] They are fairly well-educated, as 34 percent graduated from high school, compared to less than 15 percent of all those aged 65 and over at the national level (Statistics Canada 1999, p. 86).

About 30 percent of the clients receive a yearly household income of less than $15,000 and can be considered to be low-income.[17] This proportion is high as Statistics Canada (1999, p. 108) estimates that 13.4 percent of Saskatchewan seniors were living with low incomes in 1997. Another 28 percent of clients described themselves as receiving between $15,000 and $24,999. Hence, the annual household income is below $25,000 for close to 60 percent of the clients.

In terms of living arrangements, 63 percent of clients live alone, a much larger proportion than the 29 percent of seniors found at the national level by Statistics Canada (1999, p. 31). Conversely, only 28 percent of clients live with a spouse, as compared to 56.5 percent of all Canadians aged 65 and over (Statistics Canada 1999, p. 39).[18]

When asked to rate their health, half the clients rated it "excellent" or "good," 42 percent rated it as "fair," and only 8 percent reported "poor" or "very poor" health. It is difficult to compare these results with those of Statistics Canada as the scales used are slightly different. However, the top category (Excellent) was the choice of 10.2 percent of clients in this study, compared to 12.1 percent for all Canadians aged 65 and over (Statistics Canada 1999, p. 73). In addition, a small majority of clients (54 percent) say that they are "usually free of pain and discomfort." By comparison,

Statistics Canada (1999, p. 76) found that 75.4 percent of Canadians aged 65 and over are not experiencing chronic pain or discomfort. Hence, it can be said that while clients report that they are in good health, they are perhaps a little less so than other Canadian seniors.

Finally, in terms of social support, a large majority of clients have a confidant with whom they can share private feelings or concerns (87 percent), and they also have someone they can count on in case of major crisis (89 percent). However, only 64 percent of clients have someone who can help them with chores and errands. This would indicate that for more than one-third of clients, gaining regular access to informal sources of support like family and friends is difficult.

THE VIEWS OF MANAGERS AND SERVICE PROVIDERS ON THE DELIVERY OF HOME SERVICES

With the intent of documenting the nonprofit delivery of home services, and to further our understanding of the organizations studied, we conducted interviews with managers and focus groups with service providers. The "managers" included (i) the chairperson of the board of directors, (ii) the executive director, and (iii) a full-time staff member (i.e., the service coordinator or office manager).[19] Focus groups with the workers, or service providers, were conducted in Saskatoon and Regina. All service providers were invited to participate in the focus groups and a total of 14 workers accepted (six in Saskatoon and eight in Regina). What follows is a qualitative analysis of the interview and focus groups material organized around a selection of eight themes.

How the Work is Organized

There are essentially two categories of service providers in both organizations: inside and outside workers. These are also referred to as housekeepers and maintenance/yard workers. The housekeepers tend to be year round, whereas the outdoor workers are often more seasonal. An important feature of both organizations is that neither one employs a seniority-based system for assigning work; rather, the focus is on ensuring continuity of service, which means that, if desired, a client can always have the same housekeeper (and sometimes the same maintenance worker).

The intensity of work varies somewhat between the two organizations. Payroll figures show that housekeepers' hours at Saskatoon Services for Seniors range generally from 10 to 30 hours per week.[20] For many of them, working part-time or casually is their preference. However, some of the workers expressed disappointment with the limited number of work hours they were able to get. At the Regina Senior Citizens Centre, service providers generally worked between 20 to 40 hours a week. All the Regina employees in our focus group were happy with their schedules and felt they were able to determine much of it. In fact, the degree of autonomy they had in creating their own schedules seems to be key to their job satisfaction.

In Regina, the service coordinator tries to ensure that all housekeepers have full schedules before she hires another. She will then work with the new housekeeper exclusively to fill her schedule; as a result, there is only one housekeeper at any given time who is waiting for work. The Regina housekeepers also have regulars, and, once a schedule is established, the housekeepers work more or less independently, coming into the Senior Citizens Centre only to fill out their time sheets or socialize with co-workers. With regard to the maintenance workers, the service coordinator said that she sets up a schedule wherein they mow the same lawns at a specific time each week, in order that there is some continuity. In Saskatoon, by comparison, the office manager will book an appointment with the housekeeper at the request of a client, and will then notify the housekeeper of this appointment.

Hence, an important difference exists between the two organizations regarding work scheduling, which has an impact on employees' satisfaction. It seems that work satisfaction increases with the amount of autonomy employees have. At Saskatoon Services for Seniors, the office manager retains more control of the scheduling, as she takes calls from clients and informs the employees of their appointments. This does not always run smoothly. Employees are sometimes victims of scheduling errors because the system lends itself to miscommunication. One Saskatoon employee mentioned that she felt that she could definitely organize her schedule better on her own. In fact, employees probably *are* in the best situation to schedule their days in a manner that minimizes their travel time. This is the case in Regina where housekeepers develop their own schedules, and thus, only need to come into the office once a week. It is probable, but still unproven, that this greater flexibility for workers improves their capacity to respond to client needs.

Network, Environment and Competition

One important characteristic of third sector organizations involved in the delivery of human services is the tendency to work in interaction with a network of external partners (Jetté et al. 1997). Roughly, the networks of the two organizations can be mapped using a simple typology.

We can distinguish several different types of (non-mutually exclusive) relationships between organizations. The first, and perhaps most obvious one, would be a funding relationship, in which the organization receives some monetary support (and goods or services[21]) from other organizations or agencies. In the case of Saskatoon Services for Seniors, at least nine partner organizations from the public, private, and third sectors can be placed in this category: Acadia Drive Funeral Chapel, the City of Saskatoon, the Muttart Foundation, Northern Lights Casino, Saskatoon Antique Group, Saskatoon Charities Bingo Association, Saskatoon Housing Authority, the Saskatoon Foundation, and the Saskatoon United Way. At the Regina Senior Citizens Centre, respondents identified the City of Regina, the United Way, and the New Careers Corporation as significant funding partners.[22]

A second type of relationship is based on cooperation and/or cross referrals between service organizations. While the relationships with the Home Care Services of the Saskatoon District Health and Regina Health District are of prime importance, they are not the only ones in this category. Respondents from Saskatoon Services for Seniors also mentioned links with the Saskatoon Community Clinic,[23] Saskatoon Hope Breast Cancer Group,[24] Neighbour Link Saskatoon,[25] the Saskatchewan Abilities Council,[26] Veterans' Affairs Canada, and even 911.[27] Respondents from the Regina Senior Citizens Centre stressed their good relationships with public health nurses from the Regina Health District, with the Regina Housing Authority[28] and with the Regina Police Services.[29]

A third type of relationship relates to advocacy and networking activities, rather than services per se. Among their occasional or regular contacts in this category, respondents from Saskatoon Services for Seniors cited the Council on Aging, Saskatoon city councillors, local members of Parliament and the Legislative Assembly, and officials from the Department of Social Services, as well as the Chamber of Commerce. Respondents from the Regina Senior Citizens Centre also mentioned relationships with city councillors and a representative from the Department of Social Services, as well as links with the Saskatchewan Seniors' Mechanism (an advocacy organization).

In terms of the environment, one relevant question to ask is whether the development of home services by nonprofit organizations represents an unfair competition or, alternatively, whether these services can be understood as essentially acting complementarily with the offerings from other sectors? To fully answer this question would have required that we also ask the opinions of actors from the private sectors and from managers of the public Home Care Services. Unfortunately, this research relies only on views internal to the organizations studied and, as such, provides only a partial picture. Nevertheless, it is worthwhile to examine whether our key informants perceived the services of their organizations as being complementary to, or in competition with, home services from private firms and public agencies.

The respondents all agreed that the services offered are, for the most part, not in competition with, but rather are complementary to those provided by public sector homecare agencies. Part of the perception of complementarity seems to relate to the fact that public sector agencies are seen as being swamped by requests and prioritizing the heavier offerings, which are personal care and nursing services. In this context, the needs of seniors with regard to home-management and home-maintenance services are not being met adequately by the public sector. Our respondents felt that this situation creates a space wherein the activity of their organization complements publicly delivered services. By this, they did not mean that there is not some overlap of services with the public sector, but simply that the amount of unmet needs is more than large enough to justify the presence of NPO activities. In the end, some respondents viewed the fact that public homecare agencies make regular referrals to their organization as the best indication that the relationship with public services is one of complementarity.

Positions were mixed as to whether the organizations are complementing or competing with private firms. The predominant view was that these NPOs are not in competition with the services offered by private firms, either. To a large extent, this position was based on the idea that the people served by the two studied NPOs are low-income elderly who cannot afford the higher rates charged by private firms. In contrast, one respondent believed that her organization offered a higher quality of service and enjoyed a greater level of trust among seniors. From her perspective, the superior reputation of the organization insulates it, in a way, from competition. She stated that "because we are the Senior Citizens Centre, seniors know that we are there to help them." The executive director of the Regina Senior Citizens Centre pointed to the generally good relationship her organization enjoyed with private businesses. As an example, she cited the fact that on occasion, her organization has referred clients to private firms: in cases of heavy snowfalls or when the jobs requested were too big and thus, out of the scope of activity of the organization (e.g., painting a whole house). Two respondents from Saskatoon, however, clearly recognized the possible presence of competition with private business with regard to certain services. The strengths of the organization (its lower rates, its community-based character, the level of trust it enjoyed, and the mix of services it offered) were cited as competitive advantages. In sum, respondents tended to see their organization as complementing the service offerings of the public sector and, at least in some instances, as competing with some services offered by private firms.

Role of the Employee – "We do the dirty work"

During the focus groups, some employees stated that they go far beyond what a public or private homecare worker would do, including some very dirty work. It was said that most public home health-care providers will not even enter a client's home if it is very dirty. Hence, employees we spoke with thought that the work they do can sometimes make it possible for the clients to receive public homecare services they need.

Employees showed exceptional commitments toward the clients they served and expressed the view that they would do anything that they were asked, within reason. For instance, one Regina employee discussed a situation in which she entered a woman's home and had to deal with dozens of dying, dead, and decomposed mice in traps all over the home. While another agency's homecare worker might have refused to deal with such a situation, this employee simply cleaned all of the mice out of the house. Housekeepers also report that they occasionally help clients with the organization of financial documents (e.g., balancing a chequebook). Hence, these employees clearly perform some tasks that fall outside the scope of a *normal* private sector housekeeper.

The homemakers from the two agencies studied become, in some ways, an integral part of the seniors' support networks. More than one employee mentioned that they had noticed something amiss in their clients' lives or environment, and had contacted the necessary parties to take action. This might have involved calling the client's daughter, or calling (public) Home Care Services or Regina Housing to request their services. Additionally, homemakers often sit and socialize with their clients as part of their weekly visits, which is not generally seen with private sector homecare workers. The home-maintenance workers tend to have somewhat less contact with the clients, as they mainly work outside, and can generally do their work whether or not the client is home. Nonetheless, some of the outdoor workers did report socializing with clients, and one Regina home-maintenance worker even mentioned that he had telephoned a client's daughter in order to discuss the need for a plumber.

A Fulfilling, But Not Well-Paying Job

Most of the employees at both organizations identify working with an elderly clientele as the primary benefit of their work. Many enjoy the feeling of being able to help the seniors, and enabling them to maintain their independence. Additionally, the workers acknowledged a strong social component to their work. Often they enjoy "checking in" with their clients, to see how they are faring. They know that many of the seniors look forward to their weekly visit, as it is sometimes the only company that they receive, and they will have tea and talk with them.

Of course, not everything in this line of activity is a "walk in the park." For instance, some outside workers at Saskatoon Services for Seniors commented on the poor state of the equipment that the organization provided for them. Specifically, they mentioned that the shovels were unworkable.

As a result, most of these employees preferred to purchase their own shovels to use at work. Regina's indoor workers, in turn, noted that sometimes a client's cleaning equipment was poor or broken, but said "there's nothing you can do. The work has to be done — you just make the best of it." Similarly, some Saskatoon homemakers recounted some difficulties with cleaning houses which had poor equipment (e.g., a broken vacuum cleaner), but said that this was better than the alternative, which is bringing their own equipment to each house, often on the bus.[30]

Other problems in Saskatoon included difficult clients who make dangerous or unreasonable requests, such as asking home-maintenance workers to shovel snow from a garage roof, or asking indoor workers to change heavy storm windows. Additionally, a Regina housekeeper said that she has had requests to move heavy furniture, which she has done but does not enjoy. Although difficult requests are sometimes accommodated, employees do exercise their right to refuse.[31] Obviously, employees of these organizations are strongly committed to their work, and clearly, it is not the wages that keep them motivated. Thus, there must be some other reward that makes the job meaningful and elicits this level of dedication.

Many employees at both organizations expressed the view that it is fulfilling for them to be able to help seniors and thus help them remain in their homes. Enjoyment in working with seniors appears to be prerequisite. A Regina worker suggested that one has to be a special person to do this job — patient, caring, and willing to sit and listen. The work is more than just cleaning, it also entails having tea with clients and caring about their well-being.

Clearly, low pay is a feature that is common to the two organizations, although it should be noted that the service providers did not discuss this as much as the researchers expected. A Regina employee acknowledged that she did not think that they were paid enough for the work they do, but countered with the comment: "Is anybody?" Another worker noted the lack of opportunity for advancement in the organization and the fact that there are no benefits for employees: "When you think about it, there's no benefits, no pension plan, no sick leave. You know, we've got nothing. Nothing at all." While remuneration was an item of discussion with employees in Regina, they were not completely unsatisfied; rather, they seemed to accept their lower wages without resentment. The situation was similar at Saskatoon Services for Seniors. In sum, it is fair to say that employees are not in these organizations for the money and that the basis of their commitment toward the clients lies elsewhere.

Labour Relations

The interest employees have in the well-being of the clients they serve, coupled with their relative acceptance of low pay, facilitate labour relations from the perspective of both organizations. The office manager in Saskatoon perceives these to be "very good" and stressed that she receives no complaints, even from the "girls" who earn the minimum wage. She attributed this perceived high job satisfaction to the type of relationship that the employees establish with the clients: "Everybody seems happy because you build up a relationship with people, so it is not as if you were going to strangers the majority of times, and everybody is used to each other." For their parts, Regina workers agreed that they were comfortable approaching their supervisors with suggestions or complaints, and felt that they would be responded to appropriately. One employee noted, "if it's a good idea, they don't argue." There appears to be a level of familiarity between the supervisors and the workers. The workers are not intimidated by their supervisors. This could partially result from the fact that they interact with them regularly; additionally, the supervisor of the home-workers is herself a home-worker, so she is sympathetic to the employees' concerns.

The Saskatoon employees said that, for the most part, they would feel comfortable approaching their supervisors with concerns. They noted, however, that in most cases they try to solve problems by themselves, as the office staff seems to be too overwhelmed to deal with any extra issues. These employees were asked whether they felt that the organization would take their side in a client-employee dispute. Answers given to this question were mixed. One worker noted that a client had complained to the office about her work. The office manager asked the employee about her side of the story, which was different from the client's, and subsequently defended her to the client. Another employee, however, spent a great deal of time shovelling a client's driveway, and when he was finished, the client called and said he did a poor job. In this case, the organization told him to go back to the client's home on his own time (and without pay) to do the job again, which he did. We found it surprising that the employee in this situation did not complain or seem to think that this was unreasonable. This incident could be illustrative of the great respect workers have for their clients.

Employees at both agencies felt that the organization valued them, although this response came a little more quickly at the Regina focus group. They said that this appreciation was demonstrated to them in little ways, such as small gifts and staff parties at holidays. The Saskatoon group appreciated that the office manager had recently begun to make a point of telling employees when a client had called or written to commend their work. Hence, the labour relations in these organizations are good, but the structures in place to take into account the views of the employees remains informal (absence of unionization) and similar to what exist in many, well-run, family-type businesses of the private sector.

Strengths and Weaknesses to Face the Future

The organizations' main achievement is that, without these services, many of the seniors would have to find other places to live, as they do not have the capacity to maintain their homes. If they did elect to stay in their home without the services, they would need to find help from elsewhere (private firms, friends or family members), or see their health deteriorate as a result of insalubrious living conditions.

One clear strength is the conviction that their mission is not to simply clean houses, but also to help keep seniors in their homes and to enable them to maintain independence. In that sense, these organizations not only provide a valuable service to members, but also build trust in the community and combat the isolation of seniors. Our informants stressed the importance of social interactions with the seniors and that the housekeeping services offer information, referrals, and directions. For instance, if an individual is losing his or her sight, the agencies will refer the client to the Canadian National Institute for the Blind, and ensure that the connection actually happens. In acting in this way, the agency becomes a focal point of the senior community.

Another key strength of these organizations is the belief in the importance of the continuity of care (sending the same housekeeper to the same clients whenever possible). This was said to make the services of these organizations different from those of the public sector, where the dispatching of workers is based on other considerations such as seniority.

Among the strengths must be listed the willingness of the organization and its workers to deal with all manner of special requests, such as delivering *Ice Melt* from the hardware store for an old woman, or taking out the garbage. The managers interviewed generally believed that the flexibility of their organization is a important factor in the delivery of high quality services for seniors. This is not to say, of course, that all requests can be accommodated. For instance, service providers will not give a car ride to clients (an insurance liability issue), nor will they bathe clients, or provide other such personal care services. Hence, while there is some flexibility in the "job description" of the employees, there are also boundaries.

In spite of these strengths, some weaknesses might limit the future development of these organizations. The greatest weakness remains the lack of funding. The difficulty in raising money was the main problem or limitation identified by nearly all the informants in both organizations. One of the adverse effects of this constant financial shortage is the inability to attract and retain qualified staff. Time is another limitation, in the sense that a volunteer board of directors can spend only a restricted amount of time dealing with many important issues (such as training needs) which should be given greater attention. Fundraising is not a sufficient solution to the lack of funding because potential donors do not perceive this type of organization as the "sexiest" of causes.

Nevertheless, all those interviewed agreed that these institutions are likely to continue growing, especially with the increasing number of seniors in the community along with a decline in the disposable income of most seniors reducing their ability to meet their needs through the private sector. It is also based on a belief that changes in the formal (public) delivery system will not necessarily make services more accessible.

There is, therefore, a wealth of future projects on the drawing board. The Regina organization plans to purchase scheduling software to reduce dispatching errors. The executive director would also like to re-implement the "Friendly Visitor" program; however, this would necessitate raising $25,000 to $30,000 in order to hire a program coordinator. The organization also plans to replace some equipment and tools, and they are looking at some possible partnerships with different institutions to provide funding. In Saskatoon, the organization is looking into an agreement with a local funeral home which would recommend Saskatoon Services for Seniors as a housesitter during funerals. A partnership is also being formed with the Saskatoon Breast Cancer Support Group. Services for Seniors will provide their services to women recovering from or living with breast cancer, and the support group will pay for it. Saskatoon Services for Seniors would also like to offer more companionship services, but they would need to recruit some volunteers in order to do so. A transportation program is also being considered, which would be feasible if the Rotary Club agrees to carry the liability insurance.

Workplace Democracy and Client Participation

The social economy is often defined by reference to certain values such as a democratic decision-making process in the workplace (Defourny 1992). Researchers try to understand the input into how things are run from both workers and clients. At the two organizations, the clients seem to have some say as customers, and perhaps as members, in the way the organization delivers the services. The workers' input, however, seems to be relatively limited and is channelled through management in a direct but informal fashion, as is traditionally the case in, for instance, a small family business. The service providers have no representation on the board of directors; thus, they have no direct access to this policy-making body other than through the executive director, who has overall responsibility for human resources.

While the atmosphere in the offices is relaxed and friendly, the needs of the clients clearly come first, as can be expected in a service organization. One of the executive directors offered a clear summary of the situation in this regard:

> I take the opinions or advice from these two groups and decide what is the correct action to take. If you are asking me which group holds more weight with my decision, well, clearly I have to say the client holds somewhat more weight with my decision primarily because that is what we are here to do. We are here to serve clients ... the client's opinion is more important.

A board chairperson agreed and explained that:

> Because we don't have an assessment process, we don't decide what needs to be done. The client decides what needs to be done, and requests it from us. So the client ... is in charge.

The client is almost always right as the other executive director noted:

> I guess it's basically an economic power. The client may say simply "I don't want to deal with you" or they may not say anything and they are no longer our client.... The client has all the power over whether or not to use our services.

While there is nothing particularly wrong with the manner in which these organizations are run or their decision-making methods, there is also nothing particularly innovative to be found here in terms of democratic management or empowerment. This probably relates, at least in part, to the state of *associative life* [*vie associative*] in the organizations.

For an organization to be part of the social economy, its members should have the right to control it on the basis of the "one member, one vote" principle. In some cases, service providers can constitute the membership of the organizations (e.g., in a workers co-op). More frequently, however, the membership comprises the users of the services. In the two organizations studied, there is a membership (as in an "association"), but, as is often the case, the associative life seems to be relatively weak — leaving the board of directors and in particular, the executive director, in full control of the operations.

Nonetheless, at the Regina Senior Citizens Centre we find (at the formal level at least) the structural characteristics of a democratically functioning organization. No annual membership fee is collected,[32] but all users are automatically considered to be members and can therefore attend the annual general meeting (AGM), where directors of the board must be approved. In reality, few members show up to the AGM and the input of the membership is often channelled, on an ongoing basis, through comments or suggestions to the executive director. The democratic, associative life of the organization, therefore, does not seem to be particularly strong. Perhaps this can be expected, to a certain extent, given that the users are elderly people, many of whom are frail and have limited mobility outside their homes.

The situation is similar in Saskatoon. While there is a two-dollar membership fee, some clients refuse to pay it; thus, only about two-thirds of clients are "members." Regardless of whether they have paid the membership fee, however, all users of the services can attend the AGM to voice their concerns or run for positions on the board of directors.

The role of the membership within the two organizations is thus somewhat unclear since all clients are "members," whether or not they pay a membership fee. This suggests the possibility that the organizations may think it more important to fulfill the clients' demands, rather than be accountable to a constituent membership. This distinction may appear academic. However, the issues of membership and associative life relate to the type of governance (democratic or corporate) adopted by the two organizations; and thus, to whether they can truly be considered part of a social economy promoting the empowerment of worker and users.[33]

Unmet Needs

We would like to end this section by stressing that, according to the service providers, low-income seniors in Regina continue to have several unmet needs. For instance, it was believed that some of the homes are in need of safety inspections. One client's home was reported as a fire hazard, as there were so many piles of paper that one could not even find the kitchen table. Other employees mentioned that they had had requests for personal care, such as baths, which they could not accommodate. However, employees stated that many of their clients are also receiving public home health care, so these requests were relatively infrequent. Saskatoon employees did not report seeing a great deal of unmet need, and felt that most of their clients knew when it was time to get help or move into another living arrangement.

The situation was different at the Regina organization, where indoor workers expressed the view that approximately one-third of their clients should not be living in their own homes because their safety was at risk; however, often there is nowhere for these people to go. Employees saw many circumstances indicating unmet need, such as "an 80-pound woman trying to help a 200-pound husband to stand." One worker said that often a man wants his wife to stay at home and help him, even if he knows that she belongs in a nursing home. Many times, women end up getting sick while acting as their husband's primary caregiver. One Regina housekeeper mentioned that one of her clients had not had a bath in five years; another was extremely ill with multiple sclerosis (MS), and could barely move about her house.

According to the focus group participants, many clients also receive public homecare services which include personal care such as baths. The Regina workers have had some positive interactions with these public employees. Nevertheless, Regina Senior Citizens Centre employees reported that they had heard many complaints about the public homecare staff from their clients. They noted instances where the public homecare provider had arrived, given the patient a bath, and then watched television and smoked for several hours before leaving. One client is said to have reported that a public homecare worker even fell asleep on her couch. Others allegedly complained that the public homecare staff did not do anything, or that they did not even show up.

To complement the views of managers and service providers, an attempt was made to seek the perspectives of clients using the services offered. The findings from this exercise are summarized in the next section.

SERVICE UTILIZATION AND SATISFACTION:
THE PERSPECTIVE OF THE CLIENTS

To learn about service utilization and satisfaction from the perspective of the clients, we conducted a survey, using a self-administered mail questionnaire. We intentionally designed it to be very short.[34] After a pre-test, it was sent to 1,100 current clients in late October 1999.[35] In all, 411 usable questionnaires were returned for a response rate of 37.4 percent.[36] As we sought to protect fully the anonymity of the clients, there was no coding on the questionnaires that could enable us to identify those who responded.[37] Consequently, we do not have information on the non-respondents. Among the possible self-selection biases, we think that the clients with low literacy skills, and those with very serious health problems, were perhaps less likely to complete the questionnaire.

In general, the clients have been served by these organizations for about four years. We asked questions about the utilization of both the home-cleaning and the home-maintenance services offered. Almost 48 percent of clients used the home-cleaning service. Over one-third of all clients used the snow removal and grass-cutting services, while smaller proportions of clients used the other services.

We also have information on the frequency of use of home cleaning. The large majority of clients used that service either once a month or less, or between two and three times a month. Only 12 percent of clients made an intensive, once a week, use of the cleaning service. As for the maintenance services, we know that 40 percent of clients used only one such service, that 35 percent used two of them, and that 25 percent used three or more of these services.

The levels of satisfaction found for the services are quite high. It was measured on a scale of one to four, ranging from "not satisfied at all" (score of one) to "very satisfied" (score of four). For home cleaning, 69 percent of clients reported being very satisfied and another 25 percent being somewhat satisfied. This leaves only 6 percent of clients in the "somewhat dissatisfied" and "not satisfied at all" categories. The situation is similar for the maintenance services (taken as a whole) where 62 percent of clients say that they are very satisfied, 31 percent say that they are somewhat satisfied, and only 7 percent are either somewhat dissatisfied or not satisfied at all.

The vast majority of clients (85 percent) find the fees charged by the organizations to be appropriate ("just right"), while 14 percent find the fees to be too high, and 1 percent say that they are too low. In terms of satisfaction with regard to troubleshooting, 36 percent of clients say that they called at least once to report a problem with a service. Of those who called, just over 70 percent felt that the organization tried to fix the problem. When asked about the importance of the services for their overall health and well-being, 59 percent of clients find the services to be "very important," another 33 percent find them to be "somewhat important," and only 8 percent say that they are either "somewhat unimportant" or "not important at all." Finally, when asked what they would do if they could not use the services of these organizations, 60 percent say that they would try to hire someone else. Just over 13 percent of clients do not know what they would do, 11 percent would rely on family and friends, another 7 percent would try to move into a retirement home, and 7 percent would do their own house cleaning or yard work.[38]

As no single sector of the economy is solely responsible for the home services offered to seniors, clients often use services from more than one source. Some information was collected regarding the use of home services from places such as the homecare program of the local health board, Meals-on-Wheels,[39] private homecare agencies,[40] and other sources.[41] Eighteen percent of clients are clients of a public homecare program, nearly twice the proportion (9.9 percent) of all Canadians aged 65 and over receiving such assistance (Statistics Canada 1999, p. 35). Another 4 percent of clients received Meals-on-Wheels, and 5 percent do business with other homecare agencies from the private, for-profit sector. Finally, 13 percent say that they receive home services from some "other" places. In all, 32 percent of clients receive services from at least one of these sources, in addition to the services received from the organizations studied here (Table 1).

Table 1: Home Services Received from Other Sources (N=388)

	% of Clients
Public Home Care	18
Meals-on-Wheels	4
Private Home Care Agencies	5
Other	13
At least one of the above	32

Note: Missing Cases: 23.

Figure 2: Home Services Received from Other Sources (N=388)

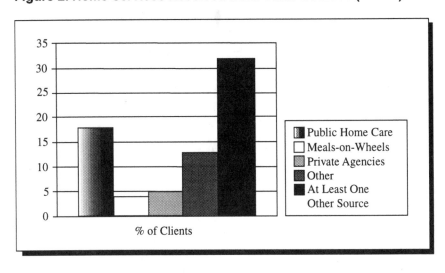

This brief analysis has shed some light on the services that clients use and their level of satisfaction with these services. Further research would be required to ascertain whether these findings would be similar or different elswhere, and whether the results would change over time. In that last case, the snapshot picture presented here could serve as a useful baseline of information. Finally, the use of alternative qualitative research methods (such as personal interviews and focus groups) would be required to further explore the clients' experience with the services used.

CONCLUSION

It is evident from our investigation that the level of funding available to these organizations is barely sufficient for them to operate, and that securing a larger and more stable funding base would be necessary for them to significantly expand their operations. The inadequate funding level has meant that qualified and dedicated personnel, including service providers and managers, receive substandard remuneration for the work they do. Insult is added to injury, as it seems that the work of these organizations is not very well known outside certain circles, and not always recognized by public authorities. It should also be noted that it is unlikely that the funding problems could be alleviated with fundraising activities alone.

While both the managers and employees agree that the work being done is gratifying — since it makes a difference in the lives of seniors — they also recognize that it is difficult work. In this context, many of the people we spoke with were concerned that the organizations are unable to provide their employees with a benefit package. This can be a problem as it is likely to impact negatively on the ability of the organizations to retain good employees, something that was identified as a key for success.

From a service delivery perspective, one of the great strengths of these organizations is that they do not use a seniority-based system for assigning work, but focus instead on ensuring a continuity of service. This means that, if desired, a client can almost always have the same service provider. This is a notable difference from what is happening in the public sector. Another interesting characteristic of these two organizations is that they are successfully working in collaboration with a network of external partners from the public, private, and third sectors. The cultivation of these relationships is likely to be a key factor in the future of these organizations.

While many employees found their work difficult, most of them were proud of being an integral part of the seniors' support network. Some service providers expressed disappointment with the limited number of work hours they were able to get. Problems with parking, transportation costs, and work scheduling were also mentioned on occasion, as well as poor equipment and other issues. While the question of low remuneration was raised, employees were generally not very demanding or militant in this regard.

In comparing the two organizations, we find a notable contrast in the level of interaction among employees. It was clear from the focus groups that the Regina employees were much more comfortable with one another. The more frequent social interaction among employees and supervisors in Regina has a positive impact as it makes it possible to relieve frustrations and to receive support. In a job that is as stressful as this, and where employees are as poorly paid as these are, it is vitally important that the employees have social support through a team approach. This seems to be lacking in Saskatoon where employees work in isolation and no one knows whether his or her job-related concerns and feelings are valid. In our view, allowing employees to have more control and autonomy over their jobs, and encouraging them to develop relationships in order to receive support are conditions for success.

An important concern to the employees was their perception that many of the seniors they serve are frail and in poor health. However, this perception was not entirely supported by the results of the client survey. It found that women in their late 70s, many of them widowed, form the majority of the clientele. While more educated than the average Canadian senior, they are also more likely to live alone, with low incomes. They report that they are in good health, but perhaps a little less so than other Canadian seniors. A large proportion of them (one-third) seem to have little or no help from informal sources to perform everyday tasks. They are highly satisfied with the services and fee structure of the organizations studied here. Further research would be required to better compare client satisfaction with these services and client satisfaction with services delivered by the public or private, for-profit sectors.

If we return to the original objectives proposed for this study, we can say that several have been reached with success. The study has documented in some detail the activities of the two organizations, has provided information on service delivery from the perspective of the providers, and has shed light on the working conditions. In addition, the research offered a profile of the clients and a preliminary analysis of service utilization and service satisfaction.

As for the current services offered, we can say that they are appropriately priced and highly satisfactory according to the clients, many of whom appear to have little access to other sources of help for homemaking and home-maintenance activities. It seems that the services mostly complement the service offerings of the public sector and partly complement certain services from private firms.

The study had less success with the identification of the unmet needs of the clients. Some of the information gathered indicates that many of these seniors suffer from social isolation and that others are in need of respite services while they are caring for an elderly spouse at home. Some homes are in need of a safety inspection from the Fire Department and that certain clients have personal care needs (e.g., bath) which are not being met. Another objective that was not fully realized is the identification of clear gaps that might exist between the public sector services and those provided by these nonprofit organizations.

The ways in which these organizations are run remain fairly traditional. There is nothing wrong or abnormal with that, but there is nothing particularly innovative either. The social economy can be defined as being made up of association-based economic initiatives, founded on autonomy, solidarity, and citizenship and advancing the principles of democratic management. Priority is given to services over profits. Like many other nonprofit sector initiatives, the organizations studied here have relatively weak associative lives and it is therefore debatable whether they should be considered as part of the social economy, or whether the definition of social economy should be expanded.

There are reasons to remain optimistic and to think (as many clients did) that the future will be one of growth for these two organizations. It remains, however, that like most social economy initiatives, they have not yet been given all the necessary tools (including financial means) they will need if we want to see a breakthrough of communitarization in preventive homecare services in Saskatchewan.

In our view, third sector organizations might represent an even more attractive vehicle for the delivery of human services when they are structured in such a way as to actively promote workplace democracy and client participation. For what we have observed in this research, this is not yet a reality in the two organizations studied. While the structure of work in these small nonprofit organizations offers an alternative to the often disparaged Taylorism of the public sector, it seems to have been simply replaced with a form of benign paternalistic management. Hence, at the moment, these organizations do not offer an adequate solution to the double deficit of democracy since they do not provide for sufficient empowerment of either workers or service users.

From our view of the Saskatchewan experience, it seems obvious that third sector organizations play a role in the delivery of home services for seniors which is still supplementary, yet not negligible, and likely to gain in importance. We feel that there is now a need for this role to be recognized and acknowledged by all actors involved, which is not yet the case.

In fact, considering the aging of the population (often living on fixed income), the insufficient public investments in homecare, and the relatively high cost of private sector services, it is easy to forecast that the demand for affordable quality home services is likely to increase over the next few decades. The number of community-based initiatives set up to meet the needs will also increase. Under what conditions will these initiatives be successful? What place will they occupy in the continuum of care? and What share of the responsibility for homecare will they take on? These are the questions still waiting to be answered.

Notes

This study was funded by the Health Transition Fund of Health Canada and by the Non-Profit Sector Research Initiative of the Kahanoff Foundation. The authors would like to express their gratitude to all those who contributed to this project. In particular, we would like to thank the managers, employees, and clients of the Regina Senior Citizens Centre and of Saskatoon Services for Seniors. We also wish to express special thanks to Fiona Douglas (University of Regina) and to Malcolm Anderson and Kathy Brock (Queen's University) for comments on previous versions of this paper. The interpretations and conclusions contained herein do not necessarily represent the views of Health Canada, the Kahanoff Foundation, the Regina Senior Citizens Centre or Saskatoon Services for Seniors.

[1]This theoretical section is largely inspired by the work of Yves Vaillancourt (1996).

[2]We use the term "human services" to cover both health and social services.

[3]We refer here to authors like Aglietta (1987), Boyer (1986), and Lipietz (1989) generally associated with the *French Regulation School*. See Drache and Gertler (1991); and Jenson, Mahon and Bienefeld (1993) for Canadian adaptations.

[4]For an overview of the community clinic movement in Saskatchewan, see Lawson and Thériault (1999*b*).

[5]On the notion of welfare pluralism, see Skelton (1998).

[6]Obviously, these four sectors do not constitute homogeneous groups. Yet, we can probably speak of different organizational cultures. The private sector does not function like the public sector which, in turn, does not function like the nonprofit, third sector.

[7]The social economy is made up of association-based economic initiatives, founded on autonomy, solidarity, and citizenship. Among its principles are democratic management and priority to services over profits (see Jensen 1998, p. 22; and Lévesque and Ninacs 1997, p. 6). In that sense, not all agencies from the third sector are necessarily part of the social economy.

[8]We define privatization as the process by which responsibility for human services is transferred from the public to the private, for-profit sector. For an analysis denouncing the effect of privatization in the field of homecare, see Shapiro (1997).

[9]It is customary to speak of one Canadian health-care system. However, there are in fact at least ten health-care systems in Canada. Admittedly, these systems are somewhat harmonized via the conditions imposed by the *Canada Health Act* and by the Canada Health and Social Transfer.

[10]By "privatized" we mean here a move toward a for-profit delivery of services that would be paid out-of-pocket.

[11]The housekeeping services of the Regina Senior Citizens Centre include spring cleaning, vacuuming, dusting, laundry, cooking, floor- and wall-washing, as well as any other activity that is necessary to ensure that a senior's home is a clean and healthy environment.

[12]SIP provides supplementary income to low-income senior citizens in Saskatchewan.

[13]Home-helpers (i.e., housekeepers) can prepare meals (short- and long-term), and run errands to do grocery shopping, banking, mailing letters, and picking up prescriptions. Finally, they offer emotional support to clients by visiting them and going for walks with them, helping them with letter-writing, reading to them, and accompanying them to appointments.

[14]Additionally, there are special committees that convene for specific items of concern such as nominations.

[15]A unique aspect of Saskatoon Services for Seniors is its "Urban Camp" program. Participants in this program are low-risk, volunteer inmates from the Saskatoon Correctional Centre, who assist Services for Seniors in peak work periods. Clients who are served by the Urban Camp program are urged to make a donation to Services for Seniors in lieu of the standard fee.

[16]More information on the survey, including technical details, can be found in the fourth section.

[17]Statistics Canada's low-income cut-off (LICO) for unattached individuals living in an urban area with a population between 100,000 and 499,999 in 1997 was $14,931.

[18]The remaining clients (9 percent) are living with other *non-spouse* cohabitants.

[19]A reviewer of a previous version of this paper noted that it might have been useful to conduct two interviews with each of the interviewees, one early in the research cycle and one after the completion of the analysis of the focus group and survey materials. We acknowledge this point and recognize that this would have been an interesting addition to the study design. However, due mainly to a tight time frame, we were unable to act upon this suggestion.

[20]The outdoor employees' output is more variable, as work is sometimes unavailable; for instance, when there is no snow to shovel.

[21]For instance, the Acadia Drive Funeral Chapel has provided promotional help for the activities of Saskatoon Services for Seniors. The Saskatoon Housing Authority's contribution takes the form of free office space. A private firm, Siecor, also makes free identification cards for the workers of Saskatoon Services for Seniors.

[22]In Regina, one respondent expressed some concerns about the risk of seeing private donors or sponsors attempt to attach certain conditions to their contributions. Such influence over policies could jeopardize the autonomy and independence of the organization.

[23]This is one of Saskatchewan's five community health services associations (Lawson and Thériault 1999b).

[24]An informal peer support group for women.

[25]A volunteer service providing free transportation for seniors.

[26]A charity organization dealing with the needs of the intellectually-disabled.

[27]Saskatoon Services for Seniors has had occasional contacts with 911 to help deal with some cognitive emergencies.

[28]Many elderly tenants living in units of the Regina Housing Authority are reported to be using the services of the Regina Senior Citizens Centre.

[29]The Regina Senior Citizens Centre has worked with the police in the area of safety for seniors.

[30]Note that little or no formal training is provided to workers. The managers acknowledge the usefulness of training activities, but say that they cannot generally afford them.

[31]A Saskatoon service provider also noted that she had encountered abusive clients, but that this was uncommon. In these situations, the organization simply refused the client further service.

[32]A $20 annual membership fee is charged for the meals and recreational activities of the Regina Senior Citizens Centre, but not for the home services which are covered by the present study.

[33]In principle, social economy initiatives tend to have their operating and governance structures managed by members of their target populations. In reality, however, participation and control levels vary widely from one initiative to the other.

[34]The questionnaire can be obtained from the Social Policy Research Unit at the University of Regina.

[35]Current clients were those having used a service during the last 12 months.

[36]The response rate in Saskatoon (41.8 percent or 209/500) was higher than in Regina (33.7 percent or 202/600).

[37]To use follow-up reminders to increase the response rate would therefore have required that we send the reminders to all potential respondents, whether they already responded or not. The executive directors of the two organizations urged us not to do this, as they feared it would confuse or upset many of their clients. We respected this wish even if it produced a negative effect on the response rate.

[38]Two percent of respondents say they would use "other" strategies.

[39]A volunteer-run type of service funded by the health districts.

[40]For example: Dial-A-Maid Inc., We Care Home Health Services, etc.

[41]This residual category might include both *formal* and *informal* sources of help.

References

Aglietta, M. 1987. "Les métamorphoses de la société salariale," *Interventions économiques*, 17:169-84.

Boucher, J. and L. Favreau. 1997. "Néoliberalisme et redéfinition des mouvement sociaux: quelques paramètres," in *Au-delà du néolibéralisme: quel rôle pour les mouvements sociaux?* ed. J.L. Klein, P.A. Tremblay and H. Dionne. Sainte-Foy: Presses de l'Université du Québec.

Boyer, R. 1986. *Capitalismes fin de siècle*. Paris: Presses Universitaire de France.

Burrows, R. and B. Loader, eds. 1994. *Towards a Post-Fordist Welfare State?* London and New York: Routledge.

Canadian Home Care Association. 1998. *Portrait of Canada: An Overview of Public Home Care Programs.* Background information prepared for the National Conference on Home Care, Halifax, February.

Chen, J. and R. Wilkins. 1998. "Seniors' Needs for Health-Related Personal Assistance," *Health Reports,* 10(1):39-51. Cat. No. 82-003. Ottawa: Statistics Canada.

Cloutier, C. and P. Hamel. 1991. "Les services urbains: le défi du partenariat pour le milieu communautaire," *Cahiers de Géographie du Québec,* 35(95):257-83.

Defourny, J. 1992. "The Origins, Forms and Roles of a Third Major Sector," in *The Third Sector, Cooperative, Mutual and Nonprofit Organizations,* ed. J. Defourny and J.L. Monzon Campos. Brussels: CIRIEC/De Boeck Université.

Drache, D. and M.S. Gertler, eds. 1991. *The New Era of Global Competition: State Policy and Market Power.* Montreal and Kingston: McGill-Queen's University Press.

Elwell, F. 1984. "The Effects of Ownership on Institutional Services," *The Gerontologist,* 24(1):709-17.

Favreau, L. and B. Lévesque. 1996. *Développement économique communautaire, économie sociale et intervention.* Sainte-Foy: Presses de l'Université du Québec.

Federal/Provincial/Territorial Subcommittee on Continuing Care. 1992. *Future Directions in Continuing Care.* Ottawa: Health and Welfare Canada.

Health and Welfare Canada. 1990. *Report on Home Care.* Ottawa: Health and Welfare Canada.

Health Services Utilization and Research Commission (HSURC). 1998*a. An Exploratory Study of the Impact of Home Care on Elderly Clients over Time.* Saskatoon: HSURC, January.

_____ 1998*b. Hospital and Home Care Study.* Saskatoon: HSURC, March.

_____ 2000. *The Impact of Preventive Home Care and Seniors Housing on Health Outcomes.* Saskatoon: HSURC, May.

Jenson. J. 1998. "Citizenship in Neo-Liberal Times: Rethinking, Restructuring, and Redesigning Responsibility for Child Care." Paper presented to the International Sociological Association, Montreal, July.

Jenson, J., R. Mahon and M.A. Bienefeld, eds. 1993. *Production, Space, Identity: Political Economy Faces the 21ˢᵗ Century.* Toronto: Canadian Scholars Press.

Jetté, C., L. Thériault, Y. Vaillancourt and R. Mathieu. 1997. *Évaluation de l'intervention du logement social avec support communautaire à la Fédération des OSBL d'habitation de Montréal.* Cahiers du LAREPPS No. 97-08. Montreal: Université du Québec à Montréal.

Lawson, G. and L. Thériault. 1999*a*. *The Evolution of Third Sector Home Care Services in Saskatchewan: A Historical Perspective, 1898–1998.* SPR Occasional Papers No. 11. Regina: Faculty of Social Work, University of Regina.

_____ 1999*b*. "Saskatchewan's Community Health Service Associations: An Historical Perspective," *Prairie Forum*, 24(2):251-68.

Lesemann, F. and D. Namiash. 1993. "Home-based Care in Canada and Quebec: Informal and Formal Services," in *Home-based Care, the Elderly, the Family and the Welfare State,* ed. F. Lesemann and C. Martin. Ottawa: University of Ottawa Press.

Lévesque, B. and W. Ninacs. 1997. "The Social Economy in Canada: The Quebec Experience." paper prepared for the conference on "Local Strategies for Employment and the Social Economy," Montreal, 18-19 June.

Lipietz, A. 1989. *Choisir l'audace. Une alternative pour le XXIe siècle.* Paris: La Découverte.

Marshall, V.W. 1989. "Models for Community-based Long Term Care: An Analysis Review." Unpublished paper. Ottawa: Health and Welfare Canada.

Picard, A. 1999. "Behind Closed Doors: The Struggle over Homecare (Part II)," *The Globe and Mail,* 22 March, pp. A8-A9.

Quarter, J. 1992. *Canada's Social Economy: Co-operatives, Non-profits, and Other Community Enterprises.* Toronto: Lorimer.

Rimer, S. 1998. "Gap in Long-term Care Coverage for Elderly Seen as Growing Threat," *The New York Times,* 8 June.

Shapiro, E. 1997. *The Cost of Privatization: A Case Study of Home Care in Manitoba.* Winnipeg: Canadian Centre for Policy Alternatives.

Skelton, I. 1998. "Welfare Pluralism: Perspectives on Potentialities," *Canadian Review of Social Policy,* 21:45-54.

Statistics Canada. 1999. *A Portrait of Seniors in Canada,* 3d ed. Cat. No. 89-519-XPE. Ottawa: Minister of Industry.

Vaillancourt, Y. 1996. "Sortir de l'alternative entre privatisation et étatisation dans la santé et les services sociaux," in *Société civil, État et Économie plurielle,* ed. B. Eme, J.-L. Laville, L. Favreau and Y. Vaillancourt. Paris: CNRS.

Vaillancourt, Y. and C. Jetté. 1997. *Vers un nouveau partage des responsabilités dans les services sociaux et de santé: Rôles de l'État, du marché, de l'économie sociale et du secteur informel.* Cahiers du LAREPPS No.97-05. Montreal: Université du Québec à Montréal. [In particular, see section 2 on *"Les services à domicile"*].

_____ 1999. *Le rôle accru du tiers secteur dans les services à domicile concernant les personnes âgées au Québec.* Cahiers du LAREPPS No. 99-03. Montreal: Université du Québec à Montréal.

Contributors

Caroline Andrew, Professor, Department of Political Science and Dean, Faculty of Social Sciences, University of Ottawa

Tim Aubry, Associate Professor, School of Psychology and Director, Centre for Research on Community Services, University of Ottawa

Keith G. Banting, Stauffer-Dunning Professor of Policy Studies and Director, School of Policy Studies, Queen's University

Kathy L. Brock, Associate Professor and Head of Public Policy and the Third Sector, School of Policy Studies, Queen's University

Suzanne Brown, Social Planner, Social Planning and Research Council of Hamilton-Wentworth

Marney Cuff, Research Assistant, McMaster University

Christine Holke, Senate of Canada and former student, Department of Political Science, University of Ottawa

Luc Juillet, Assistant Professor, Department of Political Science and Senior Fellow, Centre on Governance, University of Ottawa

Justin Longo, PhD student, Centre for Public Sector Studies, School of Public Administration, University of Victoria

Erin MacLachlan, Project Coordinator, Family Councils of Ontario and former Research Assistant, Department of Family Relations and Applied Nutrition, University of Guelph

Darcy Mitchell, Adjunct Faculty, University of Victoria and Royal Roads University

Janet Mrenica, Internal Auditor, Consulting and Audit Canada

Jack Quarter, Professor, Ontario Institute for Studies in Education, University of Toronto and Program Officer, Trillium Foundation

James J. Rice, Professor, School of Social Work, McMaster University

Betty Jane Richmond, Research Officer, Ontario Institute for Studies in Education, University of Toronto

Sandra Salhani, RSA Security, Vancouver

Debbie Sheehan, Program Manager, Department of Family Medicine and Assistant Clinical Professor, School of Nursing, McMaster University and Child Health Manager, City of Hamilton, Social and Public Health Services Department

Jorge Sousa, PhD student, Ontario Institute for Studies in Education, University of Toronto

Luc Thériault, Assistant Professor of Social Work and Senior Researcher, Social Policy Research Unit, Faculty of Social Work, University of Regina

Shirley Thompson, PhD student, Ontario Institute for Studies in Education, University of Toronto

Joseph A. Tindale, Professor, Department of Family Relations and Applied Nutrition, University of Guelph

Kelly Vodden, PhD student, Department of Geography and Researcher and Instructor, Community Economic Development Centre, Simon Fraser University

Queen's Policy Studies
Recent Publications

The Queen's Policy Studies Series is dedicated to the exploration of major policy issues that confront governments in Canada and other western nations. McGill-Queen's University Press is the exclusive world representative and distributor of books in the series.

School of Policy Studies

The Dynamics of Decentralization: Canadian Federalism and British Devolution, Trevor C. Salmon and Michael Keating (eds.), 2001   ISBN 0-88911-895-7

Innovation, Institutions and Territory: Regional Innovation Systems in Canada, J. Adam Holbrook and David A. Wolfe (eds.), 2000   Paper ISBN 0-88911-891-4 Cloth ISBN 0-88911-893-0

Backbone of the Army: Non-Commissioned Officers in the Future Army, Douglas L. Bland (ed.), 2000 ISBN 0-88911-889-2

Precarious Values: Organizations, Politics and Labour Market Policy in Ontario, Thomas R. Klassen, 2000 Paper ISBN 0-88911-883-3 Cloth ISBN 0-88911-885-X

The Nonprofit Sector in Canada: Roles and Relationships, Keith G. Banting (ed.), 2000 Paper ISBN 0-88911-813-2 Cloth ISBN 0-88911-815-9

Security, Strategy and the Global Economics of Defence Production, David G. Haglund and S. Neil MacFarlane (eds.), 1999   Paper ISBN 0-88911-875-2 Cloth ISBN 0-88911-877-9

The Communications Revolution at Work: The Social, Economic and Political Impacts of Technological Change, Robert Boyce (ed.), 1999   Paper ISBN 0-88911-805-1 Cloth ISBN 0-88911-807-8

Institute of Intergovernmental Relations

Federalism, Democracy and Health Policy in Canada, Duane Adams (ed.), 2001 Paper ISBN 0-88911-853-1 Cloth ISBN 0-88911-865-5, ISBN 0-88911-845-0 (set)

Federalism, Democracy and Labour Market Policy in Canada, Tom McIntosh (ed.), 2000 ISBN 0-88911-849-3, ISBN 0-88911-845-0 (set)

Canada: The State of the Federation 1999/2000, vol. 14, *Toward a New Mission Statement for Canadian Fiscal Federalism,* Harvey Lazar (ed.), 2000   Paper ISBN 0-88911-843-4 Cloth ISBN 0-88911-839-6

Canada: The State of the Federation 1998/99, vol. 13, *How Canadians Connect,* Harvey Lazar and Tom McIntosh (eds.), 1999   Paper ISBN 0-88911-781-0 Cloth ISBN 0-88911-779-9

Managing the Environmental Union: Intergovernmental Relations and Environmental Policy in Canada, Patrick C. Fafard and Kathryn Harrison (eds.), 2000   ISBN 0-88911-837-X

Stretching the Federation: The Art of the State in Canada, Robert Young (ed.), 1999   ISBN 0-88911-777-2

Comparing Federal Systems, 2d ed., Ronald L. Watts, 1999   ISBN 0-88911-835-3

John Deutsch Institute for the Study of Economic Policy

The 2000 Federal Budget, Paul A.R. Hobson (ed.), Policy Forum Series no. 37, 2001 Paper ISBN 0-88911-816-7 Cloth ISBN 0-88911-814-0

Room to Manoeuvre? Globalization and Policy Convergence, Thomas J. Courchene (ed.), Bell Canada Papers no. 6, 1999   Paper ISBN 0-88911-812-4 Cloth ISBN 0-88911-812-4

Women and Work, Richard P. Chaykowski and Lisa M. Powell (eds.), 1999 Paper ISBN 0-88911-808-6 Cloth ISBN 0-88911-806-X

Equalization: Its Contribution to Canada's Economic and Fiscal Progress, Robin W. Boadway and Paul A.R. Hobson (eds.), Policy Forum Series no. 36, 1998 Paper ISBN 0-88911-780-2 Cloth ISBN 0-88911-804-3

Available from:
McGill-Queen's University Press
Tel: 1-800-387-0141 (ON and QC excluding Northwestern ON)
         1-800-387-0172 (all other provinces and Northwestern ON)

E-mail: customer.service@ccmailgw.genpub.com